Getting Naked for Money
An Accidental Travel Writer Reveals All

Edie Jarolim

The Invis ble Press

Also by Edie Jarolim

Am I Boring My Dog? And 99 Other Things Every Dog Wishes You Knew

Frommer's San Antonio & Austin

The Complete Idiot's Travel Guide To Mexico's Beach Resorts

Arizona For Dummies

The Collected Poems Of Paul Blackburn (as editor, with introduction)

PART ONE

🐪🐪🐪

THE ACCIDENTAL TRAVEL EDITOR

CHAPTER 1
THE NAKED TRUTH
Palm Springs, September 2003

It was a balmy autumn afternoon in Palm Springs. My friend Nikki and I were lounging near a sparkling blue pool, reading magazines, chatting lazily, and applying sunscreen. Lots of sunscreen. Nikki and I aren't especially light-skinned, nor did we travel to California from sun-deprived cities: She lives in Phoenix, I in Tucson. But exposure was definitely an issue.

We were naked, you see, guests at a high-end nudist resort.

Mind you, Nikki and I weren't nudists. Far from it. Until a few hours earlier, we had not been on attire-free terms, nor had we been prone to disrobing in public. But I had an assignment from *More*, a glossy women's magazine aimed at the over-forty set, to write a first-person piece on nudist travel. I was to go undercover and underclothed—as in none at all.

I had been flattered to be approached by *More*. The publication was one of my more deep-pocketed clients, and I was usually the one doing the pitching. It was worth severing all sartorial bonds, I decided, to hold on to a good writing gig. Put another way, in pursuit of a paycheck, I had agreed to be a whore for *More*.

That's the short version of how I ended up naked in Palm Springs. The longer story of happening into the travel-writing career that brought me to this pass will unfold over the course of this book. Spoiler alert: This is no chronicle of pluck and perseverance in pursuit of a long-coveted goal. If anything, it often serves as a cautionary tale.

When offered the assignment, however, I had no time for ethical quandaries or existential angst. I had practical matters to attend to. My editor wanted an article outline, stat. *More* was shelling out for me to take a friend, and I needed to find someone willing. I also had to find a destination that would suit *More*'s demographic of upscale professionals and not turn out to be a retreat for naked trailer trash. And I had to come up with a rationale for going *au naturel* other than the actual one: that nudism was trendy, so a magazine was paying me to undress.

Two out of three of those tasks turned out to be surprisingly simple to accomplish. One of my travel journalism sub-specialties was dining. When Nikki, a fellow food writer, had phoned with a question about a Tucson restaurant, I brought up the subject of my *More* assignment. "I know this isn't exactly your area of expertise," I said, "but how would you approach the subject?"

"We're constantly bitching about how it's so much tougher than it used to be to lose weight after one of our food-review pigouts," she mused. "Hanging around with people who don't give a damn what they look like unclothed might be a way to get past that self-consciousness."

Hmmm. Nudism as an antidote to the quest for body-image perfection. I could work with that.

And then she uttered the magic words: "I don't suppose you need someone to come with you?"

Much as I liked Nikki, it hadn't occurred to me to ask her. She and I were primarily phone friends; we'd consult about restaurants in our respective culinary territories, and then end up dishing about our current love interests or complaining about our freelance careers. The half-dozen times that we'd met to share a meal, clothing had always been involved. But, hey, if Nikki was game to get naked with me, I wasn't going to look a gift stripper in the mouth.

So after only a single phone call, I had both an angle and an accomplice. Now all I needed was a place that would work for Nikki and me as well as for *More*. Neither of us wanted to go too far away (what if we needed to escape?) or stay too close (what if we ran into someone we knew?), which eliminated Cap D'Age, an entirely naked city in the south of France, and Shangri-La, a nudist ranch near Phoenix. We weren't interested in a naked pick-up scene like Hedonism II in Jamaica; I'd met a former manager of the all-inclusive resort, who told me he'd left because he had grown tired of having to hose down couples having public sex on the lawn.

Nor were we keen on a totally family-oriented place like Cypress Cove near Orlando. Who wanted to hang around a bunch of kids wearing nothing but Mickey Mouse ears?

I finally landed on the website of Desert Shadows in Palm Springs, possibly the only nudist lodging in that town that didn't cater primarily to gay men. It was a four-hour drive from Phoenix, far enough to avoid unwanted encounters with acquaintances, near enough to offer an exit strategy. It billed itself as family-friendly, but wasn't too close to anything Disney. And *More* was sure to approve its So Cal-meets-the-Mediterranean setting: swaying palm trees, soothing pink buildings, dramatic mountain backdrop...the whole chic shebang.

Still, I wanted to make sure we wouldn't feel out of place—or any more out of place than two women posing as nudists would feel surrounded by the textile-challenged. Going along with *More*'s instructions that I not reveal I'm a journalist—Why? What would the resort do? Make people put their clothes back on? Import ringers with better bodies?—I naturist program? I hoped not. That's not what *More*'s readers would want to hear.

We decided not to investigate further that evening. Dinner at the resort that night was a buffet, and we weren't ready to risk any close encounters with chafing dishes. Throwing on our clothes, we hightailed it to downtown Palm Springs, where everyone at the seafood restaurant we chose was more or less dressed.

🐫 🐫 🐫

We'd planned to have breakfast at Desert Shadows the following morning, a Monday, even though the idea of the staff accidentally spilling scalding coffee in my lap sounded no more appealing than brushing up against hot buffet stations. Finding the dining room shuttered, we went to the front desk, where we learned morning meals were served only on weekends. We would have to fend for ourselves until lunchtime.

In fact, we were told that if we wanted to dine chez Desert Shadows in the evening, we would have to order our entrees in advance, and they would appear on our bill whether or not we turned up to eat them. Odd. Even odder: The only two main course options were steak and salmon. Didn't naturism and vegetarianism go hand-in-hand? Proto-nudists Adam and Eve had followed a plant-based diet before losing their innocence. Then again, they would have been better off on a strict Paleo regimen, eschewing the apple and sautéing the serpent instead.

Dinner order placed, Nikki and I got dressed and headed for a nearby coffee shop, picking up a few supplies for lunch too.

Finally, determined to survey a larger nudist sample, we took the plunge into the activities pool, which wasn't very to share a meal, clothing had always been involved. But, hey, if Nikki was game to get naked with me, I wasn't going to look a gift stripper in the mouth.

So after only a single phone call, I had both an angle and an accomplice. Now all I needed was a place that would work for Nikki and me as well as for *More*. Neither of us wanted to go too far away (what if we needed to escape?) or stay too close (what if we ran into someone we knew?), which eliminated Cap D'Age, an entirely naked city in the south of France, and Shangri-La, a nudist ranch near Phoenix. We weren't interested in a naked pick-up scene like Hedonism II in Jamaica; I'd met a former manager of the all-inclusive resort, who told me he'd left because he had grown tired of having to hose down couples having public sex on the lawn.

Nor were we keen on a totally family-oriented place like Cypress Cove near Orlando. Who wanted to hang around a bunch of kids wearing nothing but Mickey Mouse ears?

I finally landed on the website of Desert Shadows in Palm Springs, possibly the only nudist lodging in that town that didn't cater primarily to gay men. It was a four-hour drive from Phoenix, far enough to avoid unwanted encounters with acquaintances, near enough to offer an exit strategy. It billed itself as family-friendly, but wasn't too close to anything Disney. And *More* was sure to approve its So Cal-meets-the-Mediterranean setting: swaying palm trees, soothing pink buildings, dramatic mountain backdrop...the whole chic shebang.

Still, I wanted to make sure we wouldn't feel out of place—or any more out of place than two women posing as nudists would feel surrounded by the textile-challenged. Going along with *More*'s instructions that I not reveal I'm a journalist—Why? What would the resort do? Make people put their clothes back on? Import ringers with better bodies?—I phoned. "A friend and I are considering a naturist vacation," I said, using the approved vocabulary term gleaned from the Desert Shadows website, "but we've never tried anything like this before." I added, "We're both single and just looking to relax. Would we feel comfortable there?"

The front desk manager was reassuring. "We have a strict policy here," he said. "If anyone says or does anything that makes you feel uncomfortable, just report it, and we'll ask that guest to leave." He also explained that many areas of the resort were not clothing-optional. "We expect you to be nude in the main public areas, like the pools, so the other guests won't feel like you're ogling them," he elaborated. In the other parts of the property, such as the dining room, your attire or lack thereof was entirely up to you.

I was dying to know what the dress code was at reception, but asking the manager what he was or wasn't wearing seemed like a porn-hotline question. I couldn't afford to be asked to leave before I had even arrived.

Satisfied that I'd found the right place, I booked a two-bedroom villa for two nights. Nikki and I would get to know a lot more about each other than we might want, so separate sleeping quarters were a must, and a two-night stay seemed more than sufficient. The rooms were pricey, the magazine's budget was tight, and our *chutzpah* had a limited shelf life.

Nikki and I began telling people about our upcoming trip, in large part to find out how they would react. Many of the women laughed and exclaimed, "You're brave. I wish I had the nerve to do that." Others snorted, "I could never…"

The male reaction was uniformly enthusiastic. Most of the men I'd met through dating sites didn't have a clue about what freelance writers do and hadn't been especially interested in finding out until now. Disclose that you're going to take your clothes off in public, especially with a female friend, and guys suddenly start drawing you out like Oprah: "Oh, so does being a freelancer involve lots of assignments like that?" "What else do you write about?" and "When are you getting back?" They also enjoined, "Take lots of pictures."

Thus equipped with a new lexicon–"nudist resort" not "nudist colony," "naturist" or "nudist" not "exhibitionist" or "perv"— but very little in the way of luggage, Nikki and I found ourselves ringing the bell of a large, unmarked wooden door in Palm Springs. I loved the intrigue. This was very James Bond in the buff.

We didn't have to wait long before we were buzzed in and my question about staff attire was answered. The two people at the reception desk were indeed dressed, casually, but covering all the bases. Just beyond a glass door, however, there they were: naked people. They were clustered in lounge chairs, splashing around the pool, strolling around and looking unconcerned, as though they weren't completely starkers.

I stifled my giggles while the manager toured us around the grounds, but it was tough. When Nikki and I finally got into our villa we collapsed, guffawing, onto the living room couch. Then Nikki mused, "I wonder how many bare butts have rested on these couch pillows." We quickly jumped up.

We took the tour: kitchen, living room, one bedroom, outdoor shower downstairs, a smaller bedroom with indoor shower upstairs. The furniture was utilitarian; other than the outdoor shower, a nice touch, this looked more like an upscale motel suite than a villa. I wondered how the resort could get away with giving that name to these accommodations—or, for that matter, how the entire place could designate itself a resort.

But I knew the answer: Who was going to stop them? I'd been working in travel publishing for more than two and a half decades, on both sides of the editorial desk; if there were restrictions on terminology, I hadn't noticed them. Hotels and restaurants—think "Chinese bistro"—could pretty much call themselves whatever they thought would sell.

We were stalling. We couldn't hide indoors all day, avoiding permeable surfaces. I had research to conduct. Besides, the weather was gorgeous and the pool looked inviting. We scuttled off to our respective rooms and came out dressed for the occasion: Not. After a round of bolstering ourselves up—"C'mon, we've gotten naked with lots of guys we didn't know very well, what's a few more?" and "None of these people will ever see us again"—we ventured out, armed only with the large towels that, throughout our stay, would do double duty as security blankets and sanitation guards.

The *al fresco* walk to the pool and search for lounge chairs turned out to be easier than we'd expected. Sure, people looked at us, but the reception wasn't much different than the one you get when you show up at any pool: Everyone checks you out and then goes back to their books or conversations.

Everyone, that is, except Nikki and me. We positioned ourselves under a tree, several yards back from the main activities pool, and carefully monitored the scene.

We observed a wide range of shapes, from totally toned to way overweight, and ages, from teenagers to septuagenarians. The men seemed to care less about their appearances than the women did; at least a far larger proportion of them had far larger proportions. Mostly, though, I was riveted by the display of male genitalia. I felt like I was in the produce section of an exotic supermarket—no poking or squeezing, please.

Voyeurism gets old surprisingly quickly. We soon tired of lounging around in the altogether, pretending to read magazines. Nikki wanted to swim laps, so we wandered over to a quiet pool in the back of the hotel complex. Wow—the cool water felt great against my unencumbered skin. I was beginning to think there might be something to this nudity thing, that officially sanctioned skinny-dipping wasn't such a bad idea.

It struck me almost simultaneously that taking a cool shower on a hot day feels just as good and offers the advantage of not putting your boobs on public display. And part of the kick of skinny-dipping is that it's forbidden. Why strip stripping of its naughtiness?

I noticed a couple perched on the steps of the pool's shallow end. I disliked striking up conversations with strangers, and this felt like a classic anxiety nightmare: You're at a cocktail party, you can't get served, and you realize you're not wearing anything. But I had a job to do. I put on my journalist's hat—figuratively speaking, of course—and, smiling bravely, splashed over to the duo.

George, middle-aged and paunchy, was a real estate developer from Connecticut. With her neatly coiffed do, his stay-at-home wife, Clara, looked like she belonged in a 1950s sitcom. I flashed on an image of *Leave It to Beaver* done entirely in the nude, then chuckled to myself at the hairy pun of the show's name. I get goofy when I'm nervous.

"We've been nudists for quite a while," George explained. "After several years of trying it on the occasional trip, it just became the way we wanted to vacation." Clara chimed in, "You meet the nicest people in these places."

Judging by George, I wasn't so sure. He not only told an offensive story about a rowdy neighbor—"Well, he was Italian, so what could you expect?"—but kept staring at my breasts. I changed the name of my imaginary 1950s sitcom to *Father Knows Busts*.

Nikki noticed the ogling, too. Was this just a fluke, we wondered when we get back to our room, or was it part of the naturist program? I hoped not. That's not what *More*'s readers would want to hear.

We decided not to investigate further that evening. Dinner at the resort that night was a buffet, and we weren't ready to risk any close encounters with chafing dishes. Throwing on our clothes, we hightailed it to downtown Palm Springs, where everyone at the seafood restaurant we chose was more or less dressed.

🐫 🐫 🐫

We'd planned to have breakfast at Desert Shadows the following morning, a Monday, even though the idea of the staff accidentally spilling scalding coffee in my lap sounded no more appealing than brushing up against hot buffet stations. Finding the dining room shuttered, we went to the front desk, where we learned morning meals were served only on weekends. We would have to fend for ourselves until lunchtime.

In fact, we were told that if we wanted to dine chez Desert Shadows in the evening, we would have to order our entrees in advance, and they would appear on our bill whether or not we turned up to eat them. Odd. Even odder: The only two main course options were steak and salmon. Didn't naturism and vegetarianism go hand-in-hand? Proto-nudists Adam and Eve had followed a plant-based diet before losing their innocence. Then again, they would have been better off on a strict Paleo regimen, eschewing the apple and sautéing the serpent instead.

Dinner order placed, Nikki and I got dressed and headed for a nearby coffee shop, picking up a few supplies for lunch too.

Finally, determined to survey a larger nudist sample, we took the plunge into the activities pool, which wasn't very active. Many of the weekend disrobers we'd observed the day before had defected, leaving only the hard-core nudists, mainly men in their forties and up. I was relieved not to have to chat with any naked teenagers, but sorry that the current range of interview subjects was so narrow.

Still, the natives were friendly. Nikki and I easily fell into conversation with a number of naked guys. We learned that we'd arrived too late on the previous day to catch the pool volleyball game (darn!), and that we'd missed in-the-buff karaoke on Saturday night (double darn!). The revelation that we were nudism newbies brought out the solicitousness in the men, who expressed several variations on the theme of "You'll never want to go back to wearing clothes again."

But maybe it wasn't solicitousness so much as salaciousness.

We eventually settled in for a chat with Wayne, who, sunning atop a rubber raft, looked like a beached pink whale with nipple rings. He told us that when he and his wife, Doreen—not currently accompanying him—weren't doing the naturist circuit, he worked as an assistant manager at Walmart.

After a few minutes of small talk, Wayne asked us if we wanted to join him in a drink. It was 10 a.m., but what the heck—booze might improve my interview skills.

Wayne clearly had the routine down. He returned with three ice-filled Solo cups, a bottle of tonic, and a half-bottle of gin. Nikki and I found an area of the pool where we would be mostly covered but have our arms free to hold cocktails. Let happy hour begin!

The conversation soon began taking a personal turn. Wayne confided that he and Doreen both had their nipples pierced to celebrate their twenty-fifth wedding anniversary. Ouch. And more pain was on the way. For their twenty-sixth,

Wayne was planning to pierce his scrotum and Doreen was going to have a ring inserted in her clitoris.

Whatever happened to saying it with flowers?

Wayne mentioned too that he and Doreen shaved off each other's body hair each week—his balls *did* look strangely shiny—and that all this kept their sex life zinging. I figured that getting drunk and talking about your balls with naked female strangers didn't hurt it, either.

Wayne eventually got around to confessing that he'd initially assumed Nikki and I were lesbians, but now realized we weren't. I wasn't sure how'd he arrived at this conclusion. Neither of us had shared the slightest bit of personal information with him. Was it because we hadn't begun fondling each other during the conversation? Because we hadn't hauled off and belted him as soon as he started discussing his scrotum?

Why hadn't we, Nikki and I later wondered with respect to the second question, or why hadn't we at least dog-paddled madly away? We were both seasoned souses; alcohol alone wasn't a sufficient excuse. We agreed that we'd been perversely fascinated by the Secret Life of a Walmart Assistant Manager.

Still, research-wise, the morning was a nonstarter. We'd wandered into *Hustler* territory. No way *More* readers would go for an in-the-buff discussion of lesbianism and body-piercings with a not-so-buff guy.

But it was still early.

I suggested walking across the bridge that linked the resort with the affiliated nudist condo complex on the other side of Chaparral Road, a main Palm Springs artery. The world's first nudist span, the Lee R. Baxandall Bridge had been a hot topic on late-night comedy shows when it debuted, particularly because it had been draped in not-entirely opaque material. The topic of the traffic hazards posed by motorists looking up in the hopes of catching a glimpse of skin seemed slightly risqué but not off limits. If Jay Leno could use the shtick on *The Tonight Show*, I could probably adapt it for *More*.

But by the time Nikki and I got to Desert Shadows, the bridge of thighs, as one waggish newspaper dubbed it, was covered in completely nontransparent canvas up to about head height. We could peer into the cars below, but they could only view us from the neck up. As I stood overlooking the traffic zipping along Chaparral Road, I could feel a slight stirring in my own thighs.

Great.

I began compiling a mental checklist of topics I could cover for *More*. Second-hand report of naked karaoke and volleyball, yes. First-hand encounter with Mr. Shiny Nuts, no. Naked bridge walking, yes. Enjoying exhibitionism, no.

To add injury to insult, when Nikki and I returned to our rooms in the late afternoon, we discovered that we'd been overexposed, and not in the media sense. Nikki was sore in a spot where the sun hadn't shone before. "Look," she cried. "I have a burning bush!"

I clearly hadn't applied sufficient sunscreen to my heretofore hidden regions, either. "Just call me Robin Red Breast," I countered.

Those 10 a.m. gin and tonics really take it out of you. Sunburned and tired, we headed over to the resort's dining room. It was our final night, our last chance to scope out the nude restaurant scene. Besides, the meal would turn up on our bill, no matter if we ate it or not. Ditching it, even at *More*'s expense, would have been too guilt inducing.

Although the restaurant was clothing-optional, there was no question of our getting dressed. Underwear would have chafed our reddened bits—not to mention that, after scrutinizing a stranger's scrotum together, Nikki and I had no claim to modesty left.

No problem. The photo on Desert Shadows' website of a naked couple eating by glimmering candlelight notwithstanding, the dining room turned out to be more glorified coffee shop than upscale restaurant. After a quick visual sweep, during which we noted that only the servers were clothed, Nikki and I returned to our default food-critic mode. We were far more interested in dissing what was on our plates—overcooked fish and tough meat, which would explain the pay-in-advance policy—than in checking out what our fellow diners weren't wearing.

🐪 🐪 🐪

Our final morning, we couldn't resist the pool entirely, but tried to keep to the shade as much as possible. Shiny Balls Wayne had decamped, but a few other people we'd chatted with in the last couple of days remained: Dave, a retired dentist wearing only a boater (hats were big, in every sense, here); Joe, a handsome financier from Pebble Beach by way of Russia, whose equally good-looking wife, Sara, was decked out in a transparent sarong with fringes; and Eliot, a pudgy computer tech from LA.

We exchanged farewell pleasantries. Joe, squatting down at the edge of the pool to talk to us and positioning himself so that his privates were, literally, in our faces, said to me, "If you're ever in the Pebble Beach area, look us up," using the plural to include his other half, Sara Sarong. Then, gesturing to the magazine I'd left on my lounge chair—a copy of *More*, as it happened—he whispered, "I'll put a slip of paper with our number on it for you." What was with the secrecy? Was this how offsite *ménages à trois* were arranged?

Dave the dentist left his card for Nikki.

"Nikki," I said, as we took our final splash around the pool, "I'm screwed. This place is just a subtler version of Hedonism II. What am I going to write about?"

Had it all been kind of sleazy, or was I imagining that?

"Neither of us ever felt harassed," I argued, playing devil's advocate. "Or at least no more so than we tend to feel when we're dressed. Having equal visual access to a guy's assets pretty much levels the playing field."

Nikki, citing the incident of the dangling poolside genitalia, countered, "I bet having women check out their equipment is part of the kick for some guys."

She conceded that everyone made a conscious effort not to be overtly sexual; Wayne may have been talking trash, but he never actually hit on us. Nor, technically, did Joe or Dave.

Still, we couldn't deny that, had we wanted to report everyone who'd said or done something iffy to the propriety police at the front desk, Nikki and I could have depopulated the place. Maybe nudism isn't necessarily about sex, just like supermarkets aren't necessarily about cooking. But when people of opposite genders—or, in the case of most of the naked lodgings in Palm Springs, the same one—let it all hang out together, it's like unpacking your groceries and bringing them over to the stove.

Perhaps as a reward for that honest assessment, the goddess of sell-out journalists took pity on me. As Nikki and I were leaving the pool for the last time, still in full undress, computer tech Eliot approached me and said, "I hope you won't be offended by my saying this, but you have a really nice smile."

Yes! I had an ending for the piece—funny, and inoffensive.

CHAPTER 2
PORTRAIT OF THE ARTIST
AS A YOUNG NEUROTIC
Brooklyn/Manhattan/Many Foreign Countries, 1970s–1985

I want to be as accurate as possible here. I've suggested that I stumbled into a travel-writing career rather than marched decisively toward one, and that's true, strictly speaking. But for as long as I can remember, I secretly wanted to be a writer. At the same time, I fantasized about visiting far-flung lands. It just never occurred to me that I could combine those aspirations— and convince an editor to pick up the tab.

The early signs were not auspicious.

My parents weren't keen on travel, at least not the voluntary kind. Refugees from Nazi-occupied Vienna, they were in no rush to head back overseas. Nor did we jaunt off on any all-American road trips. We didn't have a lot of money, and we didn't have a car.

That was okay. We were far from outliers in Flatbush, a largely Jewish and Italian section of Brooklyn. My girlfriends and I spent lazy summers at Brighton Beach Baths, giggling over cute lifeguards and sneaking smokes behind the paddleball courts; it cost a quarter to share a pack of Tareytons. My butt still has sense memories of the itchy faux-straw seats on the BMT subway line.

But I came of globetrotting age in the early 1970s, the heyday of cut-rate charters and budget carriers like Icelandic. I lived at home and earned enough money from after-school jobs to cover airfare and several weeks of hostel hopping. The *New*

Yorker cartoon showing a vast void between Manhattan and the West Coast was dead-on. I'd been to Europe twice before visiting California, and didn't think to stop anywhere in between.

The lure of the exotic ramped up in my last year of Brooklyn College when I met Lou, an aspiring photographer who was teaching in an inner-city school to avoid the Vietnam War draft. We both had summers off and were similarly inclined toward adventure and—I admit it—one-upsmanship. We dubbed our forays to places where none of our friends had been "travel coups." By the time Lou and I got married, when I was twenty-one, we had Morocco, Tunisia, Yugoslavia, Bulgaria, and Guatemala under our belts, along with more on-the-beaten-path places like Mexico, Spain, and Greece. On our three-month honeymoon, we went overland from Istanbul through Iran, Afghanistan, and northern India to Nepal, returning home via Uzbekistan, Moscow, and Leningrad to Frankfurt.

That's right. We honeymooned in two out of three countries in what was later dubbed the "Axis of Evil" by George W. Bush.

Of course, at the time, the West-friendly Shah ruled Iran, and no one had ever heard of the Taliban or ISIS. Touring the Middle East wasn't particularly gutsy. Our sense of ease in those countries was also fed, at least in part, by cultural ignorance. When Lou and I drew applause for a quick, thoughtless kiss on a bus in Afghanistan, and were encouraged by the male passengers to kiss again and again, we assumed it was just a friendly appreciation of young love. Who knew we were putting on the Afghan equivalent of a live sex show? And when my butt was grabbed one time too often in Meshad, Iran—in spite of its being obscured by a long hippie skirt, my nod to modest attire—I took off after the most blatant offender, beating my fists against his back when I caught up with him. A crowd gathered, Lou pulled me away, and we had a good laugh.

If touring the Middle East was no big deal in the early 1970s, visiting the Soviet Union was bold. Lou and I were certain that our government's Cold War rhetoric was pure propaganda. We firmly expected to encounter cadres of cheerful Communists lacking only blue jeans; we'd heard we could make a killing on these, so brought along several extra pairs to sell. Instead, the people we met seemed dispirited, grim, and uninterested in buying the heavy denim pants we had schlepped through Asia. We began worrying that we were being followed by the KGB. By the time we left, we were convinced that the Russians were trying to poison our bodily fluids, à la *Dr. Strangelove*. Not until much later did we discover that it wasn't safe to drink the water in Leningrad, and that our wracking stomach distress was caused by amoebas in the Neva River, not enemy agents.

For several years, we traveled really well together. And then we didn't.

There's a name now for our six-year relationship: "starter marriage." I cared very much for Lou, but not with an abiding passion. What I wanted truly, madly, and deeply was to get out of my parents' apartment. When our out-of-town adventures ceased to be more enjoyable than our life in Brooklyn, Lou and I parted ways, without much rancor. We stayed friends and, occasionally, lovers, until I moved to Tucson in the early 1990s.

The fact that I enjoyed sex with Lou a great deal more when it wasn't matrimonially sanctioned, both before and after we were married, should have given me a clue that I wasn't cut out for a traditional committed relationship. It didn't. Even in feminist circles, being single wasn't deemed a desirable choice.

help that the subject of my dissertation, the twentieth-century American poet Paul Blackburn, was a "dead white guy," academia-speak for someone representing the increasingly beleaguered establishment. My untrendy specialty would consign me to the boonies before I could—maybe, possibly, who knows?—snag a job in a decent city.

Most of all, I didn't want to give up my Greenwich Village apartment.

I had finally acquired what every bridge-and-tunnel brat aspired to in the days before the boroughs became hip: a rent-stabilized place in Manhattan. Call me crazy, but I didn't want to move someplace I didn't want to live to do something I didn't want to do.

🐫 🐫 🐫

I turned to Lynne Palmer, one of several employment agencies in New York dedicated to finding publishing jobs for unskilled English majors.

The agency had gotten me my first such gig out of college at Plenum ("The Language of Science"). The division I worked for was devoted exclusively to Soviet academic journals translated—very badly—from the Russian, journals like *Metallurgy*, which regularly featured smiling, overalls-clad workers competing for "Smelter of the Month." The pay was so low and the work so tedious that the decision to quit Plenum to go to graduate school was a no-brainer.

Now, a decade and a PhD later, I was back at Lynne Palmer.

One day, I got a call to come in to take a blind editing test. The potential employer didn't want to reveal its identity, my Lynne Palmer liaison said, lest unscreened applicants besiege them, but I would definitely be pleased.

She was right. When the call came that I'd aced the editing test and should report for an interview at Prentice Hall Travel (PHT), a division of Simon & Schuster, I was elated. Among other series, PHT published the Frommer's guides. *Europe on $25 a Day* had been my bible on my first college trip overseas. I recalled the immense satisfaction of ripping out a chapter and tossing it every time I finished touring a country, thus lightening my backpack load. I associated the company with carefree, youthful adventure.

I was also excited at the idea of getting my foot in the door at Simon & Schuster. Who knew what connections I could make there?

My interview with Jaclyn Forrest, the editorial director, went pretty well, I thought—at least at first. Trim and petite, with a trace of her London origins in her clipped tones, Jaclyn was very smart but easy to talk to. At the end, when asked if I had any questions, I inquired how much time editors were given to visit the destinations their authors were covering. Suddenly brusque, Jaclyn informed me that the vacation allotment was the standard two weeks.

"Editors don't do any on-site research," she elaborated. "That's the author's responsibility."

She dismissed me by saying I would hear within a week, one way or another, whether I'd gotten the job. The end of the first week came—*nada*. By the time the second drew to a close, my cuticles required reconstructive surgery. By the middle of the third, I was wondering whether I could score some Quaaludes.

Then the call came. I was in!

A year or so later, Jaclyn confided that she almost didn't hire me because of my interest in extra-office activities. "You needn't ever be afraid to ask for more money," she explained. "People respect you for having self-confidence and they can always say no. But asking about time off during an interview implies you're not going to be dedicated to the job."

I was horrified to learn about the gaffe that had almost cost me my employment, though far less starry-eyed about travel publishing by then. But I'm jumping ahead. When I got the nod from PHT, I took it as a sign that I'd been rescued, that I could finally put academia behind me without any qualms. Perhaps I should have worried more about a position at a travel publisher that didn't involve travel, but my usually keen Jewish radar for potential problems, real or imagined, was on the fritz. I was sure I'd nabbed a dream job, and no one could have convinced me otherwise.

CHAPTER 3
FROMMER'S FOLLIES
Manhattan, 1986–1988

It was 10 a.m. and I was sitting in a tiny mid-Manhattan office, contemplating penis sheaths. I'm not talking about the latex variety, though my fantasies of spontaneous, sweep-the-papers-off-your-desk sex always seemed to end with me worrying about sexually transmitted diseases.

No, I had just started reading the manuscript of *Frommer's Dollarwise South Pacific*, the first book at Prentice Hall Travel (PHT) I was assigned to edit from scratch. On the second page, I came across a description of "steep mountain valleys inhabited by peoples still wearing nothing more than grass skirts or penis sheaths." Hmmm.

I was no prude. I'd had more close encounters with penises, sheathed and unsheathed, than I cared to recall. But in the mid-1980s, privates were more private and male members didn't tend to turn up in travel guides.

More to the point, it had only been a couple of months since I'd started working as an associate editor at PHT. I didn't want to screw up.

There had to be a precedent for this, I thought. I contemplated *National Geographic's* photographs of bare-breasted native women, which thrilled adolescent boys everywhere. But the Frommer's guides seem less, well, ethnographic. And it was more acceptable to talk about female body parts than it was to discuss male organs.

Some things don't change.

Not only didn't I know the rules of editorial decorum, but I also didn't know whom to consult about them. Not Bill Goodwin, the South Pacific guide's author; I wanted him to feel confident in my editing chops, even though I doubted them myself. Not Jaclyn Forrest, PHT's editorial director and the one who'd entrusted me with the manuscript. I wasn't ready to talk about penises with my boss.

I definitely didn't want to ask Gracie Rubio, the greasy-haired editor and mapmaker who was assigned to train me. She'd nitpicked every bit of work I showed her, preying on all my feelings of inadequacy. In addition, because of her poor personal hygiene, she emitted puffs of BO when she waved her arms to point to places on the page where, she claimed, I messed up. Not until later did I discover that she had far exceeded her mandate to show me the ropes, and that she was a pathological liar (never a good quality in a mapmaker). At this point, I just knew to avoid Gracie if at all possible.

I decided to take my dilemma to Gloria McDarrah, the most experienced of the three editors in my division and the one with whom I'd formed an instant bond.

In some ways, New York is a small town. When I told Gloria that I had edited *The Collected Poems of Paul Blackburn*, she revealed she was married to Fred McDarrah, the longtime *Village Voice* photo editor who had photographed Blackburn and other downtown writers for *The Beat Scene*, an essay collection that had helped me establish Blackburn's New York milieu. Tall and soft-spoken and—as I later discovered when I met Fred—an elegant Jewish yin to her husband's fiery Irish yang, Gloria quickly became a dependable office ally.

Gloria wasn't sure about the penises, however.

I decided not to take the risk, so I called the author.

More than twenty-five years later, Bill still remembers that conversation. "We spent quite some time on the phone trying to come up with a euphemism or another way to explain [the sheaths], without any luck whatsoever," Bill emailed. "For example, we couldn't say 'private parts' because that covers only one of the three private parts. And if we said it covers one of the private parts, we had to explain which one!"

We ultimately decided, after consulting Jaclyn, to leave the penis sheaths alone.

Bill wrote, "I believe it was the first time the word 'penis' appeared in a Frommer's guide. A historic moment!"

It's hard to know what Arthur Frommer would have made of this landmark. He had no say in the matter. My second big surprise, after learning that I was to work for a travel publisher that didn't allow its editors to travel, was that Arthur Frommer was not involved with most of the books that bore his name.

Guidebooks have been around since ancient times. Pausanias's *Guide to Greece* dates back to the second century CE. The Italian Renaissance poet Petrarch put together an itinerary for pilgrims headed to the Holy Land in the fourteenth century. Europeans on Grand Tours in the 1800s toted around John Murray's and Karl Baedeker's handbooks. Michelin (1900) and Fodor's (1932) are the best known of the guides that debuted overseas in the early-twentieth century.

Frommer's Europe on $5 a Day, published in 1957 and inspired by Arthur's stint as a GI in Berlin, was groundbreaking for aiming its sights on American readers and for focusing on budget travel. Its nitty-gritty advice on how to economize on the road spurred a travel publishing empire, with more than

250 titles. At one time, Frommer's guides controlled some 25 percent of the market.

In 1977, Frommer sold the company to Simon & Schuster. It wasn't until 2013, after Google declined to publish any of the books in the imprint it had acquired, that an eighty-three-year-old Arthur bought back the use of the Frommer name and began publishing the guides again, this time with his daughter, Pauline.

I only caught glimpses of Arthur, a stocky whirling dervish, on the rare occasions when he turned up at the Gulf + Western building, an asbestos-ridden nightmare on Columbus Circle that made strange whistling sounds; it was later gutted and reincarnated as Trump International Hotel & Tower. Arthur was still involved with the Europe guide that had started it all—by then up to $35 a day—but he was no longer the primary updater. An Austrian assistant did the bulk of the on-site research.

The only book that Arthur was genuinely engaged with, from beginning to end, was *The New World of Travel*.

Too engaged, in fact.

Like the early $-a-Day guides, this book was ahead of its time. Long before spiritual and educational tourism were trendy, it proposed travel alternatives like staying at ashrams or attending language schools. But Arthur kept revising it, endlessly. This wasn't so bad when it was in manuscript. He continued, however, to try to make revisions in "blues"— blueline proofs, the final stage before a book was sent to press, and a time when making any changes, and especially those that might mess up the layout and page count, was very expensive. Worse, it had been promoted heavily in all the Simon & Schuster catalogs. Missing the publication date would have been a disaster.

By the end of the production process, Jaclyn was on her last nerve. "That book has got to go to the printer," she said. "I'm going to call down to the front desk and tell them not to let Arthur upstairs."

I'm pretty sure she was kidding.

🐫 🐫 🐫

During my first year at PHT, editing the expanding series of Frommer's guides took up the bulk of my time. PHT distributed other travel directories, including prestigious names like American Express, Economist, Insight, and Mobile, but they were produced elsewhere, often overseas. The New York editors generally saw them only briefly, if at all, before they were sent out to warehouses or chain bookstores along with the books that we created in-house.

I occasionally worked on new titles like the South Pacific book, but mostly focused on guides that existed in earlier editions. This gave me a good feel for the series format and style, as well as an introduction to the care and feeding of authors—something of keen interest to me, since I wanted to be one.

Frommer's writers were all over the map, as it were.

The vast majority of them were hardworking and conscientious, and cared a great deal about the books that bore their name, as well as about the destinations that they covered. But some phoned it in—literally. Google did not yet exist, nor were there tourism websites from which to cadge information. I suspected some writers of doing research by long-distance calls, if they did any at all. Sometimes I could tell from errors in the listing—references to attractions that had burned down, for example, or restaurants that had gone out of business years earlier—that, before it reached my desk, the text hadn't been looked at by human eyes.

Still, if some writers were lazy and tried to get by with doing the minimum, no one came close to spa expert Judy Martin for sheer *chutzpah*.

Although most of the guides published under the Frommer's name were destination-oriented, PHT occasionally put out books on niche topics that cut across geographical lines. Destination spas were just taking off in the mid-1980s. It was the ideal time to get ahead of the pampering and wellness trend.

I was charged with vetting the proposal Judy sent in for a spa guide. Her sample chapter and outline were excellent, well organized and authoritative, and I could find no other books that covered the topic as thoroughly as Judy's would. Jaclyn agreed that the book had huge potential. I was pleased to be chosen as its editor.

Sadly, Judy was not destined to lead Prentice Hall into the promised land of spa-book market share.

Soon after she set off on her first research trip, Jaclyn and I began getting phone calls. "Your writer demanded the secret formula to our rejuvenating mud," one spa director fumed. "She threatened to leave us out of the book if we didn't give it to her." Another reported that Judy wanted an unreasonable number of pricey spa treatments "for comparison purposes," and that she didn't tip the staff. A resort general manager informed us that Judy was charging gourmet meals to her comped room, claiming that PHT would pay (no way).

It got so we knew Judy's itinerary based on the irate phone calls that followed in her wake. All the messages we left for Judy to cease and desist her unprofessional behavior went unanswered, all warnings unheeded.

The spa book was finally cancelled. I don't think PHT ever commissioned another one, certainly not under the

Frommer's imprint. I can't find it on Amazon, which suggests it doesn't exist.

🐪 🐪 🐪

It wasn't until the following year, when I was tasked with shepherding the newly acquired Gault Millau guides to press, that I was introduced to the art of food writing—and the craft of fact-checking.

If the Frommer's guides were past their prime by the time I arrived at PHT, these roadmaps for food lovers were revolutionary, though few people knew them outside of Europe.

Henri Gault and Christian Millau, French journalists who met in the 1950s, collaborated on their first guide to Paris restaurants in 1962. Joined by the more business-oriented Andre Gayot in 1969, they began publishing European restaurant directories that rivaled Michelin in prestige and savvy but that were far more irreverent. They were also more inclusive in their definition of dining excellence. Credited with coining the term "*nouvelle cuisine*," Gault Millau celebrated this lighter, more casual style of cooking and touted the pleasure of tables beyond those in France and Italy—including Asia and the US.

In the early 1980s, the publisher contracted with PHT to distribute two titles translated from the French, *The Best of Paris* and *The Best of France.* This was followed by an agreement to produce the first original Gault Millau guides to US cities, starting with New York, Los Angeles, Washington, DC, and San Francisco. The books were coordinated for Gault Millau by a Los Angeles–based freelancer, Colleen Dunn Bates, but I did much of the editing in New York.

In her mid-twenties and fresh faced, Colleen was the quintessential California girl, unpretentious and laid-back, though she took the work very seriously. She was the ideal person to teach me the mysterious ways of Gault Millau. She explained the shifting power hierarchy of the members of the Gayot family, who were all involved in the books' production. She also helped familiarize me with the vocabulary of fine dining—in the kindest possible way.

Even though I was a decade older than Colleen and a native New Yorker, I couldn't hold a candle to her restaurant sophistication. I had not been able to afford to dine at nice places, and I hated to cook. But what I lacked in discernment, I made up for in enthusiasm. Food was not only a passion for me; it was a form of rebellion.

My parents didn't strictly follow all the Jewish dietary rules—we didn't have two sets of dishes, for example—but they eschewed pork and shellfish and didn't mix milk and meat in a single meal. This was par for the course for most of the Brooklyn Jews I grew up with.

But there was a way our family differed from many others I knew: We never went out to eat.

Finances were one reason, yes. But I don't think we were much—if at all—poorer than the families of friends who "went out for Chinese" once a week, even though they kept kosher at home. (This works on the same principle as "Whatever you eat while you are standing at the kitchen counter doesn't have any calories.")

My parents' rationale was more tribal: You couldn't be sure what they put in the food. By "they" I don't mean *goyim*. We didn't go out for kosher deli either. I always got the sense that eating out was dangerous, potentially detrimental to my health.

Everything changed in the sixth grade, when I met Julie Schwartz. Julie was not only pretty and well dressed, but she was exotic. For one thing, she was a twin. For another, she had a mother unlike the mothers of all my other friends. Mrs. Schwartz was stylish, a Jewish Audrey Hepburn (okay, maybe not so thin; let's say Liz Taylor). Even more shocking, she was a divorcee in an era of marriage-as-sacred sitcoms.

I was flattered that Julie wanted to be my friend. And when she invited me to lunch at the Italian restaurant owned by her mother's boyfriend—her mother had a boyfriend! he wasn't Jewish!—there was no way I was going to turn down that invitation.

My mother, reluctantly, gave me permission to go, even though she had not met the dubious-because-divorced Mrs. Schwartz, who was leading me into the foreign land of Food Prepared by Strangers.

I was both excited and terrified when I found myself seated in what must have been a standard Brooklyn Italian restaurant, staring at a menu that could have been in Mandarin for all I could decipher of it. I had no idea what to order.

Mrs. Schwartz must have seen my discomfort—she was kind as well as sophisticated—so she offered to choose for me. I gratefully accepted.

Then I heard her say to the waiter, "Veal parmigiana."

I didn't know much about Italian food, but I knew two things: Veal is meat and parmigiana is cheese. And I wasn't supposed to be eating them together.

I was in a panic, questions flooding in. Was it going to taste horrible? Would I be able to finish the dish without throwing up and humiliating myself? Or was I going to be sick later that afternoon and have to confess what I had eaten to my mother so she could administer a cure? Would I then have to listen to endless "I told you so's" about the dangers of eating out?

You already know how this ends. The veal parmigiana was delicious, far tastier than any of the bland fare produced by my mother, who was strictly a duty cook. I arrived home from lunch feeling full but far from sick.

My parents had deceived me.

I was desperate to make up for lost time. As soon as I could afford to go out with my friends, I indulged in all manner of forbidden foods: stealth cheeseburgers, on-the-sly shrimp cocktails, covert Cobb salads with bacon.... After I began to travel abroad, my tastes became more eclectic and more openly *traif*. Still, my graduate school and entry-level publishing budgets didn't permit dipping into anything that could be termed cuisine, either nouvelle or haute.

Enter the Gault Millau guides.

If my veal parmigiana epiphany sparked my culinary interests, the Gault Millau guides fanned the flames. They expanded my literary horizons, too. As with travel, I hadn't thought of food as a topic worthy of serious consideration. But these guides were not only entertaining; they also drew upon a deep well of knowledge about all things culinary, from the history of individual dishes to the chefs' former venues.

And they were extremely accurate.

Because of a libel suit brought against the company in the early 1980s by the owner of Mr. Chow, an Upper East Side Chinese restaurant in Manhattan, Gault Millau was fastidious about the content of its reviews.

The initial jury verdict against the company was overturned in appeal, the judges unanimously ruling that expressions of opinion are constitutionally protected and citing a lack of malice, but no one at Gault Millau wanted to go through the stress and expense of another court case.

As Colleen recalls, "Gault Millau did not back down on being funny and critical, but we did have rules. Basically it's fine to give impressions and mocking metaphors, but the facts had to be scrupulously correct." It was okay, for example, to say that a restaurant "smells like a school of fish died here last week," but not to assert "the restaurant serves week-old fish."

I don't usually pine for the good old days, but I do miss the pre-*Yelp* era.

Some authors were better at following the rules than others. Among those who mastered the lawsuit-avoiding lingo was Phyllis Richman, the *Washington Post's* restaurant columnist and the main dining contributor to Gault Millau's *Best of Washington, DC*. Her reviews were clever and clean—that is, in need of virtually no editing—and they always arrived punctually. Phyllis herself was a delight to work with, down-to-earth and friendly. I didn't think in those terms at the time, but Phyllis became my yardstick for the consummate professional writer, someone with a distinct voice and style who also understood the value of deadlines.

Edward Guiliano, the dining writer for the New York book, was not nearly as congenial a work partner.

No question, Edward knew the local restaurant scene. Darkly handsome and stylish, he went everywhere that was anywhere, a consequence of being married to Mireille Guiliano, spokeswoman for Champagne Veuve Clicquot; she later became President and CEO of Clicquot Inc. and wrote the best-selling *Frenchwomen Don't Get Fat*. Edward loved to talk about all the trendy spots he frequented, and especially about how his home away from home was Le Cirque, at its peak of popularity then. It was the top-rated restaurant in Gault Millau's New York book.

I liked Edward, in spite of his cavalier attitudes toward deadlines and his tendency to treat me like the help; he just assumed that it was my job, not his, to craft reviews out of his haphazardly presented observations. When, after much delay, the New York book was finally sent to press, Edward suggested that we go to celebrate at any place I liked.

I chose Le Cirque.

In addition to wanting to dine at the best restaurant in New York, I admit that I also I wanted to see if Edward was really as cozy as he claimed with Le Cirque owner Sirio Maccioni, chef Daniel Boulud, and all the other *culinarati.*

Edward seemed surprised at my request—he probably expected me to suggest someplace a bit more modest—but he agreed with good grace. And when we got to Le Cirque, everyone did indeed know Edward.

But I don't think that's why I was treated as well as I was. One of the reasons that Le Cirque garnered all the accolades it did was its wonderful service. No matter that I wouldn't have recognized a fish knife had it swam across a finger bowl and hooked a Spanish anchovy; I was tended to, not condescended to, by the staff. The ability to make the most unsophisticated customer feel treasured became the standard for all my future evaluations of service, even—especially—in big cities like New York, and even in these more casual times.

I don't recall what I ate but I know the food was superb too, beautifully presented and perfectly prepared. I had a wonderful evening, the best introduction to the world of haute cuisine I could have hoped for.

But for sheer surprise and delight, that dinner at Le Cirque couldn't hold a candle to my first forbidden plate of veal parmigiana at a red-sauce Brooklyn Italian restaurant.

🐪 🐪 🐪

Over two years, I moved up the ranks from associate editor to senior editor. I didn't have the proverbial corner office, but my workspace was large and airy. Gracie no longer tormented me and, as the travel department expanded, Jaclyn hired several congenial new editors.

But, predictably, I grew tired of editing books on exotic locales that I could only visit on my own time—and my own dime.

Though I'd abandoned my Francophile fantasies after working with the Gayots for a while, I'd gotten into the half-joking habit of asking representatives of other overseas publishers that PHT distributed if they needed an on-site American editor.

To my surprise, one of them said "yes."

It was Rough Guides, a fledgling London company whose travel books were just taking off in Europe. The first one, a guide to Greece, had been published six years earlier, in 1982.

It helped that I had an in. Ethan Williams, one of the Rough Guides' founders, had dated a friend from graduate school, Renee. Renee knew that the company was looking for a US distributor.

In turn, I knew that Jaclyn was seeking a youth-oriented series to compete with Harvard University's bestselling "Let's Go" line. With their sections on traveling with kids, suggested itineraries, and discount travel club, the Frommer's guides were cost-conscious but no longer adventurous.

In a bit of corporate matchmaking, Renee told Ethan that she had a friend at PHT; I told Jaclyn I had an in at Rough Guides.

Sure enough, they were attracted to each other, though not without reservations.

The powers-that-be at PHT wanted to change the series name. They didn't think an American audience would understand that a "rough guide" refers to a sketch or overview, or that roughing it was a good thing to the target demographic.

I wish I had kept a list of all the odd contenders for the Rough Guides' rechristening. All I have is a lousy tee shirt that reads:

Don't Just Say
"Let's Go..."

Demand
THE REAL EUROPE!

THE REAL GUIDE
PRENTICE HALL
SIMON & SCHUSTER, A PARAMOUNT
COMMUNICATIONS COMPANY

That's a lot of words to put on even a well-endowed chest.

Unfortunately, this was at least a decade before terms like "virtual reality" and "reality TV" became pop-culture staples and before the phrase "get real" might have been used successfully as a slogan. At the end of the 1980s, metaphysics wasn't hip—and neither were the Real Guides. The debut of the first eight Real Guides caused barely a ripple in the sea of guidebook sales, and the distribution deal was severed shortly thereafter. There's no mention of the series in Wikipedia's history of the Rough Guides, now part of the Penguin group.

But that was all to come.

I hadn't been in on any of the meetings that the PHT mucky-mucks held to hammer out the distribution deal, but Renee and I were invited to the celebratory dinner thrown at an Upper West Side Chinese restaurant by Ethan and his partners. Several Tsing Tao beers into the evening, I posed the inevitable question: "I don't suppose you need an American editor?"

"Hmm," Ethan mused, "we might do. Prentice Hall wants us to orientate the books to the US market. You could translate from British into American English for us." A job overseas that required only that I be single-lingual, a mistress of the American idiom, fluent in my native tongue...I was not only eager and willing, but supremely qualified.

CHAPTER 4

THE (REALLY) ROUGH GUIDES
London, 1988–89

Be careful what you wish for, especially out loud in front of someone who can make it happen. Suddenly, I was moving to London to work for a travel publisher I'd barely heard of a few months earlier. I sublet my apartment, got an expedited work visa, and went on a crash diet. The era of mini-skirts might have long passed, but images of Twiggy, the 1960s British poster girl for anorexia, were seared in my brain.

Some six weeks after I made my half-joking remarks to the directors of Rough Guides, I arrived at Heathrow with a vaguely defined job and no place to live.

Ethan, the only one of the company's four directors I semi-knew, had invited me to stay with him and his wife, Ivy, until I found a flat. On the far side of thirty, I felt a bit old to be crashing on someone's couch. On the other hand, I'd been around long enough to know that adventures never seem to come with firm mattresses.

Ivy was a pre-Raphaelite–style beauty, with thick, curly auburn hair, large green eyes, and pale, translucent skin. That's where the ethereal part ended. Far from delicate or angelic, Ivy was brusque and acerbic—at least toward me. I couldn't really blame her. I was going to be working with her husband and was friends with one of his exes. I wouldn't have been thrilled to host me, either.

I tried to keep a low profile.

For the first few evenings, I turned down invitations to go out with Ivy and Ethan, pleading jet lag. On the fourth night, however, when they asked me along to a friend's dinner party, I agreed. I'd been eager to come to London. It was absurd to keep hiding.

A dozen young up-and-comers were already gathered in a shabby-chic flat in shabby-chic Islington by the time we arrived at 9 p.m. The host, Nick, who had gone to university with Ivy, had angular, intellectual good looks, but this didn't seem to be the source of his extreme self-regard. That appeared to derive primarily from his job as an assistant producer of news at BBC-TV. He acknowledged my presence—barely. Then he and the rest of the tight-knit crew went back to talking about people and places I didn't know. So much for the good manners I'd seen on *Upstairs Downstairs,* my other key point of cultural reference besides "England Swings Like a Pendulum Do."

Having nothing to contribute to the conversation, no points of entry for me to ask questions, I only half listened. I vaguely heard the meandering chatter turn to dances and balls and then—Nick suddenly remembering me—to senior proms. He honed in like a laser. "Edie, you're an American," Nick said, as though I were a rare anthropological specimen on the order of a Tunisian snake charmer. "You must have had a high school prom. Did you go? Did you wear a pretty, frilly dress? Was it loads of fun?"

Nick's tone was so condescending and I was so irritated at having sat for so long, ignored, that something in me—my common sense—snapped. "Yes," I hissed, "I went and my dress was pretty, but I didn't have much fun. I spent most of the time puking in the bathroom because I was pregnant."

Rule to live by: Count to ten in your head when you are put on the spot and feeling upset, even if you are asked a direct question. There's a good chance that the subject will have changed by the time you are ready with a more temperate answer.

The room went silent.

"Oh," Nick finally said. "So how old is your child now?"

"Uh, I d-didn't have it," I stammered.

And so, out of nervousness and to fill the continuing awkward silence, I spilled one of my most closely held secrets to a room full of strangers: that I'd had an illegal abortion. Even my sister, who had been away working as a summer camp counselor, didn't know.

Mine was a typical story in many ways. Ignorant about the workings of the human reproductive system—my mother could barely bring herself to talk to me about menstruation—I'd gotten pregnant the first time I ever had sex, when I was sixteen and before Roe v. Wade was the law of the land.

You've probably read about girls who claimed they didn't know they were pregnant until they give birth in a bathroom stall. You've probably thought they were either lying or very stupid. I didn't reach the bathroom-stall stage of denial, but I'm here to tell you that you can be in high school honors classes and still be extremely clueless about certain things. If you're not sharp enough to know that you can get pregnant even if you haven't had an orgasm, you might not recognize the signs of pregnancy, for example. I had a sneaking suspicion about what might be causing me to throw up, but decided that since I was also upchucking in the evening, it couldn't possibly be morning sickness.

It took a trip to a physician, at my mother's insistence—her poor child had a mystery malady—to learn the truth. The doctor was very kind. He took me aside and asked if

I was sexually active. His next question was, "Should I tell her or will you?"

I bit the bullet.

All the sympathy my mother had for me instantly evaporated. She had sprung for a cab to the doctor's office. Almost the first thing she said when I disclosed the diagnosis: "We're taking the subway home."

Although my father was equally furious, we were all in agreement that I shouldn't marry my cute but doofy boyfriend, who would have been happy to tie the knot, or become a single teenage mother. Abortion was far less of a sin in my family's interpretation of Jewish tradition than not going to college.

I left out these details to the now-rapt room, picking up at the part where my mother, father, and I decamped to Puerto Rico. Even if we had wanted to go to a back-alley hack, we had no idea how to find one. My father had heard that we could have the procedure done safely in San Juan.

When we arrived, he asked the desk clerk at the Holiday Inn where a girl "in trouble" could go. We were directed to a simple but clean women's hospital with an extremely professional, nonjudgmental staff.

"Well, that was all right then," Ivy piped up, brightly. "You're a Jewish American Princess, aren't you?"

Just when I thought things couldn't get any worse.

Jewish American Princesses (JAPs) are stereotypically acquisitive, selfish, and privileged. The only thing deeper than my shame over hurting my Holocaust refugee parents and putting their university dreams for me into jeopardy was my guilt that they'd had to dip into their paltry savings for that Puerto Rico misadventure.

Now, much too late, I was speechless.

Fortunately, Ethan intervened. "I don't think you know what 'Jewish American Princess' means, Ivy," he chided. "Edie isn't one."

Somehow, the evening ended. But I spent the night tossing on Ivy and Ethan's lumpy couch, trying to come up with a plausible but non-humiliating excuse for returning to New York by the end of the week. I couldn't possibly stick out the year of my Rough Guides work permit.

The next morning, Ivy apologized profusely—for Nick, for her remark, for not being more generally welcoming. She was almost as distraught as I was. I accepted the apology, which marked the start of what would become a nice friendship. Its more immediate effect was to keep me from fleeing London instantly.

🐫 🐫 🐫

Still, I was eager to spread out my belongings in a place of my own. Two days later, I rented the first furnished flat I could afford on my salary of £12,000 a year. I was shocked at the cost of living in London; it was higher than that in New York, where I'd been making $26,000 a year at Prentice Hall. Because the pound was worth more than twice the dollar at that time, I'd assumed that my buying power would about match it in London. Economics was not my strongest subject.

More than half of my £1,000-a-month paycheck, £650 a month, procured me a one-bedroom flat on the first floor of a brownstone in the dreary north London suburb of Kentish Town. It was large, but the furnishings were worn and very 1970s: lots of avocado, orange, and brown, soiled linoleum, and shag carpeting. The layout was bizarre. The bedroom was on one side of the public entry hallway, the living room, kitchen, and bath on the other. And when I say bath, I use the term loosely. One room contained the sink and bathtub—sans shower, an American indulgence, I learned—while the toilet got its own separate space. This seemed particularly ill conceived in a country where pub crawling was a national sport. Wouldn't drunks be prone to messy peeing accidents?

There was no central heating, just a couple of space heaters, one of them sporting simulated flames. If I had been on LSD, it might have been riveting. Sadly, I was not. Worst of all, in order to get electricity, you had to insert two-pence coins into a meter in the hallway. You could either remember to keep a large supply of clunky currency on hand, or freeze your ass off in the dark.

The flat did have another advantage besides its relative inexpensiveness: It offered direct, if lengthy, access via the Underground's gloomy Northern line to the Rough Guides offices in Kennington. Yes, that's Kennington, not Kensington, which it was definitely a far cry from. The south London suburb was as characterless as Kensington was "twee"—the British term I learned to change to "nauseatingly charming" or "precious" whenever it turned up in a Rough Guide.

I began taking that ride three days later when, still unsettled in every sense of the term, I finally reported to work.

I was reintroduced to the cast of characters, the other three Rough Guides directors besides Ethan.

One large office was the domain of James Tauff and Clyde Lawson. Soft-spoken, pale, and curly haired, with delicate features, James looked and sounded more like a poet than the founder of a travel publishing company. Clyde, in contrast, was tall and stolid. I hadn't seen either of them since the fateful Chinese dinner in New York, and leaned in to hug James hello. Oops—too American. He held me off with a fishy handshake.

I waved hi to Clyde, foregoing any further attempts at physical contact.

Ethan shared the small but still roomy workspace in the back with Lewis Blake. Lewis, slightly built and with a thatch of dark hair, got up and, putting an arm around my shoulder, drew me in. "Nice to see you again," he said.

I soon discovered that the directors' greeting styles were far from the only things that divided the Fab Four. James and Clyde were middle-class, a term for which there's no exact equivalent in the US; it's several steps below royal, several steps above soccer hooligan. Ethan and Lewis were solidly working-class, and had attended schools that were not as posh as those that James and Clyde had gone to.

I'd been led to believe that, at Rough Guides, differences in class didn't matter. In fact, they were a source of strain between alpha males James and Ethan, who were each striving hard to be more equal than the other.

🐪 🐪 🐪

It was becoming head-smackingly clear that I hadn't really thought this move through.

In my quest for adventure, I'd lost sight yet again of my other goal: becoming a writer. No part of this job involved me putting words on paper, except red-pencilled corrections. Worse, I'd relinquished all my other ego-sustaining identities: respected editor, PhD, close friend, daughter...even New York Jew.

Nor did I have anyone to turn to for solace. In this era before email and Skype, phone calls to the states were prohibitively expensive. Besides, everyone envied me my glamorous overseas job. I didn't want to sound like an ingrate.

I was spending more and more time at the office, and not just to avoid my cold, creepy flat. Americanizing/Americanising the Rough Guides was more of a challenge than I'd anticipated. I thought I was just going to be changing "labour" to "labor," distinguishing between phrases like "getting pissed" (getting drunk) and "piss off" (fuck off). But I soon discovered that the cultural gulf, reflected in the guides, was as deep as the ocean that separated our countries.

Take a typical Tuesday a few weeks after I started.

Arriving at the office after a long Underground ride, I wanted nothing more than to settle in with a cup of coffee. London didn't have coffee trucks on every other corner like Manhattan did, and the Rough Guides kitchen didn't provide a coffeemaker, but its electric kettle and instant brew met my need for heat and caffeine. I'd quickly discovered, however, that it was considered impolite to head back to your desk from the kitchen, clutching your own cup. Instead, you were required to walk around asking if anyone else in the surrounding offices wanted something to drink and deliver it to them if the answer was yes.

It was like being a waitress, only without the hope of tips.

I wasn't in the mood to talk to anyone so I ducked, coffeeless, into my office, hoping someone else would get thirsty soon.

I was just about to dip into the manuscript of the France guide, the first book slated for conversion, when I realized it wasn't on floppy disk. I had the original. Before I started red penciling, I needed to photocopy it.

Personally.

Forget editorial assistants. Everyone in the office was expected to do his or her own scut work. I'd somehow landed at the publishing equivalent of China during the Cultural Revolution, sending intellectuals to work in the rice paddies.

I headed for the hall photocopier, a model that had been discontinued in the US a decade earlier in favor of those with automatic feeds. As I stood mindlessly turning over page after page—about 400 of them—for the next half hour or so, I contemplated the company's leftier-than-thou attitude. What was the connection between publishing budget travel books and contributing to the greater good of mankind?

The claim to be classless was itself dubious, based as it was on the fact that four twenty-somethings with different backgrounds had managed to bond on a Greek island. Nor was the company, founded in the early 1980s, plowing any new ground. It touted its honest opinions, budget orientation, and erudition—but that made it different from Lonely Planet, founded ten years earlier, how? Still, I gave the lads credit for symbolism. Greece was the perfect place for the myth of the Rough Guides to be created.

Finally, the duplicate was finished. I headed back to my office, twin manuscripts bundled against my chest.

I had barely sat down to read when Poppy strolled in.

I had only met her once before, on my first day, but wasn't particularly surprised to see her. Assorted authors dropped in every day to gape at *Editora americanus*. Closing my cage door to keep them out would have been considered rude.

Poppy giggled, "You're Americanising the Rough Guides. Does that mean you're going to be putting the word 'cute' in a lot?"

Ah, a new variation on the "Americans are dim" theme that ran through these visits. How clever. Lank-haired and snaggle-toothed Poppy didn't look like she was prepared to perform brain surgery, but she clearly believed that birth in an English hospital came with a certificate of superiority. "Yes," I replied. "I brought over software that does a search and replace and changes every third adjective to 'cute.' Now bugger off and leave me to it."

Okay, I didn't actually say that; I didn't even think of the search-and-replace rejoinder until I was in bed, where I replayed the scene in my head as part of the "what have I done" reel that I had begun to run nightly. Now, I just smiled sweetly. I didn't want the Brits to think that, in addition to being dim, Americans were also thin-skinned.

Was I ever going to get any of the France manuscript edited? Ralph, one of the guide's two authors, was coming in that afternoon to get my feedback. It was approaching noon, and I still hadn't had a chance to look at it.

Then Fiona, the office administrator, stuck her head in. "We're going to lunch," she announced. "Would you like to come?"

Hell yes.

Because Fiona was Irish, anti-Americanism was not her default attitude, and she was naturally outgoing and welcoming. Lunch was also one of the few communal activities I didn't mind, since it involved an outing to the local pub. The grub was good and English offices had not yet gotten the memo that you weren't supposed to drink at midday. I usually downed at least a half-pint of bitter, a pale ale that quickly became my favorite brew. In the US, I hadn't especially liked beer; here I was a born-again suds swiller.

The cast of characters changed daily, depending on which freelancers turned up and how busy everyone was. Today, it was just the regulars: James, Clyde, Fiona, and Dylan, an author with an acerbic sense of humor who was upgrading the office computer system. I suspected he and Fiona were having it off (screwing) but no one confirmed that for me. Sex wasn't ever discussed at Rough Guides.

I returned to the office somewhat more optimistic because slightly drunk. Finally, I plunged into the manuscript of *France: The Rough Guide*.

Instant buzzkill.

Bad sentence structure, incorrect spelling, faulty grammar—those, I could easily correct. But the book had a more basic problem that I hadn't encountered in the US: Socialists-with-Money Syndrome. Symptoms included renunciation of all trappings of wealth (although not necessarily wealth itself), glorification of revolution in every form, and knee-jerk dismissal of anything considered bourgeois, such as royalty or religion.

So, for example, in this book's Paris chapter, the Bastille listing was endless, while the palace at Versailles was dismissed as a "galloping excrescence." Sacré-Coeur cathedral was written off as a "carbuncle on the face of Paris."

I pared down the description of the prison, a paean to armed insurrection, and put question marks next to the Versailles and Sacré-Coeur epithets. I hadn't yet decided whether to delete them, but thought I'd try to discuss with Ralph why an American audience might want these easy dismissals of prime tourist sights to be backed up with facts. Should visitors skip them only because the author disapproved of their past-tense politics—or were they overcrowded and, in the case of Versailles, overpriced?

About an hour after I started editing, Ralph charged in and parked himself behind me. He was tall and tawny haired, with a patrician air, though he was wearing the standard Rough Guides uniform of worn jeans and ratty T-shirt. I didn't care for his permission-free, over-the-shoulder scrutiny, but at least today Ralph wasn't with his co-author, Lucinda, and her huge, hairless yellow dog. The previous Friday, when they'd all piled into my tiny office to drop off the manuscript, I'd felt extremely claustrophobic.

Ralph, who'd obviously expected me to be dazzled by the book's wit and erudition, was livid when he saw the mass of markings I'd made on every page. I tactfully tried to explain my comments and cuts, but he wasn't having any of it.

"Would you have edited Faulkner?" he raged, doubtless proud of his allusion to an author I might conceivably have heard of, since he was a compatriot.

"Yes," I countered, "I probably would have, if he had been hired to write a guidebook to Yoknapatawpha County." And I actually said this to Ralph himself, not to his imaginary nighttime manifestation.

🐫 🐫 🐫

I suspect all this would have been bearable if I had been able to turn to a tried-and-true way to relieve stress: Sex. Even if it wasn't discussed at the office, I was certain people all over the country were shagging—a term that I would have had to translate in this pre–Austin Powers era, were it to appear in any guides. Which was doubtful.

I'm no femme fatale, but I have large breasts—which, I've often been told by members of both genders, is a key asset, along with willingness. I hadn't wanted for lovers since I'd gotten divorced.

In London, however, I was bombing out.

I wasn't lacking access to men. Most of the Rough Guides authors were of the male persuasion, and some were about my age or older. Why had none of them evinced the slightest interest in sleeping with me? My accent? Maybe Brits weren't as turned on by broad inflections as Yanks were by clipped tones.

Or could it have been my ever-increasing girth?

That's another thing I didn't understand. The British could rule an empire, but managed to mangle even simple meals like breakfast. Eggs at a typical "caf" always arrived floating in grease and accompanied by soggy bacon, sawdust-filled sausage, broiled tomatoes—the only "veg" on the English diet, as far as I could tell—and slices of burnt white toast arrayed in racks that seemed designed to render them instantly frigid. Every time I'd order a so-called salad in a casual restaurant, it would turn out to involve diced processed meat and mayonnaise. The only thing leafy or green was the occasional bit of parsley.

Why was the cooking so terrific in France, just a slim body of water away? Perhaps it was a simple translation problem: The Brits thought that the French "*dégustation*" meant "disgusting."

When the food itself wasn't gross, the terms for it were. Can you think of anything more unappealing than the question, "Would you like some clotted cream [a whipped cream-and-butter blend] on your spotted dick [steamed raisin pudding]?"

I'd been assured that some of the newer, more upscale restaurants were very good, but I couldn't afford them on my salary. And, unlike at PHT, where fine dining was celebrated in books like Gault Millau, my London workplace was downwardly mobile. I would have bet the directors had the means to spring for a nice meal, but admitting to liking the finer things in life was considered damningly bourgeois on both sides of the office's class divide.

The only thing palatable I could afford in London besides Indian food or fish and chips—which were great, but not every day—was pub grub, which I happily consumed at the daily lunches. But a pint of bitter and a Stilton-and-cheddar wedge—proudly billed as containing 80 percent milk fat—on crusty French bread weren't Weight Watchers sanctioned.

Neither were the offerings at the tearooms I occasionally frequented. I loved the full cream teas, replete with fresh-baked scones and fruity jams, but they weren't exactly slimming.

Cooking for myself was not a viable alternative, either. My stove and I weren't on close terms in New York and my long work hours and unwelcoming flat in London hadn't brought out any latent domesticity. Salads? I could find few fruits or vegetables in the supermarkets that weren't wilted. Nor could I locate any healthy takeout.

It was too cold and gray to enjoy long walks around town, and the gyms I'd looked into were drab, low-tech, and high-expense affairs.

In short, between the curries, steak-and-kidney pies, and pints of bitter—not to mention my lardass exercise habits—I was packing on the pounds.

🐫 🐫 🐫

It wasn't all bad.

Slowly, I acquired a bit of a social life. One of my new friends was Shirley Eber, author of *Israel and the Occupied Territories: The Rough Guide* (not on the initial list of books to be distributed to the US, for some reason). I'd been told by more than one Rough Guider that I would like Shirley "because she's Jewish, too."

I did like Shirley, but not because of her heritage. She was funny, smart, and one of the few single women I'd met in London. I saw Shirley after work every now and then. Ivy and I got together for a meal occasionally. Maybe once every two weeks, I went out for a beer with Lewis and Ethan.

Mostly, though I would never have predicted it, I hung out with James and his partner, Vic, a wild-haired ginger (redhead) feminist; they lived together on the ground floor of the Rough Guides brownstone. A fellow outsider in England—one half of her family was from Sri Lanka—Vic and I were natural allies. And as the co-editor of Rough Guides' *Women Travel* essays—not to mention as cohabiter with James—she had some idea of my job stresses. She also knew that opportunities to meet anyone outside of Kennington, where I spent my long, long days, were limited.

We'd progressed from small talk when we ran into each other on the second floor to discussing Vic's travel anthology; I suggested a few American women who might be interested in contributing. One day, on a whim, Vic invited me to dinner.

Possibly to our mutual surprise, we all enjoyed that evening together. I was soon freeloading meals from Vic and James a couple of times a week.

Their flat felt comfortable, with a nice, worn couch, some semi-threadbare Oriental rugs, and lots and lots of books. James, remote and standoffish in his office, changed into pointy yellow Turkish slippers downstairs, which rendered him completely unintimidating.

And all talk about Rough Guides was off limits.

Travel books rarely entered our conversation, period. Because Vic was studying psychology, we sometimes talked about the latest she'd read on cognitive therapy, meditation, or the resurgence of Freudian theory. But both James and I liked contemporary novels, so they topped our discussion list. There was this new English writer, Ian McEwan, who might interest me, James said. Would I like to borrow *The Child In Time*?

James also wanted to learn about American literary trends. Had I heard of something called "language" poetry? I had indeed. One of the key figures associated with the group was a visiting writer at the University of California, San Diego, while I was doing dissertation research there. I attempted to explain the deconstruction of the lyrical "I" to James, neglecting to mention that much of what I knew on the subject I'd learned in bed with the poet.

I was glad that the English rules of mixed-gender discourse dictated that omission. Besides, I was buoyed by James's regard for my opinions. Upstairs, in my dwarfish office, I was a dim-witted American editor. Downstairs, downing plonk (inexpensive table wine) in James and Vic's comfortable flat, I was transformed back into an intellectual with an advanced degree from a good university.

🐪 🐪 🐪

The beginning of the year even brought a promise that things might be looking up at work.

By mid-December, my attempts to turn Rough Guides into Real Guides seemed more hopeless than ever. The snarkiness of the France book was the least of my problems. Several Rough Guides were missing large chunks of information, from major tourist attractions to major cities; others were wildly inconsistent in style. There was no way I could get eight books to press in six months—or sixty—on my own. James had grudgingly agreed to consider using freelance editors, but only after I'd nagged him ceaselessly.

During these first three months, no one at PHT was aware that I was tearing my hair out in London. When Jaclyn Forrest phoned from New York to see how things were going, I usually just said, "Fine." Jaclyn hadn't been thrilled about my defection, even though I'd assured her I would still be working on PHT's behalf, just on someone else's payroll. I didn't want her to know that I regretted my decision, or have her think I couldn't handle the workload.

But one relentlessly gray December day, her call caught me right after a heated discussion about freelancers with James. Upset and stressed, I had poured out the truth—that the books were a mess, and in no shape to go to press on schedule. She had listened, asked lots of questions, and then said, "Let me see what I can do."

Jaclyn phoned the next day with good news: In mid-January, she was sending in reinforcements. Janet Lawler was heading to London to check on the Real Guides situation.

Jan, who had started at PHT about a year earlier, was perfect for the job at hand. By now I felt frazzled and irredeemably ethnic. Jan was imperturbable and irreproachably WASP. And she wasn't even American; she was a Canadian working in the US on a green card and thus had British-empire cred.

Jan was all business when she turned up at 9:30 a.m. sharp in Kennington. She made the rounds of the second-floor offices, shaking hands formally. She had only met the Rough Guide directors in passing in the Prentice Hall corridors, but even if she had dined with them, gotten dead drunk, and ended up in an orgy with all four, she wouldn't have tried to hug them hello that morning. At work, Jan was always the consummate professional.

Preliminaries dispensed with, Jan followed me into my office, sat down in the visitor's chair, and started skimming the pile of manuscripts I'd laid out for her on my desk. Her face was impassive while she read, giving nothing away. I was on tenterhooks. What if too much photocopying and too many anti-American remarks had gotten me addled? What if I had misjudged the awfulness of the manuscripts, and Jan had crossed an ocean for nothing?

Finally, after about half an hour, during which I devoted a great deal of energy to not screaming, "Well, what do you think, already?" she turned to me. "Wow, these really suck," Jan decreed.

Vindicated!

For the first time, I had an ally for the morning editorial meeting. James sat po-faced—sour and disapproving, I would have translated—during my rundown of the scheduled books. After I'd finished, he stated, in a low but steely voice, that he didn't believe the last four books were as terrible as I'd made out. Jan, equally low-toned and steely, countered that she begged to differ, based on what she'd just read in my office.

Having reached an impasse, we agreed to break for lunch.

Gradually, the pub worked its magic. Some two hours and several gallons of beer later, when we reconvened in the office, the atmosphere was far more amicable. Everyone agreed to pitch in on editing the Rough/Real Guides whenever possible. And if they were too busy and schedules started slipping again, James promised to shell out for freelancers, without putting up any resistance.

For the rest of the week, Jan and I settled in with the unedited manuscripts to figure out how to whip them into shape. We stayed late into the evening, breaking only for Indian takeout, but I didn't mind. For the first time that I could remember, my office seemed cozy, not claustrophobic.

🐫 🐫 🐫

I was sad to see Jan go after a week, but believed I finally had London life under control. Now that a firm production schedule had been established, work seemed less frustratingly nebulous. I'd worried at first that Jan's intervention had ruined my relationship James and Vic, but as far as I could tell, the firewall separating our work and social interactions was intact. James's daytime irritation hadn't bled into our evenings.

I was getting used to the English winter. The weather may have been dreary and drizzly, but it never got quite as cold or snowed as often as it did in New York.

Since London was about six months behind New York in its film distribution—oddly, not even the French imports I'd seen at home had made it here yet—I could soon look forward to viewing new movies.

Best of all, I had moved to a nice, American-style flat in St. John's Wood, a furnished sublet from a friend of a friend in California. It had all the mod-cons, including a toilet and stall shower in the same room; central heating that didn't require coins to juice it; and nice, tasteful furnishings. The rug was plush but not shag, and there was nary an orange item in sight. And because I was considered a house sitter rather than a renter, I was paying only the owner's monthly expenses. My lovely posh place was costing me less than my depressing Kentish Town digs, about £400 a month compared to £650.

Swaddled in an ill-fitting cloak of optimism, I was caught off guard by the events at lunch one day in mid-February.

It was just the core crew at the pub: James, Clyde, Fiona, Dylan, and me. I'd ordered the day's special, the spinach quiche, a dish that the kitchen did really well. The drinks, including my standard half-pint of bitter, arrived. We were waiting for the food and chatting easily when I mentioned to James that I had sent the Spain guide out to a freelancer.

He whipped around and fixed me with a glare. "You really are incompetent," he accused. "I can't believe you couldn't handle those books on your own." His tone was deeply patronizing, one a squire might use to address an estate gardener who had allowed the family's roses to die because he'd been dipping into the scotch.

And then the usually mild-mannered James began to shout at me. It was like seeing a turtle suddenly rise up and run, so startling that I couldn't focus on all the details of his tirade. He railed on about what a mistake it had been to distribute the books to the US, what an error it had been to hire me, how stupid the Real Guides title was, how Americans always overtipped and ruined everything for the English.

Some possible reasons for this outburst flashed through my head:

- All that freeloading in James's flat had finally caught up with me.
- James's father had passed along his anger about the Yanks having to come over and save British butts during World War II.
- James's middle-class instincts had kicked in and, remembering he was my boss, he'd decided I was insubordinate.
- James was yelling, in surrogate, at Ethan.
- I was, in fact, incompetent. (It was true that Real Guides was a stupid name and that Americans overtipped.)

Probably the entire pub didn't fall silent during James's rant, but it seemed to me that his was the only voice to be heard in the place. I'm certain that no one at our table said a word. Not a soul defended me, or even suggested that James calm down.

I wish I could say that I defended myself; instead, I burst into tears. Not even the imminent arrival of the excellent quiche could keep me at the table. I managed only to sob out the words, "I quit." Then I got up, walked out of the pub, and away from my dud of an overseas dream job.

CHAPTER 5

CAREENING AROUND CAIRO

Egypt, June–July 1989

"You, me, marry?" Or was that "merry"? There was a lot of gesturing going on, little English-speaking. I was fairly certain that Khalid, the nice man with the terrible teeth who had been chauffeuring me around Cairo for the past week, was requesting my hand in marriage, though I had been under the impression that he already had a wife.

I was finding Egypt a bit confusing, but also exhilarating. Which was a relief.

Yes, my London adventure in editing had been a bust. But while I'd racked up a personal worst for quitting a job— exit, sobbing—I'd never been much of an Anglophile, so I had no illusions about England to destroy.

In contrast, my expectations for my next work stint, updating *Frommer's Egypt*, were off the charts. I harbored a deep—and, at one time, forbidden—love for the Nile Kingdom.

I was a terrible Jew. This I knew even before my sixth-grade veal parmigiana epiphany led me to the wanton mingling of milk and meat. My first secret rebellion against my faith dated back to earlier Passover seders.

For the uninitiated: The seder is the interminable dinner during which the story is told of the Israelites' escape from Egypt, where our exiled kin had been forced to build the pyramids. At least that's what the Old Testament Book of Exodus tells us, not to mention Cecil B. DeMille's *The Ten*

Commandments. I later learned that scholars dispute the presence of Jews in the area, much less their role in pyramid building, which is virtually unknown in Egypt. I'll get to that.

Suffice it to say here that, according to the Passover story, the Israelites wanted out of Egypt, bad. But in mid-twentieth-century Brooklyn, one little Jewish girl very much wanted back in. At every seder, I would dutifully intone, "Let my people go" while secretly longing to return to the land of the oppressor.

I blame the Brooklyn Museum.

The cramped one-bedroom apartment where my family of four lived, on the corner of Lincoln Road and Flatbush Avenue, was in a six-story pre-War building. I vaguely remember the lobby as being dim—and vividly recall my mother's horror when I innocently asked her if I could pet the cockroach I spotted in the corner of the creaky elevator. We not only faced the traffic of Flatbush Avenue, but you could hear the elevated BMT train rattle into the Prospect Park station, less than a block away. It was a cacophony matched only by my relationship with my older sister.

My building was by no means a tenement, and this is not a tell-all about my miserable childhood. It is to say that, every other week, when my mother would walk with me to Grand Army Plaza before I was old enough to go on my own, the leafy, shaded stretch of Flatbush Avenue that passed the Prospect Park Zoo and the Brooklyn Botanical Gardens felt like a pathway to another universe. I would start to get excited when the Soldiers' and Sailors' Arch, Brooklyn's Arc de Triomphe, came into view. I didn't know its name then, or that Frederick Law Olmsted and Calvert Vaux, of Central Park fame, had designed it. Glimpsing the Arch just meant that we were getting close to the Brooklyn Public Library, where I would exchange the books I'd devoured from the previous visit for new ones. With its soaring gilded doorways, the huge Beaux Arts–style building looked every inch the sacred temple of learning that it felt like to me.

But there was more. As a special treat, every other month or so, we would walk a few blocks farther down Eastern Parkway from the library to the Brooklyn Museum.

I'm sure the serenity of the setting and the shared, sister-free time with my busy parent were part of the appeal. But I suspect the museum's high-ceiling Egyptian halls would have been intriguing under any circumstance. The busts with elegant headdresses and names like Hatshepsut—a girl pharaoh!—the imposing tombs, the clean lines of the towering statues were otherworldly, transcendent. I was transfixed by it all, except for the terrifying mummies; I would have closed my eyes when we passed them if I could have done so without tripping over my triple-E-width Buster Brown shoes.

I would stand for a long time staring at Akhenaten and Nefertiti on the Wilbour Plaque, a rare artist's slab. They were odd looking, with their elongated heads—maybe due to encephalitis, I later learned—but delicately beautiful too. Returning to the library, I scoured the card catalogues and stacks for books about the Eighteenth-Dynasty couple and about Akhetaten, the city that Akhenaten built. Especially during gloomy Brooklyn winters, his sun-worshipping brand of monotheism was far more appealing to me than that of the scolding, judgmental Yahweh.

🐫 🐫 🐫

Fast-forward a couple of decades. My passion for Egypt returned with a mummy-like vengeance when I started working at Prentice Hall Travel. Just as I used to ask foreign publishers if they needed me to work for them overseas—the habit that led to the Rough Guides debacle—I regularly tried to convince

Jaclyn Forrest that the company needed a new, more in-depth book to supplement *Frommer's Egypt*, and that I was just the person to write it. As far as I was concerned, it was impossible to have too many Egypt guides.

No new book materialized, but some six weeks after I parted ways with Rough Guides, Jaclyn asked me if I wanted to fill in for the author of *Frommer's Egypt*, who had asked to take a break from updating the guide.

There were still five months left on my work visa and, once the initial shock of the Great Pub Dressing-Down wore off, I had finally allowed myself to relax and enjoy London—or at least as much as I could relax without any visible means of income.

A trip to Egypt, the chance to write part of a book, and at a time when I was running out of money but wanted to stay overseas: There was no part of this picture I didn't like.

Except for the tight deadline. The manuscript was due in September, and this was May. I had to plan and execute a research trip and revise the guide in four months. I may have visited the Temple of Dendur at the Metropolitan Museum, but I had no idea where in Egypt Dendur was, or if it even existed in the modern world.

Ironically, Rough Guides led me to the ideal person to help with an assignment made possible by my departure from the company: Shirley Eber, of "you'd-like-Shirley-she's-Jewish-too" fame. Leaving the job hadn't put a damper on our friendship; rather, it gave me more time to spend with her. The author of *Israel and the Occupied Territories*, Shirley spoke no Hebrew but was fluent in Arabic. She had taught English in Cairo and had translated several works by Nawaal El Saadawi, one of Egypt's best-known activists/writers. Since her Rough Guide was devoted to Israel, not Egypt, working for Frommer's posed no conflict of interest.

Shirley was happy to sign on as my research associate.

With the assistance of the London branch of EGAPT, the Egyptian tourist office, we hammered out an itinerary: Shirley and I would spend the first few days together in Cairo and then go our separate ways. She would head for the more remote areas like the Suez Canal cities, Hurghada, and Sharm-el-Sheikh, where knowing Arabic would be useful. I would stay in Cairo and, after two weeks, we would regroup to travel south together.

🐪 🐪 🐪

Cairo was as frenetic as I'd imagined it would be, but it wasn't culture shock. Along with London and my hometown, New York, I had some of the world's largest cities under my belt, including New Delhi and Mexico City. I was also Middle East savvy. Having spent time in Morocco, Tunisia, and Israel, I didn't feel threatened by the surging throngs, and was accustomed to the odd mix of pushiness and ceremoniousness. In fact, though my heritage was Eastern European Jewish on both sides, something about the Middle East felt deeply familiar to me.

Still, being a tourist in these countries and working there were entirely different animals. After Shirley left, I was glad to be taken under the wing of the EGAPT representative assigned to me: Talia El Dahab, a stylishly dressed but down-to-earth woman in her mid-thirties. Luckily, I didn't learn until later that she was the wife of a general in the Egyptian army. Given my newbie anxiety and my over-inflated sense of responsibility, I would have been terrified to think that I was representing the US and all its travel writers to someone so influential.

EGAPT's London office had sent over an advance wish list of things I wanted to see and do, and when Talia and I met over lunch, she presented me with a plan. I would visit the tourist sites on my own, she said, though she would arrange for free admission and introductions to on-site representatives. Khalid, a driver who worked for EGAPT, would take Talia and me around to hotels and restaurants together.

That seemed like an excellent plan—until it got put into play.

My idea was to visit seven or eight hotels a day in all price categories; I would do a quick walk-through, exploring the public areas and peering into several rooms. Talia had made it clear up front that she disapproved of tourists staying in places the government rated with fewer than four out of five stars. I figured I'd cover the less expensive places on my own.

But when we arrived at the hotels on Talia's itinerary— all links in fancy international chains like Hilton, InterContinental, Meridien, Sheraton, Marriott, and Oberoi— I learned there was no such thing as a zippy in-and-out with her. There were people to meet, rituals to observe. We were required to sit and drink coffee and chat with the director of sales or the manager or the owner—I was never quite sure of their roles, but someone important—before a hotel tour could commence. Or, rather, Talia and the VIP would chat, in Arabic; I would drink coffee and smoke the Cleopatra cigarettes that were always offered.

I know there were other brands in Egypt, but I can't recall ever seeing anyone smoke them. The inexpensive Cleopatras were the remnants of a once-thriving local cigarette industry. Exported Egyptian cigarettes used to be so popular in Europe and the US that they inspired counterfeits like Camels, established in 1913. In their heyday, Egyptian cigarettes were made with Turkish tobacco, but by the time I encountered them, Cleopatras were fairly low quality. I returned to London with my teeth stained brown, thus fitting in with the dentally challenged Brits.

Nor were the hotel tours themselves, when we finally got to them, what I'd planned on. I was shown mostly presidential suites and conference rooms, nothing that would interest the typical Frommer's reader. I didn't need or want to look at these accommodations, but didn't know how to say so, or how to insist on seeing a standard room instead, though I tried.

There were also detours to drop off Talia's six-year-old daughter for ballet lessons and to pick her up.

By the end of the third day, I had checked out maybe seven hotels, total. As I sat in the car next to Talia en route back to my hotel, shaking with caffeine and frustration, I steeled myself to confront her. I had a job to do and it wasn't getting done. As an editor, I had been very judgmental about lazy writers. Now here I was, failing miserably at my first assignment.

Buck up, I told myself: You're a professional. I vowed that, before Khalid dropped me off at my hotel, I would let Talia know, nicely but firmly, that things would have to change.

Instead, as soon as I opened my mouth, I burst out crying.

Talia was shocked—and almost as dismayed as I was. I later learned that I was the first writer who had been placed in her care. Weeping was not on her list of likely journalist behaviors. When she finally calmed me down enough so that I could explain what I was so upset about, she soothed me in quiet, lilting tones, as she would a child. "You can do everything you need to do," she said. "Please don't worry."

And that was the start of a beautiful friendship between a nice Jewish girl from Brooklyn and a general's wife from the Egyptian countryside.

Talia understood that it had been rude to exclude me from conversations with the hotel VIPs and, while trying to show me Egypt's best face, to ignore my research needs. I in turn vowed to try to adjust to Egypt's *bukra, inshallah* (tomorrow, God willing) culture.

And so we agreed I would look at hotels as well as sights on my own, incognito, and that we would visit restaurants, shops, and markets together. Talia still used the official tourism car to drop her daughter off at ballet class, but I no longer minded. She was a cute kid and I was happy to help her practice her English.

🐪 🐪 🐪

After that rocky start, I got into a smoother research rhythm, though it was hardly bump free.

I hadn't expected Cairo to bear any relation to the sepia-toned prints of the historic books I used to pore over, but I pictured the contemporary city as being, well, more contemporary. Take the famed Egyptian Museum, home to the world's largest collection of Pharaonic antiquities. I'd imagined it would look like the Brooklyn and Metropolitan museums, only entirely dedicated to Egyptiana.

Based on that notion, I devised a plan. With only a single morning to devote to a visit and knowing it was impossible to do the place justice, I decided to hone in on the greatest hits, including the treasures of Tutankhamen's tomb. I'd lined up to see the exhibition at the Met when the boy king made his first blockbuster world tour in 1978. The idea of not having to file past the gilded mask with impatient crowds at my back was very appealing.

I picked up a tattered museum catalog at the front desk and attempted to follow the outlined route. Hmm. I couldn't find numbers on several of the rooms. I next tried to navigate via the main attractions—to no avail. At first, I blamed my wretched sense of direction, but I eventually recognized that many items were not where they were supposed to be, including Tut. I suspected he'd been moved from his original spot after he went on the road, and the museum guide hadn't been revised to reflect that fact.

When I finally located Tut, I was underwhelmed. The room was a higgledy-piggledy jumble of what looked like unrelated artifacts. Missing were the dramatic lighting, the immaculate glass cases, the bold-faced explanatory text...even the gold looked less shiny than I remembered it appearing in Manhattan.

In contrast, the Coptic Museum, which had undergone a major renovation the year before I visited, was everything I'd come to expect in a modern institution, down to the immaculate bathrooms. Financed by the city's then-thriving Christian community and highlighting its history, the museum was quiet, spacious, and low lit. It was a fitting showcase for the items I was most looking forward to seeing: the Nag Hammadi scrolls, discovered in Upper Egypt in 1945. I'd read about them in Elaine Pagels' *The Gnostic Gospels*, a book that thrilled me almost as much as the stories of the pharaohs had earlier, though in a more intellectual way. Before reading it, I'd never thought of organized religion as anything but strict and authoritarian. Pagels demonstrated how early Christianity, as disclosed in the gospels that didn't make it into the New Testament, was communal and egalitarian. Over several centuries, male priests established worshipping hierarchies and systematically excluded women from power.

And no, dear Jews for Jesus, do not take my feminist interest in the roots of Christianity as an invitation to contact me.

But I didn't conduct all my historical research indoors. One of the more memorable days of my Cairo stay was visiting the great pyramid complex at Giza—and not just because I got a marriage proposal en route.

Although I usually only saw Khalid when I was with Talia, one day she didn't need him for any other tourism duties, so she offered me his car services. I didn't mind getting around the city on my own—taxis were cheap and easy to hail—but it was nice not to have to think about finding one multiple times.

Khalid had been a friendly presence in the front seat for the first week, talking rapid-fire in Arabic with Talia but often turning around to us and smiling—thus revealing teeth that looked brown with decay, or maybe a lifetime of smoking Cleopatras. On the day that he came to pick me up without Talia, I impulsively got into the front seat of the aging, exhaust-spewing vehicle. I was an egalitarian American. I wanted to get to know the man behind the wheel and to learn a few words of Arabic.

Khalid seemed a bit surprised, but pleased and enthusiastic about the lesson. We did a lot of pointing at objects, identifying them in two languages.

And then he proposed. I think. Khalid's gestures were not lewd or suggestive. Nor were they especially romantic. Residence in the United States as my husband seemed to be his goal; the word "America" kept turning up. It wasn't much of a stretch to convey incomprehension, however, and Khalid didn't insist. He was a kind, polite man—who doubtless didn't want to lose his job with EGAPT.

The proposal, if it was a proposal, occurred during one of the constant stops we made en route to Giza. Cairo traffic was unlike any I'd experienced before or since; a line from Yeats kept flitting through my head: "Mere anarchy is loosed upon the world." Few drivers seemed to be waiting for lights to change; rather, the challenge was to slot your car into a lane that was moving in a desired direction. I would have been terrified if our speed had ever gone above ten miles an hour.

I kept waiting for the logjam of cars to thin out before we approached Giza, but it never did. Photographs make the necropolis look like it's in the middle of the desert—and of course it once was. Now, however, Giza is a suburb of Cairo, with the pyramids fringing its outskirts. Picture the Seventh Wonder of the Ancient World at the edge of Queens.

That didn't detract from the impact of viewing it in the direction of the limestone bluff on which the pyramids sit—or from my excitement at seeing camels, adorned in colorful, ornate saddles, clustered around the imposing structures.

That was another piece of the puzzle of my strange sense of kinship with the Middle East: I am a sucker for camels.

From the moment I looked into a pair of mischievous, long-lashed eyes in a crowded Tunis market, I was hooked. There was something about their unlikely shape, their ungainly gait, and their innate dignity that spoke to me. After years of ogling them from afar, and especially in zoos, I was thrilled to learn that I could ride a camel at the pyramids. Talk about a twofer.

The camels were standing placidly, chewing, looking bored, as I approached. The camel drivers next to them were not nearly as passive. A tourist actually seeking out a camel ride must have been a rarity. A group of men descended on me, pleading, "Lady, you ride my camel, she is most beautiful and gentle. For you, not expensive."

Overwhelmed, I finally just chose a camel that didn't look depressed, accompanied by a guy who didn't have a whip in his hand.

Camels are very tall, and even a kneeling one is difficult to mount; the large saddle adds to the height and bulk, making it doubly awkward to achieve access, much less to do so with any modicum of grace. When my chosen camel driver—I'll call him CD—helped me up, his hand grazed my breasts, not a part of the body generally required for leverage. I told myself it was an accident and tried to focus on the fact that I was at the pyramids, about to ride a camel.

After we plodded along for about two minutes, we came to a halt, my camel having decided it was time for a bathroom break and CD having decided it was time for a sales pitch. He said, "I have authentic antiquities, not expensive for you." I nodded and smiled blandly. "You buy?" he asked. "No, thank you," I said.

But CD was persistent and I suspected that I would be forced to sit in the midday sun, listening to his spiel and smelling camel poop, until I gave in. I looked at the statuettes he had wrapped in a cloth, and finally chose a small one for a large price. "Do not let them see it at customs," CD warned, explaining that it was illegal to take antiquities out of the country.

"Only if they're authentic," I was tempted to say. But CD was holding the reins to my camel, and I really wanted to get out of there. I stayed mum.

Ugh. As CD helped me off the camel, his hand grazed my breasts again. Maybe he was trying to authenticate them.

I would have loved to be able to rehash these events with Shirley, but we weren't scheduled to meet up for another week. Happily, I wasn't without a confidante. That night, I spilled the story of my proposal and the groping camel driver to Mick Jones, the outgoing Australian who managed the Hotel Astrid, my prime home-away-from-home in Cairo. Mick was a self-proclaimed queen, and proud of it. He knew everything there was to know about everyone in the city and he loved to dish. It was Mick who told me that Talia was a general's wife—fortunately, not until after my mini-breakdown in front of her.

I assumed Mick was in charge of the Astrid's staffing, as there were always handsome young men hanging around the hotel, and around Mick.

Many of the lodgings that EGAPT had booked me into were large and upscale. That made sense: those hotels had enough rooms to allow them to comp travel writers without turning away paying guests. And they were places I wouldn't have been able to afford on my modest Frommer's advance but that I wanted to experience.

I was surprised, therefore, to discover that arrangements had been made for me to stay for a week at the Astrid, and that it was apparently a tradition for the hotel to host the Frommer's writer.

Mine was not to question why, but if I had to venture a guess, I'd say Mick got an eager American audience for his stories, as well as the lowdown about the other hotels and restaurants in town—not to mention a sympathetic review for his hotel. Or so he hoped. Having questioned write-ups that seemed overly gushy as an editor, I held myself to a high standard as a reviewer. But I had no qualms about keeping the star next to the Astrid's listing to signal it was outstanding. The hotel had loads of historic character and a central location near Tahrir Square. It was impeccably clean and moderately priced.

And then there was the room service.

One morning, about six days into my stay, I wasn't feeling very well. Just as I didn't turn down proffered cigarettes, I rarely turned down the spiced and flame-roasted kebabs and koftas that were an Egyptian menu staple. It's easy to be vegetarian in Egypt—falafel and *fool* (fava beans with oil) were also ubiquitous—but most Egyptians who could afford it ate meat frequently and seemed surprised at Western hesitation over consuming large quantities. I felt it was my job to accept my hosts' hospitality.

My stomach finally rebelled against my carnivore carnival.

I'd come down to the hotel breakfast buffet that day for a cup of tea, unable to partake in the generous spread of breads, cheeses, meats, and fresh fruit juices; my favorite—before it was trendy—was pomegranate. When Mick came over for our usual morning confab, I explained why my plate wasn't heaped as usual. I said I was going to go back to my room to rest for a while. Only black tea was set out, and Mick offered to send up an herbal tummy settler.

I wasn't surprised, then, to hear a knock at my door about half an hour later. It was Youssef, one of the beautiful young men I'd seen around the hotel. He looked to be in his early twenties, slim, with sad eyes. I recalled that he worked in the kitchen and often brought the food out to the buffet. Youssef placed the chamomile teakettle and cup on a side table that I'd cleared of my notebooks and other clutter.

I was startled, however, to sense a slow approach when I turned around to dig into my purse for a tip. As I fumbled with change, wondering how much to give, I felt Youssef behind me, nuzzling my neck.

A hundred thoughts flitted through my mind, including "bonk him on the head with the kettle and knee him in the groin." But my own groin was not very martially inclined. Instead, it was running reels of Omar Sharif in *Lawrence of Arabia.*

Mentally building a half-hour of abandon into my schedule, I let Youssef nudge me gently over to the unmade bed.

Talk about brief encounters. I thought I would be playing a part in a bodice ripper titled *Lust in Egypt.* Instead, my coupling with a dark exotic stranger resembled a Samuel Beckett short story. The neck nuzzle was about it for foreplay; after maybe two minutes of thrusting, Youssef came.

And then he went.

"I go back to work," he murmured, giving me a quick peck on the cheek and rushing out of the room. At least that spared me further pondering over the proper tip to give for the delivery of a cup of chamomile tea.

🐪 🐪 🐪

On schedule, Shirley and I regrouped in Cairo and headed south. We'd both gotten a lot accomplished, but it was still tough to fact-check everything in *Frommer's Egypt* in five weeks. I was under strict instructions to keep the page count the same, so the time I allotted to each destination was generally proportional to the amount of space given it in the original guide.

My obsession with Akhenaten and Nefertiti hadn't abated since I first encountered them at the Brooklyn Museum, however; it had just gone underground. Page count be damned. We were going to spend half a day in Tell el-Amarna, the modern incarnation of Akhenaten's city, though it was out of the way.

Shirley and I got off the train in Minya, about 150 miles south of Cairo. As the Frommer's guide notes about the ferry crossing at the town of Deir Mawas:

When you land, you'll more than likely be greeted by a group of local children, one of whom will ask you to remember his or her name. Unless you're resistant to emotional blackmail, generally heartless, or allergic to the fanciful straw baskets they make, you'll probably buy one from 'your' child when you return to the boat.

The sights [of el-Amarna] are some distance away from the landing. One exhilarating but rather strenuous option is to take a tractor, which seats two people on the benches along the sides... If you're lucky—those tractors are hard on the spine and kidneys—you can catch the minibus that also does this run.

Here I confess to something that goes against the prime directive of So You Want to Be a Writer 101: I didn't keep a standard journal during this trip. I took copious notes about what I saw and did as it might affect visitors, from the cost of attractions to the best times of day to go, but didn't record my feelings about any of these experiences—or record any personal events, period. My quickie with Youssef, for example, has been entirely reconstructed from memory.

My rationale: I was just working on a guidebook, not a real piece of writing. I had strict notions about what constituted "real" writing. It pretty much boiled down to if I was producing it, it didn't qualify.

It's fortunate that I also have a tendency to ignore the prime directive of good housekeeping: I rarely throw out anything I've ever worked on. I still have my copy of the fifth edition of *Frommer's Egypt*, with my corrections for the sixth scrawled in the margins. Browsing that annotated book now not only unleashed a rush of memories about the trip but also made me rethink what I thought I knew about my creative path.

I looked at the sentence in the passage above about being emotionally blackmailed by the local children and thought, "Hmmm, that sounds like something I would write." Sure enough, those sentences weren't in the earlier edition. In spite of the strictures of the guidebook format, I was already finding and honing a voice, a comic perspective.

In that same passage, I'd also introduced an adjective to describe the ride across the desert plain to Tell el-Amarna that hadn't been there before: "Exhilarating."

That seems like an odd thing to say about a bumpy tractor ride in the hot sun that I don't recommend to others. Ah, yes. It was my way of sneaking in a bit of personal commentary in shorthand that barely hints at the intensity of what I felt.

Shirley and I were the only ones who boarded the flatbed trailer that day. The two men in the tractor's cab spoke very little English. I don't suppose it was very interesting for them to wait by the ferry dock in hopes of hauling around tourists with whom it was usually impossible to converse.

But Shirley drew the two men into Arabic conversation before the road noise made it too hard to hear.

As we spotted the ruins of Akhenaten's city in the distance across the isolated plain, we hit a particularly hard rut in the road. Shirley leaned forward to say something to the driver, and both men cracked up.

"What did you say that was so funny?" I wondered.

"Oh, I just asked him if he had been a cab driver in Cairo, because that's how he was driving," Shirley replied.

Many tableaus bubble up when I think of this trip—strains of music playing while I learned to belly-dance on a river cruise in Cairo, the taste of thick, bitter coffee sipped in a waterside cafe in Alexandria, the scent of flowers in Aswan—but for capturing the essence of my realized dream of Egypt, nothing came close to jolting along a dusty desert road toward the ancient kingdom of my childhood imaginings, sharing a laugh with the locals.

🐫 🐫 🐫

Not long after our Tell el-Amarna adventure, Shirley headed back to Cairo via the remote oases of Siwa, Bahariya, Farafra, Kharga, and Dakhla, where her Arabic would be particularly useful. I missed her dry wit and her language skills, but it was nice to travel on my own for a while, especially since I was headed for Luxor, formerly Thebes; I wanted to be free to be as archaeo-geeky as I liked. My excitement over visiting the tombs of the pharaohs on the Valley of the Kings was undercut only by my claustrophobia, first discovered when I descended into a crypt in Palenque, Mexico. Now I suddenly felt waves of anxiety wash over me. Still, I wasn't going to blow my chance to see the world-famous hieroglyphs in their natural setting; I just hoped the tour guides wouldn't misinterpret my heavy breathing.

In the end, my favorite forays into ancient Egypt didn't involve being enclosed underground looking at artwork that had faded with exposure to air and the moisture of tourist breathing, heavy and otherwise. Top honors, instead, went to visiting Karnak Temple at night. The result of 2,000 years of royalty trying to outdo each other with ever-taller pylons, more ram-headed sphinxes, and increasingly elaborate stelae, the 200-acre Karnak was grander than anything I could have imagined.

And going after the shimmering daytime heat had abated was a revelation. I'd always considered sound-and-light shows to be cheesy, but the one at Karnak was magical. Rather than sitting in the bleachers and having a psychedelic concert experience, sans drugs, we were led on a walk through the temple. As the towering figures loomed above, suddenly illuminated, I imagined that I was part of a sacred procession. It doubtless helped that the commentary booming through the loudspeakers was in French; the English tour was offered on a night when I was no longer going to be in town. Things always sound better in French, and I didn't know the language well enough to determine if, as was likely, the narrative was goofy or ponderous.

Another unexpected nighttime delight was exploring the intimate Luxor Museum; its hours were extended during the summer. Low-lit and with well-marked, beautifully laid-out displays—including a reconstructed wall from a temple devoted to Akhenaten and a colossal sandstone head of my favorite pharaoh—it was everything I'd hoped for but hadn't found in Cairo's lauded institution.

I returned to the capital feeling recharged and as besotted with Egypt as I'd ever been. I was even pretty proud of my guidebook-updating efficiency. Before I left Cairo, I'd enlisted Habbibah, an associate at the local tourism office, to help me gather service information. I hadn't been able to check the opening and closing hours and prices for maybe a quarter of the places in the city and figured she would be better at extracting that information by phone than I would.

The day before I was scheduled to fly back to London, I went into the tourism office, all cocky and ready to rock and roll—only to discover that Habbibah had called in sick.

I broke down crying. Again. What was happening to me? I rarely turned on the waterworks in New York, and never in public. Was I going to sob my way across the globe whenever things didn't go my way? Talk about unprofessional.

I spent many hours in London agonizing over my unverified listings until it finally sunk in: The disclaimer at the front of each book didn't only apply to natural disasters.

"Readers are advised that prices fluctuate in the course of time, and travel information changes under the impact of the varied and volatile factors that affect the travel industry."

Falling into the "varied" category: Attractions opened in Egypt, or didn't, with little regard to listed hours. Add to the *inshallah* attitude the fact that shopkeepers and museum curators were as likely as not to get stuck in traffic. No wonder Habbibah went AWOL; she doubtless thought my request for nit-picky details was insane but didn't have the nerve to tell me.

I overcame my loss of face in front of her officemates more quickly. Even while I was sipping the tea that had been hurriedly brought to me, I consoled myself with the knowledge that I was leaving Egypt the next day. Indeed, over the years, in the aftermath of many embarrassing incidents in remote places, my self-soothing mantra was, "They'll never see you again." I later amended it: "Even if they do see you again, by that time they're likely to have forgotten about the incident, no matter how large it looms in your memory. And if they do remember, they won't think it's nearly so bad as you did." I realize this is too long to be a mantra, but it's more nuanced than the original.

I was further comforted when I later learned that my crying bouts were small potatoes in the general scheme of Egypt gaffes. On a tour of Cairo to begin peace talks following the Yom Kippur War, for example, Israeli prime minister Menachem Begin declared to a large delegation, "We built the pyramids"—referring to his Jewish countrymen. Begin's Egyptian hosts were startled, then outraged. Apparently, the Exodus story is not on the Cairo curriculum. Schoolchildren are taught instead that Egyptians—and not enslaved ones—built all their famous monuments themselves. Begin's statement "spurred fury among Egyptian historians and archaeologists," according to one newspaper account. Protest articles cropped up in the Egyptian press.

Two years later, Egyptian President Anwar Sadat nevertheless partnered with Begin to sign the Camp David Peace Accord. And children all over the United States continued to tell the Passover story without questioning its basic tenets—and, in most cases, without guilt.

CHAPTER 6
THE OTHER "F" WORD, FODOR'S
New York City, September 1989–December 1991

My adventure in Egypt was excellent in almost every respect except one: It left me broke. By the time I finished paying trip expenses, paying Shirley for her research, and paying my London rent, I had just about enough left for my air ticket back to New York. It had crossed my mind that I should give freelancing a chance when I returned to Manhattan, but the more my London bank account drained, the more the idea panicked me.

Like most of my counterculture cohort, I disdained material goods. Unlike those who grew up rich, however, I rarely felt that I had enough of those goods to reject. My parents never discussed their finances with my sister and me, but they both worked long hours and I sensed their nervous, whispered conversations in German concerned money. That insecurity was deeply imprinted in me.

I'd asked for my old job back at Prentice Hall Travel after Egypt but had been rebuffed. Jaclyn said the publisher had nixed the idea because leaving had been disloyal—even though I'd been editing a series that the company was distributing, not a competitor's line. Screwed both ways, I was.

But I had one wild card.

A few weeks before the directors of Rough Guides came to New York, a headhunter had contacted me, proposing an exploratory lunch with two high-level representatives from Fodor's. I was flattered. Fodor's was a division of Random

House, and I'd heard the publisher allowed—nay, even encouraged—its editors to travel.

This led to a peculiar meal at Zarela, an upscale Mexican restaurant in midtown Manhattan. Richard (Dick) Brooks, the editor-in-chief of Fodor's, was short and disheveled—and very distracted. He rarely addressed me. He alternated between grilling his colleague, Maria, about work issues and asking the server repetitive questions about the menu. I wasn't the expert in Mexican food that I later became, but I wondered how the editor-in-chief of a major travel publisher could be so unsophisticated about south-of-border basics—not to mention so ditzy during an interview.

I left the restaurant feeling off my game, discombobulated.

The promised call to let me know either way about employment never came, which didn't surprise me. I nevertheless contacted Fodor's to inform them, as a courtesy, that I was taking a job with Rough Guides.

Dick immediately phoned and offered me the Fodor's position, and at a higher salary than the one the headhunter had quoted.

I said no, I was committed to going to London. And that was that.

Now, figuring I had nothing to lose, I wrote Dick and asked if the offer was still on the table. I noted that I had more editing and updating experience than I'd had a year earlier.

To my amazement, he said yes.

And so I embarked on my third publishing job in five years—one that I got, as it turned out, on semi-false pretenses. It didn't take me long to discover that I hadn't been headhunted for my editing skills or my powerhouse personality but, rather, for my Rolodex, the card file of Frommer's authors that Fodor's assumed I would be bringing along.

Ironically, the coveted Rolodex had never existed, at least not in its imagined incarnation. Editors at PHT had almost no say when it came to hiring writers. Jaclyn would occasionally ask my opinion about potential candidates for a new book, but the final decisions were always hers. Had I come to Fodor's directly from PHT, my dowry would have been a messy card file with contact information for only the few dozen Frommer's writers whose books I had edited over the years.

Even if a contact file crammed with PHT experts had existed, it would have been useless. With few exceptions, Frommer's guides were written by single authors, many of whom earned royalties on the books that bore their names. In contrast, Fodor's hired multiple authors, preferably with distinct areas of expertise—the restaurant reviewer at a major city newspaper would cover dining, say—for a flat rate. This focus on the local had two advantages: Fodor's could boast of the insider savvy of its writers and it could pay them less, since they were already on-site and—so the rationale went—didn't need to spend money researching topics with which they were familiar.

Hiring locals also made it easier to convey the impression that Fodor's writers weren't taking freebies, although they were.

All in all, there would have been little incentive for PHT authors to defect. It would mean going from writing and updating an entire guidebook that—at least in theory—kept on producing cash flow to receiving one-time-only fees for slices of Fodor's guides.

No matter. By the time these facts emerged, I was already ensconced in an airy office at Random House.

Anyway, what I lacked in a Rolodex of travel writers, I more than made up for with a roster of academic contacts. Friends and friends of friends from my NYU and UCSD grad school days were scattered throughout the US, cobbling together a living teaching multiple classes as adjunct instructors. Others were on scholar-exchange programs in far-flung corners of the world.

Academics tend to enjoy good ethnic restaurants, non-touristy local attractions, and hotels with character. They are also accustomed to doing labor-intensive research for next to nothing. In short, they are extremely well suited to be guidebook updaters—second only, perhaps, to CIA operatives.

Yes, those rumors were true.

I'd long heard whisperings that Eugene Fodor was a spy, but I'd also heard that about Arthur Frommer; people were always confusing the two "F"-named guidebook icons. I didn't lend either story much credence until Fodor died in early 1991 and the obituaries recapped his resume.

It all started in 1936 when, after working as a translator on a French shipping line, the Hungarian-born Fodor compiled his first travel book, the 1,169-page *On the Continent*. Published in England, but eschewing the grand tour and great monuments approach to travel of earlier British series, this breezy, conversational guide offered practical advice, including where to stay and eat and how much to tip. It also encouraged visitors to get to know the locals—a novel concept at the time.

During World War II, Fodor's linguistic skills—and his disdain for the Nazis—caught the attention of the Office of Strategic Services (OSS), which later morphed into the CIA. After his wartime service, Fodor returned to the travel-guide business and used it to provide Cold War cover to many operatives. As he later reported to the *New York Times*: "I told [my CIA handlers] to make sure and send me real writers, not civil engineers. I wanted to get some writing out of them. And I did, too."

By the time I started at Fodor's, the company had been thoroughly spy-washed. Stories of espionage were not part of the office lore.

Stories of Eugene Fodor's kindness, erudition, and wit were, however, and they were brought out in spades at his memorial service, a gathering of publishing-world luminaries. The outpouring of genuine admiration for the departed made me sorry I had never gotten to know him.

I only met Mr. Fodor—I never think of him by his first name—once, long after he had given up an active role in the company. It was a year before he died of a brain tumor at age eighty-five. I had a bit of a shock when a well-dressed, elderly man came into my office and introduced himself to me as Eugene Fodor, but he immediately put me at ease, sitting down for a few minutes to chat, asking what I was working on, if I was enjoying it. I soon realized that he was making the rounds, taking the time to talk to everyone on the floor, including all the editorial assistants. He was a real gentleman, in the best sense of that word.

🐫 🐫 🐫

The guidebooks reflected their founder's personality. Compared to Frommer's and other popular series of the day, they had a cosmopolitan tone. They combined an emphasis on culture lacking in other American guides with an engaging voice, forgoing the snark of overseas series like Rough Guides and Lonely Planet.

Just as Frommer's guides were no longer hipster-friendly, Fodor's was past its literary prime, the era when Sir Edmund Hilary wrote the introduction to the Himalayas guide, James Michener the preface to *Fodor's Hawaii*. During my time with the company, a huge program was in place to break down the more discursive, essay-style books into digestible information "nuggets"—like Kentucky Fried Chicken, the editors would joke.

Random House nevertheless felt more genteel than Simon & Schuster. Although I'd worked with top-notch writers and editors at PHT, Fodor's more closely resembled the stereotypical publishing houses of movies and literature. The editorial assistants were mostly Ivy Leaguers or had at least graduated from posh East Coast schools—so much so that I felt a bit out of my element. A PhD from NYU didn't compensate. In my head, I was still the girl who had to go to the free city school, Brooklyn College, and who couldn't afford graduate school without scholarships.

I never said any of this was rational.

But I'd been hired at Fodor's as a senior editor. This meant that, unlike at Rough Guides, those Ivy League assistants had to do my photocopying. Which was essential, given my workload. One of the first books to land on my desk was *Fodor's Europe*. It was a monster, more than a thousand pages long, with so many authors and moveable parts that the editorial duties had to be divided up between another editor and me.

There's nothing like spending nearly a decade working on a four-volume dissertation to put a mere 500 pages into perspective. I did a decent job and was comparatively calm under deadline fire. I'm guessing it was my handling of the Europe guide that led Dick Brooks to ask me to shepherd through a new Fodor's series, *The Wall Street Journal Guides to Business Travel*, even though I was still a relative newbie.

The books had been under the charge of one of my favorite co-editors, Chris Billy; he was extremely personable and funny. I can't recall what excuse he gave for wanting to offload the project—perhaps that he was an expert on the USSR, which was slowly coming apart at the seams. Chris had his hands full tracking maps and text references for *Fodor's Soviet Union* whenever another republic broke away. Up and down the halls of Fodor's, editors could be heard muttering, "Shit, are we going to have to change all the running heads?"— the short chapter titles that appear on top of every page.

Still, my experience with *Fodor's Europe*—and with my dissertation—didn't prepare me for working on the *Wall Street Journal* guides. I soon learned why Chris had been so eager to bail.

It wasn't just the scope of the project that was daunting, though it was very far-reaching. I was in charge of producing three new books covering seventy-eight business capitals: thirty in the United States, thirty in Europe, and eighteen in the Pacific Rim. A few authors took on multiple cities, but most accepted only one. All told, there were some sixty-five contributors, only a few of whom had already been hired when I came on board.

Nor were the stresses of hammering out a format for the series and of living up to the *Wall Street Journal's* reputation for excellence the prime sources of my agita, though we're getting warmer here. The heart of the problem: Dick had pitched the series to the newspaper, and that meant he was very, very involved in it.

Dick had the temperament and impulse control of a passive–aggressive teenager. Reading through edited chapters, which he did erratically, invariably inspired Dick to ask for some change in the template. "Don't you think we should add the number of conference rooms to the hotel listings?" he would ask, or "Don't you think we need to add comedy clubs to the nightlife section?" These questions were all rhetorical, of course. It was up to me to convince writers who weren't being paid a stellar rate to begin with—from $1,000 to $1,500 per chapter, depending on the destination—to make these changes for no additional compensation.

Literally adding insult to the injury of requesting unpaid changes were the critiques Dick would send to the writers unlucky enough to come under his scrutiny, many of them stringers for *The Wall Street Journal*. The scrawled comments they would find in the margins of their printed-out manuscripts were not only rude, but weird. It wasn't enough for Dick to circle a phrase and label it a cliché; for one restaurant write-up, for example, he drew a crude little bed next to the phrase "bed of lettuce."

I spent a lot of time on the phone talking down journalists who had received these critiques, urging them not to take it personally. It's possible that I used the term "deranged" in reference to my boss. By the end of this project, I'd honed my groveling and apologizing skills, though not my ability to suffer fools in authority gladly.

There were plenty of upsides, too. Not only did I work with top-rate journalists around the world—I could break up the day by chatting with writers in different time zones—but I was also able to hire freelance editors and mapmakers to work with me in-house. I brought aboard some of my favorites from Frommer's and even from the poetry world, creating a mini support group in the office.

And while I stayed late most nights and took work home on the weekends, I also carved out time to travel. Editors, like writers, were permitted to accept "help." I went to Rome, a city I'd always yearned to see, to check out the business climate. I revisited San Francisco, a blast from my hippie past, for a professional assessment. I had previously bunked in a Berkeley dorm and dropped acid; this time I luxuriated at the Drake.

In case you're wondering: Taking freebies was and is against *Wall Street Journal* policy. Writers now are only permitted to accept gifts that they can eat or drink on the spot; I'm told that many an expensive bottle of booze is consumed in one sitting as a result. I doubt that the rules were any less stringent twenty-five years ago. Call it plausible deniability. I didn't ask the writers who worked on the guides whether or not they accepted comps, but I would have bet a year's salary that many of them did. I can't imagine that anyone who lived in the US and had to travel to Beijing, say, would have been able to afford the research otherwise.

Dick's micromanaging notwithstanding, I was also proud of my newfound authority, including having a say about the books' design. The look of the Fodor's standard gold guide came courtesy of Massimo Vignelli, known, among other things, for designing a groundbreaking New York City subway map in the 1970s. The *Wall Street Journal* guides were sufficiently high status to warrant their own distinctive style. One day, Fabrizio La Rocca, the head of Fodor's art department, Dick, and I were invited to confer with Vignelli in his Upper East Side headquarters.

Luckily for me, dressing for success wasn't a prerequisite in New York publishing. I didn't wear jeans to work, but my slacks and flats weren't very stylish. Still, I wasn't entirely immune to the allures of New York fashion, and every now and then I succumbed to an urge to splurge. I took the occasion of going to one of the city's premier design firms to debut the results of one of those sprees: a long black suede coat with a black shearling lining. I felt uncharacteristically confident and chic as I entered the glass door marked Vignelli Associates.

The offices were as starkly stunning as I had anticipated, though I hadn't expected the color scheme, or lack thereof. Everything was white: Walls, desks, chairs, even the carpets created a snowscape of textures, like an early Rothko canvas.

Having a tendency toward klutziness, I found this whiteout as intimidating as the prospect of talking to the impeccably tailored Vignelli. The Milan-born designer was charmingly down-to-earth, however, personally offering to bring everyone coffee. Much as I could have used the caffeine, I was terrified of spilling a brown beverage on the white rug. I declined.

Once we settled in to discuss the design, I began to relax.

Then I looked down at my hands.

My palms were black. Everything I had touched bore light black traces. It was a good thing I hadn't committed a crime, other than an aesthetic one. My fingerprints were everywhere.

I couldn't figure it out. Then it struck me: The never-before-worn suede garment was a black-dye dispenser.

I excused myself to go to the ladies room, where I scrubbed down like a surgeon, but that still left me with the problem of the telltale marks on the conference-room table. I'd slipped my notebook over the offending smudges as soon as I spotted them, and now I tried to remove them with a wad of bathroom tissue. That damned turncoat coat. It had given me a false sense of feeling chic and in control. Here I was, surreptitiously trying to clean a table at one of the country's top design firms with damp toilet paper.

Dick was, typically, oblivious. Massimo and Fabrizio—younger and brasher, but also Italian-born and -bred—were too gallant to say anything, but I suspect they were wondering why I was re-enacting the "out damned spot" mad scene from

Macbeth. I must have looked especially insane when we were leaving and I tried to slip into my coat without touching it.

There you have it: instant karma for having told several of my authors that Dick was deranged.

🐫 🐫 🐫

Despite all our best efforts, the *Wall Street Journal* series tanked.

A good part of the problem was the Gulf War, which put a damper on business travel. Coming smack in the middle of the production schedule, the conflict proved as inconvenient to Fodor's as the breakup of the Soviet Union had been.

I would have been sorrier to see my hard work go to waste had I not been preoccupied by the fact that my mother was dying.

Rita Jarolim had been diagnosed with liver cancer, the literal outgrowth of colon cancer left unchecked. She had delayed going in for a colonoscopy until she was in extreme discomfort. Surgery revealed that what might have once been a manageable bowel tumor had spread to her liver.

Neither one of my parents was big on going to doctors. Some twenty years earlier, my father had agreed to a checkup only when he could no longer ignore his shortness of breath. He was diagnosed with an enlarged heart and prescribed pills, a prescription he neglected to fill. Some two weeks later, my father died of cardiac arrest at age seventy.

In response to her cancer diagnosis, my mother decided she wasn't interested in chemo, radiation, or any other treatments that might have prolonged her life. She was seventy-eight, she said; it was time. The doctors gave her six months to a year to live.

My mother was not only dying, but she was dying in another city, Atlanta, where she had moved to be closer to my sister and her children. The original plan had been to relocate with my father, but he'd had his fatal heart attack a month before they were scheduled to leave.

I'd often been glad that nearly a thousand miles separated me from my mother. Now I wanted nothing more than to close the distance. My mother insisted that I not take too much time off from my job, so I had to settle for phoning her from work every day and flying down to Atlanta on several weekends.

During these brief visits, I discovered that I was probably more upset about her imminent demise than my mother was. Death became her. I don't recall ever seeing her happier than she was during those last months.

She wasn't afraid and she wasn't in pain. Liver cancer is debilitating—and of course deadly—but it often doesn't hurt. My mother was not only able to live on her own until close to the end, but also to continue her regular activities. She was swimming laps in an Olympic-size pool at the local YWCA three weeks before she went in for a final hospital stay.

She did make a few concessions to her illness. She allowed herself to relax her usually fastidious housekeeping habits, just a little. She ate ice cream out of the container—more of it than she'd ever permitted herself before—and left dishes in the sink for a few hours rather than washing them immediately, though never overnight, she assured me.

Instead, she focused her energies on putting her papers in order—and on making final requests.

My mother had always been a world-class guilt-tripper. I had caused her metaphorical demise so many times—I didn't want children! I got divorced!—that I grew deaf to her complaints. Now that she was actually dying, she had my attention.

Most of her last wishes were very reasonable. She had been a staunch member of the International Ladies Garment Workers Union and regretted that she once—and only once, she would want me to tell you—voted for the union-busting Ronald Reagan. She made my sister and me swear that we would always vote Democratic.

She also wanted to be cremated, in spite of the prohibition against the practice in the Jewish faith, from which she had drifted away. "If it was good enough for my parents, it's good enough for me," she'd said, referring to the concentration camp ovens where Hermann and Ernestine Rosenbaum had likely met their fates. My father was the mordant wit in the family, but my mother had her moments.

Her doctor had promised to give her some extra morphine if she was in any pain at the end, and he was true to his word. Nine months after she had been diagnosed and two days after she checked into the hospital, Rita Jarolim was eased out of this world. She didn't often have control over events in her life, especially the tragic ones in Vienna, but she died exactly the way she wanted to. And for that I was grateful.

I was grateful, yes, and I thought I was prepared for the loss, so I was shocked by how disoriented I felt. I wasn't in a relationship and I had no close family left. As my mother had feared—but was unable to prevent, even by last-request fiat— my sister and I cut off all contact with each other almost immediately after her death. Pleading Jewish religious observance (though not, apparently, the Honor Thy Father and Mother part), my sister refused to have anything to do with the cremation. Nor would she attend the ceremonial burying of my mother's ashes next to my father's body, even though New

Montefiore, a Jewish cemetery in Queens, had agreed to the arrangement.

I adored my nieces but didn't want to put them in the middle of a longstanding sibling feud.

Also contributing to my sense of being unsettled: I had just turned forty and still didn't know what I wanted to do with my life.

Or, rather, I knew, but I wasn't doing anything about it. Unresolved yearnings to be a writer are poignant when you're a teenager, stylishly angsty when you're in your twenties. At the end of your thirties, you're in *On the Waterfront* territory, in danger of looking back and saying, with regret, "I coulda been a contender."

I no longer wanted to be a wannabe.

Freelancing had gotten even less feasible than when I'd first contemplated it. My rent-stabilized building had been converted into a co-op, which more than doubled my monthly expenses. Even if I could scrape together enough work to cover my mortgage and maintenance payments, I would also have to shell out for things like office equipment and health insurance. And working in a 450-square-foot space all day would feel confining.

This led me to a terrifying conclusion: To be a writer, I needed to leave New York.

And not just the city, and all it represented, but my friends. They were part of the problem—or I was, in relation to them. No matter how large and sophisticated your hometown is, it locks you in the vise of other people's sense of your identity. My childhood best friend recently reminded me that, when I was a teenager, I couldn't bear to return clothing to department stores because the saleswomen intimidated me.

It was hard for me to admit my literary ambitions to myself, much less to anybody else. If I was going to reinvent myself as a writer, I needed to find an inexpensive place to live, and one where I had no history.

🐫 🐫 🐫

It also needed to be warm and sunny. Seasonal Affective Disorder wasn't often diagnosed at the time, but I knew I wasn't imagining the deep funk I plunged into every winter when the gray weather arrived. Another thing I knew: There is nothing romantic about depression. It robs you of the confidence and focus that are essential to good writing, traits that are fleeting at even the best of times.

I already had a general idea of where I might go to take the sunshine cure: the Southwest. To say you are moving to the Sunbelt is embarrassing, but add the word "west" to any destination and it sounds adventurous.

In the 1980s, I'd visited the Four Corners area, where Arizona, Utah, Colorado, and New Mexico converge. It wasn't an ideal vacation. I didn't drive, so I was at the mercy of Lenore, my more automotively-abled companion. She was the type of person who needed to change restaurant tables at least four times before we could order: The sun was in her eyes, the table wobbled, she could smell cigarettes from the smoking section, the people next to us were too noisy. But over the static of Lenore's neuroses, I heard the landscape speaking to me.

I know, that sounds woo-woo, and it felt that way. But it was the same visceral recognition I'd experienced in the Middle East, only with English-speaking shopkeepers and without the camels and crowds.

So I had a region to start with. I just needed to narrow down my search to a city—one that had decent airport access and progressive politics. You can take the flaming liberal out of New York, but you can't transplant her to redneck country.

Denver was out; it snows too often there. Las Vegas is a union town, but I couldn't picture myself in Slots Central. Santa Fe was too expensive, too cold, and too far off the beaten transportation track. I put Albuquerque on the back burner, though I hadn't quite connected with the city when I visited.

The answer arrived in one of those bits of serendipity that almost make me believe in a higher power. Almost.

After I finished the *Wall Street Journal* series, I went back to editing the gold guides, including several domestic titles. Arizona was on my schedule when my mother died.

When people ask me why I moved to Tucson, I have many canned answers, some more tongue-in-cheek than others. "Sheer whim," I often laugh. But it's more accurate to say, "I was editing *Fodor's Arizona* and had a really good writer for the Tucson chapter."

The mercury topped 100 degrees F the entire week in August that I scoped out the city, and it was humid; during the summer monsoon season, the dry heat flees town along with the snowbirds and the University of Arizona students. Limited public transportation meant I had to depend on tour operators to get around. In Saguaro National Park, a piece of jumping cholla cactus embedded itself in my leg on a nature path right behind the visitors center. I required first aid for a plant attack within sight of the parking lot.

But, oh, those craggy mountains ringing the city, the tail ends of the Sierra Madres and the Rockies having a throwdown. The serene, pristine spread of the Sonoran Desert, with its strange, often irate, flora and fauna. The kaleidoscopic, cinematic sunsets. It was like nothing I had ever seen before, and it felt like home.

"This," I thought. "This is the place."

PART TWO

WESTWARD? YO!

CHAPTER 7
DRIVE, SHE SAID
Tucson/Phoenix/Flagstaff, early 1992–early 1994

My first months in Tucson, I had a recurring dream. My mother would phone and say, "Where are you? I've been trying to reach you." I would answer, annoyed, "I told you, I moved to Arizona. Why don't you come visit? It's nice and warm here." Her response: "Why would I want to do that? It's hot enough where I am now."

I knew she wasn't talking about Atlanta.

My nighttime anxiety was shadowed by its daytime *doppelganger*. I'd decamped from New York in a blur, an adrenalin-fueled sprint. The magnitude of what I had done only slowly began to sink in as I contemplated my to-do list:

- Learn to drive
- Buy car
- Make friends
- Start freelance writing business.

Learning to drive was my biggest challenge. I had three strikes against me: a phobia of getting behind the wheel of a car, no sense of direction, and a fear of heights.

It's easy to develop an aversion to driving in public transportation–happy New York City, and an inability to read maps and orient yourself in unfamiliar areas is no great handicap there; trains, buses, and taxis do your thinking for you. I suspected my directional challenges were hereditary: One day when I was with my mother in an Atlanta mall, neither of us could figure out where the exit was or find stores we had visited less than fifteen minutes earlier, even after consulting the directory. As for my fear of heights—really, of edges—I was fine as long as I avoided rotating rooftop restaurants.

It was a different story in Tucson.

With the help of a San Diego friend, I'd rented an apartment on a major bus line. I figured I would settle in and get the lay of the land before venturing into automotive terra incognita.

That plan lasted about a week, until I wanted fresh produce and other groceries of the type I couldn't get at the nearby 7-Eleven and had to take a bus to the supermarket.

It was a Saturday. I left my apartment around 4 p.m. and got to the Albertsons some fifteen minutes later. Instant panic attack.

In Manhattan, grocery stores and supermarkets are easily accessible by foot or subway and are tailored to people who go shopping several times a week to tote home a few items at a time—items that will fit into the limited storage space of New York apartments. The high price of real estate also dictates that food stores in the city be cramped, with narrow aisles.

In my new home, markets deserve their "super" designation. The average store, not just bulk wholesalers like Costco or Sam's Club, covers half a downtown Manhattan block. The selection is huge, as are most of the products. Geared toward families, not singles, they're designed for being transported away by car. Need only one roll of toilet paper? Forget it. There's a minimum of four per package—and that's the expensive size.

Shaking off my mental paralysis, I finally picked up a few items that I recognized and could easily heft, headed for the bus stop, and waited.

And waited.

The bus never came. It was getting dark, and I finally started walking. It was probably a mile and a half to my apartment. When I got there, I did what I should have done before I left: checked the bus schedule for the time of the last service. Sure enough, the bus stopped running at 5 p.m. on Saturday.

Monday morning, I opened the "Driving Schools" section of the Yellow Pages and started making calls. I finally chose an instructor based on his English accent. After living in London for a year, I knew that the Brits drive like maniacs. I figured I could learn good defensive driving techniques from him.

Gordon turned out to be a very nice man, if somewhat humorless. He kept telling me to relax. I kept telling him I was from New York and congenitally incapable of that. If he couldn't teach me to drive while I was tense, we might as well forget it. He looked more than a little tense himself after our first lesson.

I did pretty well over the six-week course, all things considered. Dual brakes and steering—and the big Student Driver sign on the sturdy sedan—tamped down my anxiety somewhat. The ultimate test of my abilities and nerves was going over Gates Pass, a narrow road that winds along the crest of the Tucson Mountains and drops precipitously into the valley below. My palms got extremely wet but weren't sufficiently slippery to loosen the steering wheel from my death grip. I didn't fall off the mountain.

Gordon gave me a thumbs-up and told me his work here was done. I just needed practice.

To accomplish that, I also needed a vehicle. I didn't think it was a good idea to total a rental, so I scoured the newspaper classifieds for a cheap used car. I settled on a seven-year-old Toyota Corolla that cost $1,000; it was in great condition, the ad said, though it had 99,000 miles on it.

I took a taxi out to the owner's home, on the far-east side of town and off the beaten bus service path. The area is completely developed now, but at the time almost all the roads were dirt. I considered asking the cabbie to wait, but from the outside, the car looked okay and I didn't want to keep the meter running. I figured I could phone for another cab if necessary.

No pressure, right?

The owner was Japanese—a good omen, I decided, since the car was Japanese too. He seemed friendly, but eager to get the test drive underway. I'd been aware that driving the car was part of the purchasing process, but somehow assumed I could do it on my own—which, of course, was absurd. Why would anyone just hand over car keys to a stranger? I thus found myself going through my driving paces next to a man who was eyeing me suspiciously, no doubt because I was sweating profusely and my hands were shaking. I wasn't about to explain that it was my first time driving an automobile that didn't have dual brakes and steering. Better to let him think I was on meth.

It didn't help that I had no clue what I was supposed to look for in a vehicle. Friends advised, "See how smoothly it drives, look to see if it pulls to one side." Great. We were on a badly rutted dirt road. In the end, I set the bar pretty low: No parts fell off when I touched them. I said I would take it. I handed over the money and drove off in the direction that I thought might get me home, in mortal terror of destroying my new purchase and/or getting lost until I ran out of gas in the dark.

🐪 🐪 🐪

Starting a freelance business was a lot easier. Although I'd struck out for the West to fulfill my writerly dreams, I knew my minuscule savings and small inheritance from my mother weren't going to give me much breathing room to pursue that goal immediately. I'd lined up some security-blanket work from Fodor's before I left—editing and, initially, updating guides that wouldn't require automotive skills.

As soon as I got a car, I wangled an assignment to update the Grand Canyon chapter of *Fodor's Arizona*. I didn't feel ready to drive on my own, but several friends volunteered to be wingmen—including my former brother-in-law, Robert.

We were doubly connected. Robert was not only Lou's brother, but also the ex-husband of my childhood best friend, Sharon. Strange but true: When we were kids, Sharon and I had sworn to marry brothers—and we did. The four of us and two other college friends spent most weekends in our early twenties stocking up on Baskin-Robbins, getting stoned, and playing marathon games of Risk. Those pot-fueled exercises in world domination ended when Lou and I got divorced. A few years later, Robert came out as gay, and he and Sharon split. I managed to stay friendly with both of them, and Robert was the road warrior of the two.

We set out early one morning for Flagstaff, the closest town to the Grand Canyon; several pages of *Fodor's Arizona* were devoted to it, and I had scheduled a stay of a few days. The Flagstaff Convention and Visitors Bureau had arranged for us to eat at a nice restaurant on our first night, and we'd planned to get to town in plenty of time to get settled before dinner. But we'd detoured to explore a Native American ruin after lingering over banana cream pie at a truck stop. Rather than the anticipated five and a half hours, it took us more than seven to reach Flagstaff, leaving us no time to find our motel and drop off our things. We had to go directly to dinner.

This worried me. Most of the route from Tucson was along I-10 and I-17, major highways with speed limits of 75 mph. I was still terrified to get behind the wheel with all those cars zooming by, so Robert had done the bulk of the driving. We'd planned for me to take my turn as soon as we got to smaller Flagstaff; finding our digs in the daylight would give me better odds of locating them again after dark. With that reconnoiter ruled out, Robert assured me he wasn't tired, that he'd get us to the motel after dinner, no problem.

But he soon began showing a bit too much enthusiasm for the chardonnay we'd ordered with our chicken Kiev. He was a good way through his second glass while I was still on my first. I ceded the rest of the bottle to him, figuring it was better to get lost than have a sleepy drunk at the wheel.

After dinner, Robert tried to guide me to our motel with the sketchy city map in the Fodor's guide I was updating. Not only were his directions less than articulate, but they also required me to find the streets he was naming. Was my night vision failing? I could barely read the signs.

I later learned that Flagstaff is an International Dark Sky city, the first in the world to get this recognition. Although the restrictions against light pollution—the excessive wattage that obscures the night sky—may have delighted the astronomers at Flagstaff's Lowell Observatory and other stargazers, they were hell on a hapless visitor trying to find her way around an unfamiliar town.

I drove slowly, veering in to peer at street corners, focusing on the task at hand. When you grow up in New York, shrieking ambulances and strobing police-car lights become background noise; you learn to filter them out. By the time Robert alerted me to the fact that a patrol car was trying to get me to pull over, I had apparently been ignoring the signals for more than half a mile.

"Do you know why I pulled you over?" the police officer asked. I said I didn't, that I hadn't been speeding. She explained that I had been weaving down the streets and then had been unresponsive to all attempts to get me to stop.

I thought my explanation, that I was from the land of loud noises and bright lights and concentrating on finding my way in a dimly lit town, would be convincing. Not so. Next thing I knew, I was being asked to walk a straight line, count backwards from ten, and touch my nose. It was cold, I was nervous, and, in a nod to dressing for dinner, I'd changed into boots with uncomfortably high heels. Although I passed the nose-touching and counting tests, I was too unsteady on my feet to convince the law of my sobriety.

The officers didn't have a Breathalyzer with them. They told me I needed to come down to police headquarters to blow into a tube. My increasingly vocal protests about being a travel writer who was meeting with the tourist bureau the next day went unheeded. I was handcuffed ("Just following regulations, ma'am") and unceremoniously escorted into the back of the police cruiser. Robert, who assured the police he was fine to drive my car, was given directions to the station.

By the time we got there, it had been nearly three hours since I had my single glass of wine. My blood alcohol level was about 0.001. I was released without an apology ("Just following regulations, ma'am") into Robert's care. By then he was sober enough to deliver us to our motel without further incident.

🐫 🐫 🐫

Fortuitously, my reputation as the travel writer who got hauled off to the Flagstaff hoosegow in handcuffs didn't precede me when I later arranged to meet Penelope Peterson, my main contact at the Arizona Office of Tourism (AOT).

I'd first spoken with Penelope when I was editing *Fodor's Arizona* in New York. We'd talked on the phone again to discuss my Grand Canyon itinerary from Tucson, but we hadn't yet had a face-to-face. Since I wanted to dip my toes into the Phoenix area, home to the AOT office, I jumped at Penelope's suggestion that we have lunch at a resort in Scottsdale, where I could then spend the night.

I was still afraid to drive on I-10, especially the busy 90-mile stretch between Tucson and Phoenix, so I decided to take the scenic back route, Highway 77 to Highway 79 to Highway 88 to Highway 60 to...

Damn. I can't stand being late and expect others to turn up on time, too—at least in the US. But I was used to appointments in the same city, to building in time for subway and bus delays; I'd never had to account for long-distance road traffic. After turning off twice to find a gas station with a pay phone to call Penelope—cell phones were not yet in common use, though happily Penelope had one—and getting lost near Scottsdale, I was nearly two hours late when I finally arrived.

I was completely frazzled, though Penelope kept reassuring me, as she had over the phone, that she'd been happy to relax by the pool and get some paperwork done. I soon began to unwind, too. Penelope proved as warm and friendly in person as she'd sounded over the phone. She encouraged me to order whatever I wanted for lunch and, since I wasn't going anywhere, I started with a glass of wine.

Penelope looked at me a bit warily. Uh, oh, I wondered. *Faux pas?* I wasn't planning on more than one glass, and I didn't order anything expensive, but Penelope seemed a bit put off throughout the meal.

She regained her enthusiasm during the resort tour, but when she accompanied me to the front desk to check in, her sunny face clouded over again. When the desk clerk asked for my credit card for incidentals—telephone calls, room service, mini-bar charges, valet parking, and other things not included in the comped room rate—Penelope said, with more emphasis than the situation warranted, that I needed to give over my credit card. This wasn't my first comped-room rodeo; I knew the drill. Penelope looked visibly relieved when I didn't balk at the desk clerk's request.

Not until we met again, several months later, did Penelope explain her odd mood swings. The travel journalist she'd played host to right before me was Judy Martin, the blackmailing writer who had to be yanked from the Frommer's spa guide. Apparently, Judy hadn't mellowed in the half-dozen years since the Great Massage Meltdown. During her lunch with Penelope, she had insisted on talking to the hotel chef, even though she wasn't writing a dining story. When he came out, she'd demanded to know the preparation and ingredients of every dish. And she had been reluctant to turn over her credit card for incidentals.

Because I was also from New York City and the experience with Judy was fresh in her mind, Penelope had been very, very afraid.

Even paranoids have enemies. Usually when I worried about representing the entire genus of travel writers, I was overinflating my importance. Not this time. I was happy to have the chance to prove that New Yorkers could be professional and respectful, even though we might not always be punctual.

🐪 🐪 🐪

It was also far easier for me to make friends in Tucson than it was to learn to drive, and I had Terri, the onetime marketing director at the Flandrau Science Center and Planetarium, to thank. Flandrau was one of several excellent museums and exhibition spaces on the University of Arizona campus, and I'd toured it on my first scope-out visit to Tucson.

Terri was unlike any PR person I'd ever encountered before. She was as well put together as the rest, wearing a tailored gray dress and heels, though more diminutive than most at four foot ten inches and without an ounce of extra fat. As I later learned, this was not the result of delicate eating habits. Terri could down a steak with all the fixings faster than I could. But she was like a hummingbird, in constant motion. If I wasn't aware that she occasionally forgot to eat—something that never, ever happens to me—I could almost believe she burned off more than her weight in food each day through sheer energy.

A lot of people tasked with showing journalists around know the basics about the sights they represent, but flounder when asked in-depth questions. Not Terri. She knew everything there was to know about the Science Center, especially the gem, mineral, and meteorite exhibits. It turned out her father had run a rock shop in Tucson; one of her brothers sold high-end fossils and minerals; and another brother was internationally famed for being a meteorite hunter. Terri hadn't gone into the family business but definitely knew her way around open-pit mines and other dirt piles.

She was also unusually outspoken for a PR person— actually, for a person, period. Terri was a one-woman no-spin zone. At one point during our Flandrau tour, she stopped in front of a tired display and said, "This really sucks." She swore that the new exhibit that was going up soon would be a lot better.

To use a favorite Terri-ism, she was a hoot.

After our tour, I told Terri that I was thinking of moving to Tucson and asked her if I could call her if I did. She said, "Sure," though she looked at me a little squinty. I was one of those notoriously unfriendly New Yorkers. I don't think she believed I would ever move to Tucson, or contact her if I did.

I would have been hard-pressed to explain to Terri why I was certain I would be in touch if I didn't chicken out and stay in Manhattan. It was partly, of course, because I liked her. But she was also a character in the feminist fantasy I had constructed about the West, the embodiment of the gutsy, funny, and progressive women I was hoping to bond with in Tucson.

Good thing I didn't confide in Terri about my imaginary future pals. She would have set me straight, post haste, and I might have missed out on a major friendship.

Terri was funny and gutsy, yes. Progressive? Not so much. The discovery that she kept a gun in her glove compartment was the first tipoff that we might disagree about a few things. But by the time I realized that my politics and hers were diametrically opposed, it didn't matter. Terri and I had more in common, including a love of single-malt scotch and an interest in writing, than we had dissimilarities.

Only occasionally did our differences make a difference. It was the late 1990s, and I was waiting for Terri at an upscale restaurant I'd been assigned to review; the magazine was footing the bill. Looking out the window, I spotted her driving up in a pickup truck sporting an "Impeach Clinton" bumper sticker and parking next to my Toyota. Annoyed, I told Terri she wouldn't get a free meal from me unless she moved her vehicle far enough away from mine so that no one seeing us leave together would think I shared her views. It was an idle threat. Once we settled in with a glass of wine, the only talk about sexual peccadilloes involved her current love interest and mine. I couldn't be bothered to make Terri go out and give me political cover.

🐫 🐫 🐫

Terri also indirectly helped me find a house, though I wasn't really looking for one.

I had a six-month lease on my public-transportation-adjacent apartment and was planning to renew it until I could drive well enough to decide where I wanted to live—and to furnish the place. I'd left most of my belongings with my subtenant in New York and rented furniture, which I didn't even know was a thing until I heard about it in Tucson.

But as soon as I bought my car, Terri sent me to her insurance agent, Steve. After we finished the paperwork on the policy, Steve said, "It was a pleasure doing business with you. What else can I sell you?" I joked, "When I buy a house, you can insure that."

Rule to live by: Do not joke about an interest in real estate if you don't wish to be pursued. Nearly everyone you encounter—and especially people in the insurance business—is likely to have a real estate agent among his acquaintances.

The next day I got a call from Jackie, Steve's real estate agent friend.

What the heck, I thought. It can't hurt to look. I was curious about the Tucson neighborhoods I'd glimpsed when I was checking out the town. I was especially fascinated by housing complexes with faux Spanish names like Alta Vista, in a neighborhood that had no vistas, high or low, and Rancho Sin Vacas, Ranch without Cows, which pretty much went without saying in midtown. I fantasized building a retirement complex called Alta Caca (*altacocker* is Yiddish for "old fart").

Jackie showed me about eight houses in a University of Arizona neighborhood she thought I'd like, based on our brief phone conversation. I turned them all down, some because they were outside my price range, others because they weren't my style.

I felt like a realtor's nightmare, but Jackie said my direct approach was far easier to deal with than dithering. She called about a week later, claiming, "I've got your house." She was right. I could afford it and it fit my Southwest character requirement: It was a swirled-stucco adobe with a red-tile roof, built in the early 1940s. Jackie was a little concerned that I might not like the busy street on which it was located but—as my experience in Flagstaff attested—noise and lights didn't bother me.

My initial issue with the house was one that Jackie had never encountered before: It was too big. I live alone, I told her. What was I going to do with four bedrooms, two baths, a dining room, and a separate guesthouse just slightly smaller than my New York apartment?

"You'll figure it out," she laughed.

I did, though it was disconcerting at first. I had never lived in a house before, much less owned one. And this one not only came with a guesthouse, but with its tenant, Frank, a scary-looking skinhead. I rarely had to deal with him more than once a month, when he brought over the rent, but I always dreaded our encounters. His most mundane statements were profanity-laced and angry. He would say, "It's so fucking hot outside" in a way that suggested this was somehow my fault.

I was relieved when Frank gave me notice about nine months later. Terri and I were sitting in the yard when Frank was preparing to leave. He came over carrying several kitchen utensils, including a large knife. He asked if I could use any of them, with an undertone of, "Or I could just embed them in your chest." As soon as Frank was out of earshot, Terri said, "No matter what that guesthouse looks like, you give him back his security deposit, no questions asked." I did.

For the most part, I soon grew to love my home. I had a yard with peekaboo views of the Santa Catalina Mountains, where I could sit out with a beer and watch the sunset; a guestroom with its own bath, so visitors didn't have to sleep on a foldout sofa and pass through my tiny sleeping alcove when they needed to pee; and my own washer and dryer.

This last was the biggest kick. I'd hated doing laundry in the creepy basement of my Manhattan building. I could never remember to collect quarters and knew I would find my underwear dumped on the table if I was five minutes late retrieving my wash load. More than two decades later, I still experience a frisson of pleasure at being able to do laundry whenever I like, without fear of interference. Sometimes I leave my wet clothes in the washing machine longer than I should, just because I can.

🐫 🐫 🐫

My anxiety dreams eventually stopped. I woke up one morning and realized I was living the American dream, or at least a version of it that doesn't involve a partner and children. I had a car and a house, and I was slowly carving out a freelance business. Even my mother might have approved, I thought.

It wasn't until I started writing this book that I realized something else: I'd been following in her footsteps.

I'm embarrassed to admit that I was a bit ashamed of Rita Jarolim when I was growing up. She was thirty-nine years old when she had me, much older than most of my friends' mothers. Because she had prematurely gray hair, she was often mistaken for my grandmother. My friends had stay-at-home female parents. Mine worked outside the house as a seamstress.

Just as I wanted store-bought clothes, not the ones she made me, I wanted a bold American "mom." My mother had a strong Austrian accent and she was overprotective, imposing curfews much earlier than those my friends had. Her fearfulness dated back to her childhood, she once confided. A shy only child, little Rita was often teased for being a scaredy-cat by her uncles, who were all butchers. One of them thought it would be funny to present her with sheep eyeballs in a nicely wrapped gift box and watch her squeal with fright.

It hadn't sunk in that, at age twenty-three, my mother had journeyed solo from Vienna to New York to escape the Nazis, leaving her parents and everyone else she loved—sadistic uncles included—behind. Only a distant relative, a stranger who had been paid to sponsor her, awaited her on the other side of the Atlantic. She didn't speak the language. She met my father, another refugee from Vienna, in English school in Brighton Beach.

My move to Arizona was a dim echo of her exodus. It was brave only by today's pop culture standards of self-actualization.

I don't doubt that mother would have been worried about my uprooting. She would have fretted that I would be lonely in Tucson, that I wouldn't have enough money. But she would have been proud of my achievements. And, my nightmare scenarios notwithstanding, she would have loved the city's warm weather.

I'm certain she would have balked at getting into a car that I was driving. I would have balked at having her as a passenger. I can just picture us: she telling me to slow down, I telling her to stop nagging. It would have been stressful, two directional dyslexics trying to find our way. But we would have managed, and far better than anyone might have had a right to expect.

CHAPTER 8
FINDING MY FREELANCE MOJO
Tucson/Las Vegas/Mexico, 1992–1994

Getting settled into my new Tucson life meant growing accustomed to being unsettled. I barely had time to unpack before I had to fly off to Las Vegas for Fodor's.

I was psyched. I'd never been to the city before and was eager to peer behind the cinematic curtain, the romantic song-and-dance fests of Elvis and Ann-Margret and the glamorous gangsters of *Oceans 11*. This was before the era of films riddled with grisly mob violence or those depicting Las Vegas as a place where dreams go to die, but I had the vague sense of the city as seedy. I imagined a kind of Bowery in the Desert, Times Square with the hookers dressed like showgirls.

One of the first things that struck me when I arrived was how clean Las Vegas was, even the old downtown area. I'd pictured sidewalks littered with cigarette butts and strewn with drunks. That couldn't have been further from the truth, and not just because the drunks mostly stay inside the casinos.

It's knee-jerk for sophisticates to dismiss Las Vegas as soulless and superficial, but I was drawn to it from the start, even before its incarnation as a foodie mecca offered a snob-resistant rationale for my affection. Like most people, I enjoy natural light and a ka-ching-free environment; there's a limit to the amount of time I can spend inside casino hotels. But I immediately liked Las Vegas's energy, its excess, its kitschy sense of humor—not to mention its Jewish gangster roots. Tales of colorful mob bosses like Bugsy Siegel and Meyer

Lansky, who ushered in an era of Hollywood-style glamor with the 1946 Flamingo Hotel, became a guilty pleasure, a bracing antidote to the faceless victimized Jews of World War II.

In the early 1990s, Las Vegas was beginning a major shape-shift. The smaller, older hotels on the Strip had not yet been superseded by ultra-luxe palaces such as the Bellagio, vast theme hotels like Paris and the Venetian, or glitzy reincarnations rising from dramatic demolitions, including the Aladdin. The huge, upscale Mirage, where I was staying, had opened in 1989, to be joined in 1993 by Luxor, Treasure Island, and MGM Grand. Over the years that I covered Las Vegas regularly—first for Fodor's and later for *Brides* magazine—I witnessed several of its metamorphoses: as family-friendly, as a place for upscale weddings or girlfriend getaways, as a convention hub, as a celebrity chef magnet... That may be another reason the city endeared itself to me; I was also working on an image reboot, on reinventing myself as a freelancer.

The first person I met professionally under my new guise was Myram Borders, the chain-smoking, harlequin glasses–wearing head of the Las Vegas News Bureau. I'm not sure that she actually smoked when I met her, but because of her deep, gravelly voice and her no-guff attitude, she is seared in my memory holding a cigarette. She'd been the manager of the Las Vegas bureau of United Press International for two decades before transferring over to media relations in the 1980s, and she knew the city beat inside out, from gaming, politics, and organized crime to celebrity headliners. She also knew what would interest particular journalists. I was researching the hotel scene, and Myram was able to tell me exactly what was being built and when it was opening—and to predict future trends.

It was Myram who asked if she could connect me with Ian Abernathy, a journalist from Scotland who was looking to share a rental car so he could tour the area. I was slated to research day trips for Fodor's, so I jumped at the opportunity. It turned out that Ian was seeking someone to share driving duties as well as rental expenses. He was disgruntled to learn that I couldn't help out on that first score. But he wanted the company and didn't mind the money.

I soon discovered that "disgruntled" was Ian's default mood. Grouchiness in others brings out my own inner grinch; Ian and I were soon bickering about where to go. We finally settled on Oatman, a former gold mining town about two hours from Las Vegas in Arizona, on the longest extant stretch of Route 66. Ian wanted a genuine Old West experience, and Oatman seemed likely to provide it.

Those two hours in the car together felt interminable. When Ian wasn't complaining about the fact that I didn't drive—apparently he had never met a New Yorker—and the many, many things he disliked about Las Vegas, he was bragging about the various female editors at *Conde Nast Traveler* and *Travel + Leisure* who had the hots for him (apparently he had met some New Yorkers; he just hadn't tried to rent a car with one). Maybe he thought that talking about how powerful women desired him would spur me to competitively want to bed him, but it had the opposite effect. I kept thinking, instead, "So what am I, chopped liver?"

I was, anyway, dubious about Ian's claims to be a lothario. With his thick head of white hair and rugged features, not to mention his Scottish burr, Ian would have been attractive in a silver fox kind of way if it hadn't been for one thing: luxuriant snowy tufts growing out of his ears. Some women like hirsute men, but most I know draw the line at hairy orifices.

Being a captive audience to his bragging and grousing wasn't the only thing making the journey drag. Ian was a horrible driver.

As a perpetual passenger, grateful for being toted around, I was tolerant of pretty much every style of driving. But Ian stopped and started with no method behind his braking madness as far as I could tell, even on the freeway. I was tempted to keep my eyes closed on the hairpin curves of the Black Mountains on the first Route 66 leg in Arizona, but it might have exacerbated my car sickness. Instead, I focused on trying to decode Ian's eccentricities. Maybe a rare form of Tourette's was behind both his bouts of sexual braggadocio and his jerking-foot-on-the-brake syndrome. The more likely explanation: Most of the driving he did was in the UK on the other side of the road. This would also explain Ian's eagerness to find someone to share the wheel.

It was a relief to arrive in Oatman, a quirky former boomtown where burros roam the streets; according to legend, their progenitors hauled gold ore at once-thriving mines. Oatman is now artsy craftsy, but at the time, there were only a couple of shops, including one selling carrots and burro feed, and only one place to eat, the restaurant in the 1902 Oatman Hotel. Oatman still promotes the rumor that Carole Lombard and Clark Gable honeymooned at the hotel in 1939, though the couple actually spent the night at nearby Kingman.

No movie stars would be likely to bed down there anymore, but the Oatman Hotel had a certain rundown charm. What struck both Ian and me was how crowded the dining room was. Neither of us had realized that it was St. Patrick's Day. As a result, all the beer on tap was green, and corned beef and cabbage was on special. Ian griped about how ridiculous it was to come to the middle of nowhere and find this tourist travesty, what a waste to dye good beer and bowdlerize a traditional Irish dish, blah blah blah. As a Scot, Ian was only Ireland-adjacent. I dared not imagine his hue and cry if a restaurant had assaulted his national pride by trying to serve an inauthentic version of haggis. Then again, I've never seen any version of haggis, inauthentic or otherwise, on a US menu. You'd need some mighty strong single malt to make sheep-innards-and-oatmeal go down.

Since I wasn't driving—ha, ha—I drank several green beers, which made me more tolerant of Ian's curmudgeonly ways. In fact, I began to find his complaints pretty funny. And I was sufficiently relaxed to nod off on the return trip.

Maybe I seemed mellower by the end of the day, or maybe Ian hadn't noticed my general lack of geniality earlier on; whatever the case, when we returned to Las Vegas, he seemed genuinely surprised that I didn't want to meet him for a drink later that evening. I did want to see more of the city and, especially, the bars, but I'm not that much of a masochist. I pleaded a writing deadline, the journalist's unassailable excuse.

Some months later, Ian sent me a clip from *The Scotsman* of his story about our excursion. It was beautifully written and warmly humorous. Had I missed that side of his personality, hiding, hedgehog-like, beneath the prickles? I chuckled at his take on our experiences, including the description of me as "the only woman west of the Mississippi who didn't have a driving license." But when I got to the part about our St. Paddy's Day lunch at the Oatman Hotel, I was startled to discover that he'd made it seem as though we had gone as a couple, that we were romantically linked. At first, I was annoyed, but the more I thought about it, the more it made sense. I had become part of the stable of powerful women who desired Ian, the Fodor's editor with whom he'd had a Las Vegas tryst. Maybe I wasn't chopped liver, after all. Ian just hadn't yet mythologized me when we were together.

🐪 🐪 🐪

Mexico was next on my Fodor's schedule. As soon as it had been clinched that I was going to be living less than two hours from the border, I volunteered to update the Copper Canyon (Barrancas del Cobre) chapter of *Fodor's Mexico*. As the book's editor, I'd been intrigued to read about a natural wonder in northern Mexico that was billed as the country's Grand Canyon—only four times as large.

Why had I barely heard of the Copper Canyon? Probably because there were no direct flights from New York to anywhere nearby. It was all part and parcel of the East Coast–centrism I was becoming aware of, the historical slant that had forced the Puritans on me from the day I learned to draw my first Thanksgiving turkey, but kept me in the dark about the Spanish padres. I knew more than I ever wanted to about Increase and Cotton Mather, but until I moved to the Southwest had never heard of Junipero Serra and Eusebio Kino. Not only were the Spanish missionaries slightly less cruel than the pilgrims to the native peoples they encountered—they built agricultural communities rather than just mooching food and spreading smallpox—but their names were a lot more mellifluous.

I was nervous about going to Mexico. For one thing, I didn't know the language. Like many New Yorkers who dream of a *pied-à-terre* in Paris, I'd studied French in high school and college. For another, although I'd been to Mexico many times as a tourist, I was now going as a professional. Things—I wasn't sure what exactly, but many of them—would be expected of me.

I calmed myself with the knowledge that I had a bit of menu Spanish, that *Fodor's Mexico* was well known throughout the country, and that I was far from inexperienced in the ways of guidebook research. I had made several advance arrangements for free hotels and tours under Fodor's aegis.

Intensive worry was—still is—one of my pre-travel rituals, an integral part of my preparation process. No matter how many trips I took, how familiar I was with the destination, how many checklists I made (and invariably misplaced), I had to put in a requisite number of obsessing and stressing hours. I understood why my job seemed enviable to others. But I was always daunted by travel logistics, and having my income depend on them only compounded my anxiety. If you miss your flight, you're not just missing a day of vacation, annoying as that may be. You're falling down on the job.

It was a typically sunny day in late March when I flew from Tucson International Airport into Los Mochis, an agricultural town-turned-train hub near Mexico's Pacific coast. Felipe, a representative of a local tour company, was waiting for me with a sign on the tarmac of the tiny Los Mochis airport. He was middle aged, trim and neat, like David Suchet's *Poirot,* only less fussy.

I've mentioned the impressive dimensions of the canyon, but the engineering feat that allowed visitors to traverse it was equally mind-boggling. Completed in the early 1960s, the Chihuahua Al Pacifico rail line required laying 410 miles of track, blasting eighty-six tunnels, and building thirty-five bridges in a rugged, remote region.

I was scheduled to catch the Copper Canyon train early the following morning and wanted to check as many Fodor's listings on the western end of the route as possible. Felipe took me on a whirlwind tour of Los Mochis, where most people board the train at the crack of dawn, and of Topolobompo, the seaport that became the center of railroad-building activities. The town's name, which means "watering place of the sea lions" in the language of the indigenous Mayo people, is now far better known by most Americans as a Mexican restaurant in Chicago. I like to think that celebrity chef/owner Rick Bayless chose the appellation so he could amuse himself with its mispronunciations, though I have not a smidge of evidence for this theory.

The train also made a stop, an hour later, at the nearby colonial town of El Fuerte, named for the fort built by the Spanish to fend off attacks by the aforementioned Mayo Indians. That's where Felipe and I ended a long day of visiting every place Fodor's readers might want to see and everywhere they might want to sleep or eat. Felipe was wonderfully knowledgeable about the entire Copper Canyon route, clueing me in on the bad and the ugly as well as the good.

He was also very kind. At my hotel in El Fuerte, where he treated me to a margarita and *botanas* (snacks), I tried to take a photo and discovered that the battery for my Olympus point-and-shoot was dead. I'd brought several extra rolls of film, but had neglected to remember extra batteries. Panicked because I was heading into the canyon early the next morning, I asked Felipe where I could buy some replacements. "Relax," he said, "I'll go get you new ones." I tried to give him the only Mexican money I had to cover the cost, a very large bill. "Don't worry about it," he said.

He returned half an hour later, batteries in hand.

When it was time for Felipe to leave, I was in a quandary: Was it appropriate to tip him? He was nicely dressed and looked middle-class. I wasn't sure if he was an employee of the tour company he represented or its owner. If the former, would the company cover all his expenses? I still only had the very large peso bill I'd gotten from the airport currency exchange desk, and I thought giving him dollars might be rude.

So I shook his hand and thanked him profusely for his help instead of tipping him.

Felipe didn't look angry or even reproachful. He just looked a little crestfallen.

It's funny, the things that stick in your mind—and your craw. All these years later, I can still picture that sad look. I felt like running after Felipe and saying, "Wait, I'll try to get some change." Or, "Would giving you dollars be okay?"

Rule to live by: When in doubt about tipping, always err on the side of generosity. A few Mexican-specific corollaries: Foreign money is better than no money; when you go to Mexico, bring small American bills. I don't know why this is so, but over the years I discovered it was really hard to get tip-size denominations of peso bills. The coins are easier to find, but heavier to tote.

The next morning, I boarded the train and forgot about Felipe and tipping.

The Mexican train system, Ferrocarriles Nacionales de Mexico, was in terrible shape by the time I experienced it in 1992. The government had merged the five regional rail lines, which had been nationalized after the Mexican Revolution, but the system was too deep in debt to be salvaged; it was later privatized and mostly scrapped. The Copper Canyon route was a cash cow, so it was better maintained than the other lines, but even its first class was hardly luxurious. It wouldn't have mattered—this was, after all, a day trip—except that the windows were cloudy and it was too chilly to stand between cars, ogling scenery, for very long.

I got off the train in Divisadero, a postage stamp of a place known mainly for being on the Continental Divide and having the most impressive canyon views—comparatively speaking. Although the Mexican gorges stretch out for miles longer and are deeper in spots, for the most part they don't look as dramatic as the Grand Canyon. The stark geological layers of erosion, carved by six rivers over millions of years, are often obscured from sight by thickets of pine trees. By any other metric, however, the Copper Canyon is a knockout. I'd booked an overnight in the tiny town in order to get the full-on visual experience.

I quickly learned that scenery has its limits.

It took me about an hour and a half to check out the other three lodgings besides the one where I was staying. It was cold and I felt sluggish. I had been at sea level that morning. Now I was at the highest point of the train ride, an elevation of almost 8,000 feet. It had been sunny and 75 degrees F in Los Mochis. It was gray and 35 degrees F in Divisadero.

But even if the weather had been warm, I would have been antsy just lounging around. I had a chapter to update. There are only so many adjectives to use—breathtaking! spectacular! awe-inspiring!—to describe the views. The next train going east toward Chihuahua wasn't due for another twenty-two hours.

I confided my dilemma to three fellow train passengers from England, who were lounging in the lobby of my hotel. One of them suggested I take a horseback ride to Bacajipare, a Tarahumara village near the bottom of the canyon—where, as a bonus, it would be warm.

Why not, I thought. I was interested in the culture of the Tarahumara people, who lived in and around the canyon, and this was an activity I could report on. I went to the front desk and booked a guide for after lunch.

As the time approached, I began to question my sanity. I hate being cold, and sitting still on the back of a horse was not likely to warm me up, at least not for the first part of the trip. I'm a New York Jew. Horseback riding came even less naturally to me than driving. And there was my fear of heights. I figured I would be terrified all the way down unless I closed my eyes, which would defeat the main purpose of the ride: ogling scenery.

I should have trusted my instincts and bailed, but I had my pride, as well as the reputation of Fodor's to uphold. I was also in full view of the three Brits who had recommended this activity. I retained a Rough Guides–inspired need to prove that Americans are not wusses.

At the appointed time, I went to the front desk to meet my guide.

No one can accuse me of ageism, even in the days before I was in danger of being subjected to that prejudice. I've always maintained that older people have a lot to offer, intellectually speaking. Athletically speaking—less so. I was appalled to be introduced to José, a frail, stooped man who looked to be in his seventies. His coughing fits did not inspire confidence.

Oh yeah, and he didn't speak any English.

Against my better judgment, I headed out with José and two horses that looked as geriatric and as unhealthy as he did.

I thought, "How bad could it be?"

Let me count the ways.

Start with the paths. As far as I could tell, they didn't exist. I kept waiting for the trees to clear so I could see the trail that lay ahead but I saw nothing except pine forest.

Then there were the horses. You've heard about the sure-footed mules of the Grand Canyon? These animals weren't remotely related to them. My ride kept tripping.

At one point, when José could no longer ignore the shuddering noises I made every time the horse stumbled, he pointed to the ground to indicate the ice and then gestured for me to dismount.

Ok, fine. I figured my feet might be surer than the horses' hooves and that maybe a little hiking might warm me up.

Ah, then, the *coup de grâce*. José's hand grazed my breast when he helped me down.

Jeez. This geezer looked like he was on the last legs, yet he had summoned the energy to grope me.

Maybe I was imagining it. I was wearing a lot of clothing.

But no. After we had descended into the canyon a short way, the air felt warmer and there were fewer patches of ice. José gestured for me to get back on the horse. As he helped me up, there was that pressure again.

My Cairo camel guide was not José's sole precursor in perversion. Years earlier, a snorkeling instructor in Cancun groped me and my friend Marilyn. Third time's a charm—or a pattern. I was beginning to think there was a passage in the International Instruction Manual for Tour Guides that said American women like to have their breasts touched when you are assisting them with activities.

If you ride the New York subway regularly, your personal space is constantly being invaded. Unless you feel any thrusting or rubbing by the people pushed up against you—at which point an elbow jab or toe stomp is in order—you accept uncomfortable contact as a part of city living. Encountering it in a remote Mexican canyon was disheartening but hardly life shattering. Almost the worst part was my sense that José's heart wasn't in it.

For a while, we soldiered on. Then the trees began to clear and I saw the vast canyon vistas spread out before me. I didn't see any clear trail, however.

That's when my fear of heights really kicked in. We were about an hour into our two-hour descent and I'd had it.

Because José didn't speak English and I didn't speak Spanish, I had a hard time conveying my fervent desire to turn back. I repeatedly wrapped my arms around myself, pointed up the mountain, and said, "*Returnamos, por favor. Es muy frío,*" trying to indicate that I was cold. Of course "returnamos" is not actual Spanish and, for all I know, José might have understood *frijoles* instead of frío and thought I wanted beans, or that I'd eaten beans in the hotel restaurant and needed to find a bathroom.

Whatever the case, José chose to ignore my peculiar gestures and pidgin utterances. He kept directing the horses downward. I tried to focus my mind elsewhere, willing the experience to be over. At least it got warmer as we descended, which meant there was no more ice for the horses to slip on and I could close my eyes when we were on particularly precipitous overlooks.

When we finally arrived in Bajicipare, we were met by—surprise, surprise—people selling stuff.

In addition to being famed for their speed as runners, the Tarahumara people are known for their baskets, pottery, and ironwood carvings. I like the idea of being able to buy Mexican folk art directly from craftspeople. Just the idea. In practice, I hate having to choose between eager-looking vendors. It didn't help that I suspected that José got a kickback from the village artisans, which would explain his determination to deliver me to them.

Add to that, I still had a week left on my trip and didn't want to drag around anything bulky, breakable, or heavy. Ironwood is amazingly dense.

Bottom line: I'd expended most of my vast quota of guilt on not tipping Felipe in Los Mochis. I wasn't about to buy any pity trinkets.

When he finally realized that I wasn't in an acquisitive state of mind, José reluctantly started back. Whew. Going up a slope is far less stressful for me than going down; you can't see the overlooks. And the first hour was fine. But the mercury dropped again as the elevation rose. The horses started slipping again. José gestured for us to dismount again.

Now I had something else to worry about besides boob grabs.

On our descent, I was able to avoid contemplating José's health, except during his hacking coughing fits. As we started to ascend on foot, however, he added heavy, raspy breathing to his repertoire of unpleasant noises.

Great, I thought. My guide is going to have a heart attack. I'll be stuck in a far-off Mexican canyon with two klutzy horses and a dead guy. My own corpse won't be found until months later—if ever.

My supply of empathy, like my allotment of guilt, was about depleted.

But I lived to tell the tale to the three English tourists, who greeted me in the lobby where they were still sitting, now having beers. After I finished the story, one of them said to me, "Oh I would never have gone down with that guide. He looked like he was about to keel over."

Thanks for sharing that—after the fact.

🐫 🐫 🐫

The following winter, I returned to the Copper Canyon with my friend Terri in tow. She was a northern Mexico maven, having traveled down from Tucson with her family for as long as she could remember. I told her I'd pay for gas and for any hotels that we couldn't get comped if she would take the wheel. It was a deal.

I hadn't been able to cover everything I'd wanted to see on my previous research trip, especially Batopilas, a town at the bottom of Batopilas Canyon. Founded by the Spanish conquistadores in the early eighteenth century, it had been one of Mexico's top producers of silver, turning out some 300 million ounces of ore over the centuries. One guidebook described the town as having a subtropical climate year-round, lush with orange and mango trees and home to parrots, deer, and the occasional jaguar. It sounded irresistibly romantic. When I learned that a converted hacienda called the Canyon Lodge had just opened there, my determination to go was cemented.

I phoned the owner of the lodge, a Michigan-based entrepreneur named Tug Malone, and told him I wanted to check out the hacienda for Fodor's. He said he would be happy to comp me and a friend, but explained that there was usually a minimum three-night stay in the Batopilas hotel and that it was sold as part of a package with his Forest View Lodge, on the canyon's rim. I would be glad to stay in his other place, I said, but wouldn't have time to spend more than a single night there plus two nights in Batopilas. Tug agreed to that truncated schedule, while cautioning that we might feel rushed.

And so Terri and I set off for Los Mochis in her sturdy SUV. We spent the night in Alamos, a tiny Colonial-era town about eight hours south of Tucson. Popular with Arizonans who want to combine a getaway in the nearby beach resorts of Guaymas and San Carlos with a bit of culture, Alamos was impeccably clean; housewives swept the streets each day at the crack of dawn. It was also very quiet, with a couple of homey restaurants, a few inns, and a small museum. I would have been happy to poke around Alamos for another day to see if I could find any nuggets to add to the Fodor's guide, but we had a schedule to stick to and Terri was bored. She who controls the vehicle controls the timetable.

We departed early the next morning for El Fuerte. There, we left the SUV and caught the train to Creel, a backpackers' mecca at the eastern end of the Copper Canyon; its main street is lined with modest hotels and restaurants. I'd spent a day there the previous year gathering recommendations from budget travelers.

I'd spent a night there the previous year having a fling with Enrique, the thirty-something manager of one of those modest hotels.

Enrique had invited me to dine at his hotel's restaurant and, a few *cervezas* into the evening, started giving me meaningful looks and compliments. He had a nice face, not exactly handsome, but friendly, and a good, solid build. It was clear where this conversation was leading—upstairs, together— and I was more than willing to follow. The sex, the Mexican version of my Cairo quickie but without the added turn-on of surprise, was not very satisfying, but I welcomed the physical contact. I should say the "wanted" physical contact, as opposed to what I'd experienced a day earlier on the horseback ride from hell.

My encounter with Enrique would have been blissfully zipless had the Copper Canyon train not been thirteen hours late the following day. Enrique kept abandoning his hotel manager's post to come over to the station and check in on me.

I appreciated his gallantry, though I imagine the guests at his hotel didn't. I'm sure I would have been annoyed had he left me entirely to my own devices all day, but we didn't have much to talk about and Enrique wouldn't believe my assurances that I would be fine reading my novel and working on the Mexico guide. It's not easy being a sexually liberated woman in Mexico—or, I should say, it's even harder than it is in the US. I had to try to make conversation or sit with Enrique in uncomfortable silence whenever he came by.

Terri's presence this year meant an affair to forget would not be on the agenda.

The Forest View Lodge sat just outside of Creel, in a piñon pine thicket near Cusarare Falls. Our rustic-chic room, blending Spanish Colonial–style furnishings with modern tiled baths, had only a wood-burning stove for warmth and kerosene lamps for light. Terri and I didn't mind the lack of electricity. The setting was lovely, the communal dinner included in the lodging package hearty and collegial.

The stove didn't hold enough wood to remain lit all night, and the temperature dipped, which made it hard to get out of bed the next morning. But we roused ourselves early to meet Carlos, the guide assigned to drive us to Batopilas. Talk about déjà vu. Like Señor Handsy in Divisadero, Carlos looked frail and geriatric. I wondered whether toting tourists into the canyon was a duty reserved for retirees, or whether these guides were actually far younger than they appeared and had gotten worn out by riding up and down all day on bumpy, unmaintained roads.

This time, our guide's taciturnity couldn't be blamed on a language barrier. Terri is fluent in Spanish and couldn't manage to get more than monosyllabic grunts out of Carlos. Our vehicle looked as inadequate to the task of the long descent into the canyon as the tired horses of the previous year had. It was open on the sides, faded red with patches of rust. Not only was it lacking shields against the dust, but it seemed to be missing springs and shocks. I get carsick when trying to read on anything that moves, even when the ride is smooth, so I was very glad to have Terri to talk to for five and a half kidney-jolting hours.

At last, we were deposited at the Canyon Lodge. The gorgeously restored hacienda did indeed evoke Batopilas's glory days—in some ways. For a stretch in the late-nineteenth century, Batopilas was the only place in the country besides Mexico City that had electricity. Thus there was a certain irony to the fact that the rooms were outfitted with an odd mix of kerosene lamps for reading and electrical outlets for hairdryers. I suppose it's better than the reverse: No one likes a kerosene-powered hairdryer. But while the creature-comfort deficit was a good fit with the cool, piney sister lodge where we had stayed the night before, it seemed out of place in an elegant hacienda in a town known for its fabulous wealth.

The decor was quirky too—charming, but not consistently Mexican. One room featured vintage Elizabeth Taylor posters, for example, while another paid tribute to Marilyn Monroe.

Still, all the guest quarters had large private baths and lots of hot water. After Terri and I took turns showering off the road dust, we were ready to take on Batopilas.

The ride into town hadn't led us to expect much, but we were still unprepared for the complete absence of lushness we encountered. Terri later recalled, "We had a laugh about the 'tropical paradise' as expressed by two forlorn-looking orange trees, a dusty banana tree in a pot, and a palm tree or two... It didn't look like it had rained in YEARS. There were no shops, nothing to do but watch little kids and chickens running around." So much for the deer, parrots, and jaguars.

We spotted a lanky, nice-looking man wandering around the main square and scribbling assiduously in a notebook. He had a friendly American air, but we didn't try to engage him in conversation. We had been somewhat revived by our showers, but Terri and I agreed that we needed a proper meal and some strong drink before being civil to strangers.

I suppose it shouldn't have been a surprise that the stranger turned out to be staying at the Canyon Lodge; it was the nicest accommodation in town. But what were the odds, Terri and I later wondered, that he would turn out to be another travel writer, Joe Cummings from northern California? And that Joe would be the only other guest at the lodge besides us?

Curiouser and curiouser: The three of us were greeted at dinner by another Californian, a genial, sunburned man who called himself Barranca Bob; he was from the southern part of the state and looked like a surfer. He explained that he had been hired at the lodge as a hiking guide, but during owner Tug Malone's absences—which were frequent, especially in the winter off-season—he doubled as the inn's informal manager.

He was thrilled to see us. Most of the guests Bob encountered were rich, spoiled Americans, he said. Now he had three freeloading but non-spoiled Americans for company, two of them travel writers eager for his insider knowledge.

After a down-home Mexican dinner prepared by the housekeeper, we settled into the living room to talk. When we'd run into him in town, Joe told us, he had been drawing a map of Batopilas for the second edition of his *Northern Mexico Handbook*, published by Moon. He emailed, "I was absolutely obsessed with the nine northern [Mexican] states back then, mainly because they were so little visited by foreigners. No one ever covered northern Mexico in such detail, before or since. A friend who knows Cormac McCarthy said *Northern Mexico Handbook* was one of McCarthy's references for locations in his *All the Pretty Horses* and *The Crossing*."

Joe wasn't nearly as articulate about his guidebook that night. None of us was very articulate about anything after a while. We were all shit-faced.

Barranca Bob had decided that part of his job as host was to ply us with alcohol. Both the Forest View Lodge in Cusarare and the Canyon Lodge were on the honor system: You wrote down what you drank and paid for it afterwards. Bob kept pouring premium spirits from the liquor cabinet without keeping track.

Whenever one of us expressed concern that he might be pushing the limits of the owner's largesse, Bob would say, "Oh, Tug wouldn't mind. You're travel writers."

For maybe the first time since I started freelancing, I felt like a genuine member of that community, gossiping with Joe about the many people in the guidebook world we knew in common, comparing notes on what we'd seen and thought was worth recommending in the area. Bob promised to take us all on a hike to some of the more interesting remote spots the next day. Eventually, we all teetered off to our respective rooms.

In spite of a massive hangover the next morning, I was looking forward to the hike. Terri, however, had other ideas. She was determined to depart, deaf to my reminders that I had promised Tug that we would stay for two days—and that was pushing it. She'd suddenly remembered something she urgently needed to do in Tucson at a particular time. We had to head back, she insisted. Immediately.

Much to the astonishment of everyone—including the staff, Carlos the driver, Joe, and Bob—we announced we had to leave. Our ride back up to the rim was mostly silent. The headache and nausea caused by the previous night's overindulgence weren't improved by the ruts in the road—and by my fury. The lesson I'd learned in Alamos was reinforced: She who has the keys to the vehicle controls the schedule.

Terri and I eventually made it up, but I never did find out why she'd insisted on going. When I asked her about the trip some twenty years after the fact, she recalled our hasty retreat as a mutual decision.

Maybe she had been bored by our travel writer shoptalk or felt left out of the conversation. Maybe she didn't want to spend another minute of her life in Batopilas. Ah well; time to let it go. In memory, as well as in tipping, it's always best to err on the side of generosity.

Joe and I continued to be in touch for a long time, though he doesn't remember much about that evening except the reason that he doesn't remember much about that evening. We ran into each other at travel writers' conferences for many years until Joe moved to Thailand—the subject of his first Lonely Planet guide and the source of many royalties. Joe is one of the few people I know who made serious money in the guidebook business. Only one of the major players in that boozy Batopilas gathering has been lost to time: Barranca Bob, displaced So Cal surfer dude. Did Tug fire him? Did he drink himself to death at the bottom of the canyon, *Under the Volcano*-style? I didn't ever learn his real name, so not even Google can reveal his fate.

CHAPTER 9
STRADDLING THE EDITORIAL DESK
All Around Arizona, 1992–1995

How to annoy a guidebook writer: After she returns from a week of rushing around, peering into hotel rooms, checking museum hours, and chatting up tour operators, ask her how she enjoyed her vacation.

The initial kick I got from going on the road for assignments was quickly tempered by the hectic schedule, the need to gear my research toward a guidebook template, and the low pay.

Especially the low pay.

The expression "traveling on someone else's dime" came pathetically close to describing my freelance earnings from Fodor's. I got a flat fee, based on the page count of the section I was assigned, with no extra allotment for expenses.

Take the Copper Canyon chapter of *Fodor's Mexico.* I was paid $1,000 to update eighteen pages. My hotels and some meals were comped, but if you subtract $325 plane fare to Los Mochis, $40 to ride the Copper Canyon train, $150 for additional meals, $50 for activities, and $40 for taxis to and from the Tucson airport, that leaves $395. And that's a low estimate of my expenses. I spent eight days on the road and at least a week inputting all the information, a total of fifteen days. On average, I work 6.5 hours a day. Multiply 6.5 by 15 and divide $435 by 95.5 and you get $4.14 an hour. Even by Tucson's low cost-of-living standards and adjusted for inflation, that's pitiful.

There was also a clause in my contract that said I could be docked $200 for every week I was late. I never knew it to be invoked in all my time as an editor at Fodor's, but it existed, as did many other onerous, potentially bankruptcy-inducing legal stipulations.

The horseback ride at Divisadero, the fling in Creel, hanging out in Batopilas the following year...these adventures all came courtesy of a Fodor's gig, sure, but more typical was the day spent checking hotels and sights in Los Mochis the first year. And back in Tucson, nodding with boredom at my desk, inputting addresses, telephone numbers, number of rooms, opening hours, amenities, admission fees, price categories, accepted credit cards—I often wondered what the hell I was doing. I'd left New York to become a writer, not a hotel room inspector or a fact checker. I rationalized that I was establishing myself as an expert in the Southwest US and Mexico and gathering story ideas to pitch to magazines.

This turned out to be true, though I'm not sure this particular form of dues paying was a great fit for someone with my compulsive work habits. I spent far more time than I should have trying to get every last detail correct. But given my connections with guidebook publishers and my initial lack of confidence in approaching magazine editors, it was the path of least resistance.

Happily, I also got a lot of editing work from Fodor's.

In an odd inversion of economic logic, updating was far more labor-intensive and time-consuming, but editing paid the bills. My fees ranged from $1,500 for editing a smallish US book like *Fodor's San Diego* to $4,500 for a large foreign guide like *Fodor's Mexico*. And, unless I wanted to visit places to familiarize myself with them—or, in the case of San Diego, where I did my dissertation research, to see my friends—I didn't have any travel expenses.

It might take me from three to six months to complete each book but I always had breaks between editing phases—hiring writers, reading submitted copy, looking at final proofs—during which I could leave town. And I was able to work quickly and efficiently. By now, guidebook editing was second nature to me and I generally enjoyed it, especially when I worked with writers who managed to include some local color, who were conscientious about the service details, and who met their deadlines.

Writers like me.

Straddling both sides of the editorial desk gave me a newfound appreciation for what went into producing a clean update—one that didn't require me to correct weird syntax and grammar or send back a lot of queries requesting clarification or additional information. I thought back on my previous interactions with contributors. I'd often sent only a terse "Got it, thanks" note in response to receiving assignments. I could justify this when I was too busy to look at a submission, but how long would it have taken to get back to an author later and say, "Great job"? I rarely did that, and not only because I was distracted. I foolishly assumed that writers who were professionals knew they were good and didn't need me to praise them. Offering them more work was sufficient proof of my approbation.

It didn't take long for that bit of editorial karma to bite me in the butt when I started freelancing. To this day, if an editor doesn't say anything positive about my work, I'm convinced she hates it. This fear partly stems from congenital insecurity, but it's also based on insider knowledge of the workings of at least one editor's mind. I wasn't only stinting when it came to praise, but cowardly when it came to criticism.

When I was hiring writers for Fodor's *Wall Street Journal* series, for example, I told an applicant who had submitted a few excellent clips from prestigious publications that I was almost certain she would get the assignment, but that I wanted to see some articles that had not yet been professionally edited. Most editors don't have time to look at original samples; it was a fluke, or maybe intuition, that I did so this time.

When the manuscripts arrived, I was dismayed by their poor quality, though hardly shocked. It's a self-perpetuating process: Editors clean up the prose of a mediocre writer to make it publishable, and *voilà*—the writer acquires a nice portfolio of clips to send along to the next victim.

I didn't know how to tell the writer that her work was unacceptable, so I didn't. I didn't tell her anything at all. I just avoided her calls and emails until they stopped coming. I forgot about the incident fairly soon, but she never did. Years later, when I signed up for a travel writing conference and checked off the box indicating my interest in a roommate, the writer posted on the conference forum about me: "I would never share a room with her. She's a liar." Guilty—at least of the sin of omission. I should have found a kind but clear way to let her know why I didn't want to hire her after I'd more or less promised her the assignment.

I spent the conference—a large one, fortunately— avoiding her. Again.

Maybe my most important bit of freelance consciousness-raising was a newfound sense of urgency about getting "my" writers paid. I didn't have anything to do with financial matters at Prentice Hall Travel but at Fodor's it was part of my job to make sure that the company met its financial obligations to authors. Facilitating payment wasn't a priority, however, and I got annoyed when writers bugged me. Didn't they have a cushion to fall back on when there was a short check delay?

Talk about hubris. Would that every editor was required to spend a minimum of six months freelancing before working in-house. I've had to dip into my insubstantial savings to cover an unexpected expense many, many times. It would be hard to count the number of days I've spent biting my nails, waiting for a check to arrive. As soon as I realized the error of my ways, I worked hard to light a fire under the accounting department's bureaucracy. Along the way, I discovered it was easier to bug the New York office to get someone else paid than it was to ask for what was owed me.

Why this should be so is a question for a therapist. Or a feminist sociologist. And I digress.

Probably my largest, most lucrative project in those early freelancing years was developing a new series, *Fodor's Bed & Breakfasts and Country Inns*. I was in charge of compiling the first three regional guides: the Southwest, California, and the Pacific Northwest. I liked the challenge of being in on a project from the ground up—even one under the watchful eye of Dick Brooks, Fodor's editor-in-chief and the bane of my existence when I worked on the *Wall Street Journal* guides. Being a few thousand miles from Dick made a huge difference. He could no longer pop into my office and suggest inane changes whenever it struck his fancy. It takes far more time and effort to mess with your employees long-distance.

And by the time the project got into its research phase, I was able to drive and had gotten assigned several sections of *Fodor's Arizona* to update. I finagled a sweet deal: I would write some of the Arizona listings in the Southwest B&B guide and thereby amortize my travel expenses over two books.

Fodor's Bed & Breakfasts and Country Inns would have been a plum except for one thing: I loathed B&Bs.

🐪 🐪 🐪

True, I'd had rather limited experience with them up to this point, but that was by design. My idea of a good way to start the day didn't include socializing with strangers.

Mind you, I am a morning person, as I was shocked to discover when I moved to Tucson. I'd had inklings of this personality quirk in Manhattan, where I used to beg friends to meet me for dinner earlier than the fashionable 8:30 or 9 p.m. And I always felt better if I managed to fall asleep before midnight, which was rare, since I stayed up to watch the local news at 11 p.m. I often spent half the night tossing, worrying that I'd be exhausted at work the next day if I didn't get some sleep. Which I was.

In southern Arizona, where summer is the uncomfortable season and life is geared toward beating the heat, I discovered my circadian rhythms were in sync with the local custom of going to bed by 10:30 p.m. and rising by 5:30 a.m. Go figure. My head thinks I'm a city sophisticate; my body believes I am a farmer.

But just because I like getting up early, that doesn't mean I wake up chirpy or willing to chat with people I don't know.

Pre-caffeinated social interactions were not my only gripe with B&Bs. Victorian-era furnishings were minefields for a klutz like me. I was in constant fear of breaking the spindly little legs of those delicate Queen Anne–style chairs, dislodging a frilly antimacassar from the arm of an uncomfortable fainting couch, or accidentally smashing a set of priceless china that belonged to the innkeeper's beloved great aunt. And don't even get me started on the thousands of pillows that tend to get piled on the beds. What are you expected to do with them when you want to go to sleep? Place them carefully on the single armchair in the room where you've already draped your clothes because your nano-closet contains only two spindly wire hangers? Fling them on the floor?

B&B plumbing made me nervous, too. The last thing I needed to worry about while on the road was someone else's toilet. And I could have happily lived without ever climbing in and out of a claw-foot tub, especially because I'd much rather take a shower than sit soaking in my own grime and skin flakes.

Did I mention the thin walls? Talk about enforced intimacy with strangers.

Also, I don't do ghosts. For some reason, many B&B frequenters think it's a treat to have the disembodied disturb their sleep; a resident haunt is deemed a selling point. An innkeeper to whom I confided my lack of interest in spectral visits said, with great authority, "The dead only come to those who wish to see them." Would that the living were as considerate.

I know, not all B&Bs are Victorian, not all their plumbing is dodgy, and not all are spirit-friendly. But no matter what era they're channeling, inns tend to feature themed rooms that highlight historical figures, the innkeepers' dearly departed, Hollywood stars—you name it. If I wanted themes, I'd go to Disneyland. And when your room has a name, it's impossible to feel relaxed in it. I wouldn't want to leave strands of my hair on Emily Dickinson's sink, but I can go crazy with my comb in Room 305.

Perhaps what I disliked most about these romantic retreats—or so they're often billed—was dealing with couples.

I've read that many women on their own feel safer at inns than they do at motels. Me, I feared eating with people who were paired off far more than I did walking down long, dim corridors. The reactions to finding a solo woman at the breakfast table ranged from condescension toward me ("Don't you get lonely all by yourself?") to resentment toward their partners ("You like talking to her better than you like talking to me!").

Rule to live by: If you are in a relationship, even a decent one, don't assume that single people envy you. The odds are good that we're regarding you with pity or relief that we're not similarly entangled.

Taking along a friend would have smoothed over any awkwardness at breakfast. But the more comfortable I became with driving, the more I saw the advantages of traveling alone—and that's not even factoring in the potential of companions like Robert the Tipsy Designated Driver and Terri the Intransigent to reflect badly on me. I wanted to be free to have business meals with tourism reps and to take offbeat detours at whim. At the Tombstone Courthouse State Historic Park, for example, I was fascinated by the barbed-wire display, a window into the role that fencing played in the West. When you're with someone who is hungry for lunch and not especially interested in history, it's awkward to say, "Wait, I just need a few more minutes with the barbed wire."

For another thing, B&Bs are often not platonic pal-friendly; many only offer rooms with one queen or one king bed. On a couple of occasions, when a female friend and I requested a rollout cot, we got an eye roll first: The innkeepers assumed we were trying to hide the fact that we were lesbians. Ironically, on my research trip with Robert, who is gay, no one looked askance at our request for an extra bed. Apparently, it's okay for straight couples not to want to have sex, but same-gender couples are expected to rut like ferrets.

I had also discovered the exhilaration of driving along Arizona's back roads, singing off-key and at the top of my lungs to the Dixie Chicks' "Wide Open Spaces," and had tasted the freedom of stopping to find a bathroom whenever I damn well felt like it. There was no turning back.

🐪 🐪 🐪

I took the potential to be discomfited by fellow B&B guests for granted, but—over-solicitousness aside—I wasn't expecting owners or staff to be troublesome. Surprise.

I had a strategy: If I came downstairs early, I could stake out my seat at the breakfast table and either go over my schedule notes or talk to the innkeeper, uninterrupted. If I were already planted at a table, I wouldn't be calling attention to myself in the same way as I would if I were making a late arrival, and could ease into conversations. But one Sedona B&B I visited, newly built in characterless faux-Southwest style, was larger than most. The dining room held two long, family-style tables in the center and two tables for four by bay windows with red rock views. When I walked in, a couple was sitting at one of the tables for four. I smiled and nodded at the two, then headed over to one of the communal tables, grabbing a seat at the end for easy escape.

The B&B manager, Kathy, rushed over to me and asked if I would mind joining the pair at the bay window instead. "Yes, I would mind," I said. "What's the problem with my sitting at this empty table?" She replied, "Most of our guests are couples, and you might mess up the seating arrangement."

Here I'd thought I was being considerate by not bogarting the other scenic-view table, as I had been tempted to do. I was livid. "I wouldn't want to mess up your seating arrangement," I said. "Why don't you just bring me my breakfast upstairs in my room?"

Kathy backed off. I sat stewing in my chosen spot, watching as two friends joined the original bay-window duo— the manager had not bothered to ask them whether it was okay for me to disturb their *tête-à-tête*—and as the communal table filled up, though not quickly enough to inconvenience any couples.

This type of thoughtlessness was not as uncommon as you might imagine, nor was it limited to this type of lodging. I often encountered the attitude that, since I was getting a free room, I shouldn't expect any other extras—you know, like friendliness. It took me a while, and lots of discussions with fellow writers and PR people, to realize that if the staff didn't understand that it's smart to be nice to the travel press, they might not get the principle of being nice to paying guests, either.

Then, too, not everyone saw the benefit of having their business listed in a guidebook—sometimes known as a "directory"—as opposed to sexier consumer magazines like *Condé Nast Traveler* or *Travel + Leisure*.

Consider a B&B in Ajo, a former mining town in southwestern Arizona. Penelope from the Arizona Office of Tourism (AOT) had phoned the owner to explain that I was working on two prestigious guidebooks for Fodor's and asked her if she could host me. AOT had no authority (read: budget) to help with the tab, as a local chamber of commerce or convention and visitors bureau might have had—if sleepy Ajo had had a local chamber of commerce or convention and visitors bureau with a budget. Penelope's advance call was a favor to me but had no teeth.

I followed up the call from AOT and the owner agreed to comp me. When I arrived at the inn, however, she started waffling, grumbling that she didn't understand what I was doing, even though I showed her the previous edition of *Fodor's Arizona*, in which her B&B was listed. "Who uses those books?" she asked. I resigned myself to paying. That was okay. The room wasn't very expensive, and I was only going to be there for one night.

The next morning, three women who had traveled together from southern California came down to breakfast a few minutes after I did. When they discovered that I was there to update *Fodor's Arizona* and to work on a new B&B guide, they were as excited as they might have been to encounter their favorite best-selling author. One of them whipped out her well-worn guide and asked me to sign it. I explained that I hadn't worked on this particular section of the edition she owned, but she insisted.

I snuck a look at the owner to see if she had witnessed the scene. She had. I didn't get an apology, but I didn't get a bill, either.

Then there were the business owners who saw the value of being in a B&B guide, but didn't understand that objective criteria were used for listings.

One day I got a call from Roz James, who had just opened an inn in Tucson. She'd heard I was editing a new B&B guide and wanted me to review her place. One of the requirements for inclusion in the book was that the lodging should have a minimum of four rooms with private baths; another was that it should have been open for at least a year. The four-room requirement could sometimes be waived if a place with only three rooms was outstanding, but because of the high failure rate, the one-year-open rule was hard and fast.

Roz's three-room B&B—call it Casa Antigua—didn't meet either of the two criteria for inclusion, and I told her that when she phoned me. She said it didn't matter. She was sure I'd seen a lot of different inns in the course of my research and must know what worked and what didn't.

I'm a sucker for people who think I'm an expert in something. I said sure, I'd be glad to come by and take a look.

Casa Antigua was a beautiful 1910 adobe with lots of original details, including a viga-and-latilla ceiling—rough wood beams latticed with smaller twigs. The rooms were vibrant with color and bold Southwest art. I liked almost everything about the décor, with one exception: the tinwork crosses above the beds.

I got the concept. Many lodgings in traditionally Catholic countries have crucifixes or pictures of saints over their sleeping areas; I encountered them in *pensiones* all over Italy. And a Mexican-American home at the turn of the twentieth century would have had religious icons in every room. But I had been traumatized as a kid by tales of the Inquisition—what kind of Hebrew-school teacher assigns ten-year-olds reading material with pictures of racks and iron maidens?—and still found it creepy to sleep under a cross. My lapsed Catholic friends concur, though for different reasons: They say they prefer not to be reminded of the guilt instilled by their childhood faith—especially if they're planning to have sex outside the bounds of holy matrimony.

I told Roz, in response to her repeated solicitation of my "honest opinion, really," that I loved the place but that, "Unless you're often visited by vampires, I would lose those crosses." I went on to give an interdenominational explanation, never once mentioning the Spanish Inquisition.

She bristled and proceeded to lecture me on Mexican folk art, telling me that I didn't understand the cultural context of these religious symbols.

I can usually distinguish people who genuinely want your opinion when they ask for it from those who only want their behavior affirmed, but I'd clearly missed the signs this time. No matter. I wrote off my visit to Roz as a learning experience, an opportunity to fine-tune my bullshit detector and to see the inside of a classic barrio home.

That would have been the end of the story if I hadn't had dinner with my friend Andrew Collins a few weeks later.

He had been an editorial assistant when I was at Fodor's, and we'd gotten friendly after we both started freelancing. Andrew was in Tucson to research *Fodor's Gay Guide to the USA*—a book in which, I'm proud to say, I am cited in the acknowledgments as an honorary lesbian.

Andrew had just toured Casa Antigua on Roz's invitation—the woman was up on writers who might list her inn, I'll grant her that—and reported back, "Roz told me you weren't going to include her B&B in your book because you think she's an anti-Semite."

Whoa. How did she make the leap from my advice to "lose those crosses" to my accusing her of being a Nazi sympathizer?

Andrew wasn't planning to include Casa Antigua in his book either; he went by the one-year-open requirement for lodging inclusion too, with the exception of hotels that were part of a large group like Westin, say, or Ritz Carlton. We joked that Roz would tell the next writer she lured to her B&B that Andrew didn't include it in his book because he thought she was homophobic.

We never had the chance to find out. Casa Antigua closed nine months after it opened.

🐫 🐫 🐫

I've said that editing was my bread and butter. It also gave me a rare sense of confidence, and not only because I knew I was good at it. Sure, a writer can make an editor's life miserable by missing deadlines and turning in shoddy copy, but editors hold the purse strings and the reins over future work offers. Power, baby!

I was therefore jolted when one of the best writers on the B&B guides, Tom Servant, stopped speaking to me mid-assignment.

I'd edited Tom's *Fodor's New Mexico* when I was in New York, and it was a pleasure. Tom was a fine observer and prose stylist whose work had appeared in *Playboy, Esquire,* and other major magazines. I'd also enjoyed chatting with him about life in Tucson, where he'd moved from the East Coast. It took a while for us to get together when I made my own transition, however. Like me, Tom arrived as a non-driving ex-New Yorker. Unlike me, he never learned.

When we finally met, we became fast friends, despite Tom's archaic attitudes toward women. He would wax nostalgic about the days when flight attendants (stewardesses, to him) could be rated on their looks; that became the subject of one of his *Playboy* pieces, he told me proudly. He talked, too, about lusting after younger women—even though he had a teenage daughter about whom he was very protective.

I took all this with a grain of salt, figuring he was just trying to get a rise out of me. I didn't take the bait. Tom was genial and entertaining, and we had a lot in common, including an interest in Southwest and Mexican culture. And since neither of us was attracted to the other—I was too old for him despite being more than twenty years his junior, he was too out of shape for me—there was no sexual tension between us.

I didn't mind picking Tom up and driving him home when we got together. I had accumulated a lot of schlepping-people-around debt from the years when I had lived without wheels in San Diego, and Tom never mocked my fledging driving skills, as some passengers did.

When I started assigning the Southwest B&B guide, I naturally thought of Tom for the New Mexico sections. He'd already researched a lot of the inns and was always glad to spend time in Santa Fe. I knew it could be iffy to mix business relationships with personal ones, even friendships. Still, I figured I'd known Tom first as a writer, and a good, reliable one.

One night, a few months after he'd signed on to the project, Tom invited me over to dinner with two friends: another writer, Joe, and a photographer, Gary. After dinner, we agreed, I would drive Tom to a gallery opening we all wanted to attend and then deliver him home again.

Joe, Gary, and I were sitting around and drinking the wine I had brought while Tom puttered around in the kitchen. At one point, he shouted for me to come in and chop the radishes he needed for a salad. I was comfortably settled on the couch and in the middle of telling a story. No one else was being given kitchen chores. I suggested, light-heartedly, that Tom ask one of the men. He did, and I thought no more of it.

The rest of the evening seemed off, however. Tom was acting oddly hostile. And after that night, he stopped responding to phone calls and emails. I was confused—and then upset. I wasn't especially bereft about Tom's unwillingness to socialize with me; I had other friends whose politics were more in sync with mine. His refusal to answer my queries about his B&B listings was a problem, however.

I finally left him a message: "I guess you don't want to get paid." That did the trick—sort of. Tom's answers to my questions were extremely cursory. It wasn't worth it to continue pulling teeth. I called the Santa Fe B&Bs to get the answers I needed.

Time passed. I didn't see Tom, but we were both part of the close-knit community of Mexico-phile writers who lived north of the border. I would often hear about him through the grapevine, reports about press trips he was on, the fact that a book of his essays had been reissued. After a while, the stories began taking a disturbing turn. "What did you do to Tom?" one of my friends asked. "He's saying terrible things about you." Among the more printable, from later on: my *Complete Idiot's Travel Guide to Mexico's Beach Resorts* was "an idiotic guide, written by an idiot."

I still didn't have a clue why Tom was so angry with me. Every time I asked his friend Joe, he pleaded ignorance. Finally, I got the truth out of Joe's wife, Sue, who had grown tired of Tom's Feminazi rants, his praise for Rush Limbaugh.

He had never forgiven me for the radish incident.

I couldn't believe that Tom was so petty, or that he could hold a grudge for so long. Apparently, he was fine with my professional role as his editor as long as I knew my social place: in the kitchen when summoned there. Still, I had to laugh. Of all the grievances for a misogynist to harbor, Tom's symbolism was topsy-turvy. Who ever heard of a man being upset with a woman for refusing to chop his radishes?

CHAPTER 10
MESSING WITH TEXAS
San Antonio/Austin, 1994

New Yorkers and their real estate are not easily parted.

Having grown up in a city where poring over obituaries and bribing building superintendents are competitive sports, I wasn't about to give up my 450 square feet of lower Manhattan just because I'd moved to Arizona. I had gone block-by-block, dispensing envelopes to doormen in promising high-rises near NYU in exchange for news about possible vacancies. The apartment I finally nabbed may have been too small, too dark, and—after it went co-op—too expensive to serve as a home office, but it was the perfect *pied à terre* for a freelancer looking to keep up her contacts in the world's publishing hub, not to mention her old friendships. I had no problem finding subletters who'd let me spend at least two weeks a year in my place as long as I gave them enough advance notice.

During one of these two-week schmoozefests, I had lunch with Jaclyn Forrest, my former boss at Prentice Hall Travel. I saw from her new business card that Jaclyn was now Vice President/Editorial Director of Travel Books at Prentice Hall and that Prentice Hall was under the aegis of the Paramount Publishing Consumers Group. The sower colophon—an image based on a Millet painting, intended to suggest that the publisher was planting seeds of wisdom—was the sole reminder of the company's link with Simon & Schuster.

It struck me that, aside from the meaningless "Vice President" designation, Jaclyn's job title hadn't changed in the half-dozen years since she'd hired me as an associate editor. I wondered if I would have been as excited about interviewing for a job with her at Paramount Publishing Consumers Group as I'd been about the possibility of signing on at Simon & Schuster. What the heck was a "consumers group" anyway? A gathering of imprints catering to people who bought books rather than stole them?

I put my speculation over her job title aside when Jaclyn offered me the chance to write my first book.

Over a bento box of much-coveted sushi—I was still dubious about eating raw fish in the desert, even though a Tucson friend had challenged, "I suppose all the fish you ate in Manhattan came from the Hudson River?"—I listened to Jaclyn's pitch. Frommer's wanted to expand its coverage west of the Mississippi with a few new city guides, she said, and she'd immediately thought of her transplanted-to-Tucson editor. Jaclyn named three pairs of cities PHT was considering. I can't recall two of them. She had me at San Antonio and Austin.

Austin was home to journalist Molly Ivins and Texas governor Ann Richards, the embodiment of the women I'd hoped to encounter in the West: bold, smart progressives with a wicked sense of humor. If I couldn't find Tucson versions—and it was increasingly looking like a lost cause—second best was visiting Molly and Ann's native habitat.

Although I didn't have an interest in any San Antonio residents, female or male, everything I'd read about the city sounded appealing: the bustling, tree-lined River Walk; the chain of Spanish missions, including the Alamo; and, especially, the Tex-Mex food, present and past. What's not to like about a town where women called chili queens reigned over the town plazas, ladling out picante stew?

There were only two things that stopped me from jumping on this offer.

First, I'd never set foot in either San Antonio or Austin.

I've mentioned that Fodor's and Frommer's had different hiring philosophies. Fodor's liked to divide their guidebooks up among multiple authors who were experts in different facets of a destination and who, preferably, lived in the area. Frommer's looked for trustworthy writer/researchers to cover an entire city or country; residence was a bonus, but by no means a prerequisite.

Each approach had its advantages. Familiarity breeds an inability to see things from a fresh perspective. When you live somewhere for a while, it's harder to get a fix on what's likely to confuse—and delight—those who are visiting for the first time.

Unfamiliarity breeds cluelessness, the need to start from scratch.

Jaclyn pooh-poohed my concern that I'd never been to either city. I knew the Frommer's format cold, she said, and I was good at ferreting out the essentials of a place. Fair enough.

My second reservation was more serious: I would be writing my own book, yes—but it would be a guidebook.

I harbored no illusions by this time. Guidebooks occupied the lowest rung on the publishing status ladder, along with how-to books, textbooks, and other utilitarian fare. Although they made a lot of money for companies—maybe *because* they did—these books were looked down on, their authors treated as though they were interchangeable.

They were, indeed, easily replaced.

By the early 1990s, royalties had been almost entirely eliminated for new writers. If I agreed to do the San Antonio and Austin guide, it would be on a work-for-hire basis: All rights would belong to PHT and I would get a flat fee, with no contractual guarantee that I could update the book if I wanted to.

I also knew how little would be left of that flat fee after factoring in my expenses and research time.

One definition of insanity is doing the same thing over and over and hoping for a different outcome. I'd vowed to spend less time on guidebooks, more time on articles, and not necessarily travel-related ones. I'd had several op-eds published in Tucson's *Arizona Daily Star* and had even gotten a think piece into *The Guardian* in the UK, an essay about being single by design. This last was typical of me: I submitted a story on a topic close to my heart to a prestigious newspaper, but ensured that few people I knew would read it if it was accepted; although it was my go-to paper when I lived in London, *The Guardian* wasn't widely distributed in the US, and online publishing didn't yet exist.

I enjoyed nothing more than letting my mind roam over a wide range of topics, crystallizing my cogitations in words. My aim was to get paid for it.

But a book of my own, emblazoned with my name as sole author—now there was a shiny object. Blame it on my abiding love for Egypt. I was the Queen of Denial.

🐪 🐪 🐪

I had several months to prepare for my research trip, during which I boned up on south-central Texas. I found plenty of historical resources but not much about the area's hotels, restaurants, and attractions. There were no big-name guidebooks to San Antonio and Austin, and the few general state guides available were either out of date, cut and dried (AAA), or very specialized, focusing on hiking, say, rather than providing an overview. This was good news for PHT, which would be filling a tourism void, but bad news for me. In the short term, I needed to figure out an itinerary; big picture, even if my book turned out to be hugely successful, I wouldn't earn a penny beyond my original fee.

I finally cobbled together enough information to devise a tentative schedule: two-and-a-half weeks each to explore San Antonio and Austin, another week for the nearby Hill Country towns. It was ambitious, but I figured if I could cover Egypt in five weeks, I could manage two cities and a dozen small towns in six.

I hadn't anticipated the difficulty of working without the safety net of a previous edition. And I hadn't expected a glitch in communications with one of the two major destination marketing organizations (DMOs)—the umbrella term for convention and visitors bureaus, chambers of commerce, and other entities designed to get people to come to a place and spend money—I was depending on for help.

It was an old story. Since 1896, when journalist Milton J. Carmichael founded the Detroit Convention and Businessmen's League, DMOs have had to scramble for funding. Many are supported by bed taxes, levied on lodging stays; others rely on membership dues from local businesses; and several cobble together a combination of resources. In all cases, DMOs need to account for the way their money is spent. Travel writers are vetted to ensure they are worth the investment of time and treasure, whether that means having a staff member tour them around, convincing a hotel owner to donate a room, or paying for dinner out of the DMO's budget.

It's fairly easy to assess the value of a magazine story. If it's two pages long, say, the article is worth at least as much as the cost of placing a two-page ad in that magazine; the larger the circulation of the publication, the higher the price of the ad. A journalist with an assignment to write a thousand words for an in-flight magazine, where the ad prices are high and the audience is captive, can expect to be treated really, really well.

Because guidebooks don't make their money from advertising, it's hard to quantify the value of a listing, much less that of an entire new guidebook.

Not only was I working on a project of incalculable (in a bad way) worth, but I was now a Tucson-based freelancer, not a New York editor with a title on letterhead stationery. I no longer had access to my former tourism resources, and I had no editorial assistant to track down the best contacts. I had only the general phone number and fax numbers for the Austin and San Antonio tourism bureaus and a letter of assignment from Jaclyn.

Although I phoned in advance and explained to anyone who would listen that I was writing a new Frommer's guide, it was impossible to predict on whose desk the faxed assignment letter would land. In Austin, the first city I planned to visit, it turned up in the inbox of Kara Smith, a young tourism associate who had been on the job for only a few months. She faxed back, briefly, that she would be working with me.

The lack of specificity of the "assistance" and "professional courtesies" (code for comps) requested in the assignment letter, the arrival of the letter on a newbie's desk, and the facts that guidebooks are tough for even old hands to evaluate and that this one hadn't existed before—all these circumstances converged to guarantee that my detailed request for free hotels and detailed help with my itinerary would meet with stony silence from Austin. As my visit grew close and I still had no rooms pinned down, I made desperate phone calls to Kara, who told me she was "working on it." She finally faxed confirmation of the hotels where she had arranged for me to stay. I had to take their desirability on faith.

🐫 🐫 🐫

Talk about flying—and driving—blind. I arrived at Austin–Bergstrom International Airport with no confidence in my arrangements and facing the daunting task of renting a car for the first time. I'd only ever driven my by-now-trusty Toyota. I was terrified to maneuver out of the Avis lot—wait, that's the windshield wiper, not the air-conditioner—and edge my way onto the highway.

My nerves were completely frayed by the time I finally drove up to the entrance of my assigned accommodation. Nothing I saw there calmed me down or cheered me up. The so-called resort in which I found myself—really a gussied-up motel—was in an undistinguished rural stretch nearly an hour from downtown Austin. Its draw was that it was on Lake Travis, but this was one of the more remote of the six Highland Lakes that thread through central Texas. As I pored over a local map, I had the sinking realization that the other lodgings Kara had arranged for me were equally inconvenient.

I spent two nights in a downward spiral, convincing myself that I would fail at guidebook writing and that Jaclyn would realize her faith in me was horribly misplaced.

Finally, I got a grip. I decided to drive downtown and plant myself at the Austin CVB until Kara or someone else helped me create a useful itinerary. Forget comps. If I couldn't stay at any of the city's top hotels, I would tour them and pay out of pocket for cheap rooms nearby.

While waiting to see Kara, I struck up a conversation with two interesting-looking women, one with thick, curly hair, the other pale and ethereal. I wasn't sure if they worked at the office but they looked too comfortable with their surroundings to be tourists. I'd been browsing the rack of visitor attractions pamphlets and told them I was impressed by the historical self-guided tour brochures. Many of these make history deadly dull, I said, but Austin's were vivid, beautifully written. I wanted to visit all the sites they described.

This praise seemed to please both of them—inordinately, I thought at first.

I soon learned that the curly-haired one, Julie Strong, was the head of Austin's cultural tourism division, which had conceived the brochures; poetic-looking Lisa Germany had written several of them. They wanted to know what I was doing in town, what I had already seen, what I was planning to do next. When I explained that I was writing a new Frommer's guide, they were excited. When I told them I was having a hard time figuring out my itinerary and welcomed all suggestions, they adopted me.

Rule to live by: If you are thinking nice things, say them out loud. You never know who will be listening.

Julie conferred about me with the director of the Austin CVB. Doors began opening—sometimes literally. The next thing I knew, I was checking into the opulent Driskill, a historic hotel in the heart of downtown. The tourism office helped set up other lodgings, excursions, and dinners and directed me to the most interesting shops and nightspots.

I could finally relax and delight in Austin, a quirky urban mix of whimsy and grit. It was an eco-conscious, crunchy-granola enclave that nevertheless fit many Lone Star stereotypes. I watched bats fly en masse from under the Congress Avenue Bridge from my perch at the Four Seasons' lobby lounge and then two-stepped at the Broken Spoke Saloon. I browsed indie bookstores and, at BookPeople, bought a poster of Ann Richards, clad all in white and straddling a Harley. (It was a reproduction of a 1992 *Texas Monthly* cover, with the tagline: "Ann Richards Is Riding High. Can She Be Our First Woman President?" Ahem.) I ogled a Gutenberg bible at the Harry Ransom Center, one of the many research facilities and exhibition spaces at the University of Texas, Austin, and discovered that the source of much campus culture was literally crude: When an oil well on land belonging to the university system blew a gusher in 1923, money for the arts was assured.

I also went to the O. Henry Pun Off, the annual celebration of groan-inducing wordplay, where Molly Ivins was a judge. It was fun, but Ivins seemed tired, besieged by fans. I had a brief fit of envy, wondering if I would ever have that problem, but then realized that seeing one of my favorite writers as part of an assignment was not too shabby either.

My schedule runneth over. By the end of my stay, I could see how someone unfamiliar with guidebooks might have looked askance at my requests. Kara later admitted that it had been easier to say no to me than to go in and ask her boss about a request from a journalist that she thought was outrageous. She was just trying to take the initiative, to make a decision.

Kara turned out to be far from the only one in the Texas tourism world who hadn't heard of the Frommer's guides, or at least hadn't heard the name of the series founder (FROH-mer) uttered aloud. Several times when I told people I was working on a new Frommer's guide, they'd say, "What, you're working on a farmer's guide?" A few who understood the words and had heard of Arthur Frommer asked me if I was his secretary.

🐫 🐫 🐫

From the get-go, San Antonio was far more guidebook writer–friendly than Austin. I had a detailed itinerary in hand within weeks of my first inquiry. But all the tourism assistance in the world couldn't implant in me a sense of direction or map-reading skills. Getting around San Antonio was far harder for me than getting around Austin.

I don't know which stymied me most: the old or the new parts of the city. San Antonio's downtown was typical of Western cities that pave their winding cattle paths; I could discern no rhyme or reason behind the warren of one-way streets. At least there the traffic moved slowly. Most of the major roads of Texas converge in San Antonio. I always seemed to be in the express lane to somewhere I didn't want to go, unable to make the quick lane changes required to get off. Circling endlessly around the two main highway loops, 410 and 1604, I felt like Charlie, the man who rode the MTA 'neath the streets of Boston and never returned.

I finally devised a strategy to get me through the worst of my driving stress: breakdown time. You've heard of controlled burns to prevent larger fires? I had controlled cries. Whenever I felt my anxiety level going through the roof, I would get off the freeway wherever I could, pull over, and weep. This didn't help me find the place that I was looking for, of course, but it released tension. Just mentally allowing myself a break from trying to cope worked wonders; I rarely needed the outlet.

Stowing my rental car in a downtown garage space provided by the tourist office was a huge help too. I spent many blissful days being a pedestrian and testing the public transportation.

It was on one of my walkabouts that I found the perfect research assistant, though I hadn't realized I wanted or needed one.

I'd been to visit the Alamo, which, like most people who went to school on the East Coast, I knew I was supposed to remember, but had no idea why. That Texas was an independent republic for a while is another bit of history that gets short shrift in Brooklyn classrooms. The former mission church, site of a futile battle against Mexican dictator Santa Ana, was smaller than I'd expected, and it was smack in the middle of downtown, right across the street from the Ripley's Believe It or Not museum. It was also near Booksmiths, an independent bookstore that specialized in volumes dedicated to Texas and the Southwest.

I had gathered a great deal of first-hand information by then but was still looking for the comprehensive guides to San Antonio and Austin that I hadn't been able to locate in Tucson. Here, I was spoiled for choice—indeed, overwhelmed. I asked a friendly but authoritative-looking young woman if she could make some recommendations.

Boy, could she. I was impressed by her depth of knowledge about everything on the shelves and, as we got to talking, about San Antonio in general. She, in turn, was curious to know why I needed all those books; they seemed beyond the scope of interest of even the most enthusiastic tourist. We exchanged names and professions: She revealed that she was Shannon Smithson and this was her family's bookstore. I explained that I was working on a new Frommer's city guide. Shannon thought a big-name guidebook like Frommer's would be a boon to San Antonio tourism.

And that's when, on the spot, I decided Shannon would make a great research assistant. She knew books and she knew San Antonio.

Shannon emailed, "I was managing my family's bookstore poorly and thinking about going back to graduate school. I remember you coming in, and I'm pretty sure you were wearing white capris and a Hawaiian print shirt. You asked me a lot of questions, most of which I think I had the answer for. I was excited that you might need help on a book (a real book!), because I wanted to be on the editing/publishing side of bookselling much more than I wanted to be on the selling side."

Grass on other side, greener. If only I could have dissuaded her from going to grad school.

Shannon ended up helping me with several San Antonio sections, but it was her restaurant recommendations—and her company at meals—that I valued most. Shannon became my first foodie friend.

The word "foodie" has become a cliché, but it wasn't part of the popular lexicon in the 1990s. I can't recall an earlier term for those with an unbounded yet detail-oriented enthusiasm for food that didn't have the snobby connotations of "gourmet" and "gourmand." In New York, my friends and I grazed the city's vast buffet of ethnic restaurants, but we either liked the food or we didn't; we weren't interested in dissecting the ingredients of the dishes or discussing their history. And we were too broke to eat in the type of restaurants that had identifiable owners or chefs.

The first time I met people who would have been termed foodies was in San Diego, where I was doing dissertation research in the early 1980s. I was nowhere near ready to join their ranks. Exhibit I: the dinner I attended at the home of one of the young academics in the literature department who had befriended me. When my host, Michael, announced that he had picked up arugula for the salad at a farmer's market, I wondered if he'd been hitting the cooking sherry. Assuming Michael was Anglicizing the pronunciation of "a *rugelach*," I was convinced he was trying to pass off the Jewish crescent cookie as a vegetable. (Not that I hadn't had my own fantasies along those lines; I just couldn't believe he thought he'd get away with it.)

Editing the Gault Millau guides at Prentice Hall had provided me entree into the world of the restaurant-obsessed, but fine dining remained out of my price range. Tucson's restaurants were comparatively inexpensive, but when I first arrived, the pickings aside from Mexican food and steakhouses were slim.

Now, in San Antonio, I had the means, motive, and opportunity to break out my inner foodie, with Shannon as my partner in crime. Eating our way around town, gathering chef/owner gossip, was my idea of heaven.

Shannon continued to help me with the San Antonio portion of the Frommer's guide, especially the dining section, for the next two editions. After that, she was considerate enough to move to Austin and marry someone in the restaurant business, thus expanding and consolidating her dining scope. There was no acknowledgements section in the Frommer's city guide format, but had one existed, I would have thanked Shannon in it, profusely.

🐪 🐪 🐪

Downtown was not only the locus of one of my most helpful tourism encounters in San Antonio; it was also the site of my worst. My dinner with Georgia Calloway, the marketing director of one of the top hotels on the River Walk, was a textbook example of why public relations and politics don't mix.

The meal started off pleasantly enough, but once a glass of merlot loosened her tongue, Georgia could not stop railing against Bill and Hillary Clinton, who had just been installed in the White House. She was especially obsessed with Hillary, who was going to be a guest at the hotel after giving a talk on…I can't recall. Georgia's diatribe was too distracting. I knew that Hillary's comment about not staying home to bake cookies had earned her the title of evil radical feminist in some circles, but this was the first comprehensive summary I'd encountered of her shady land deals, her complicity in the murder of Vince Foster, her lesbian affairs—or was it an affair with Vince Foster and the murder of one of her lesbian paramours?

I'm pretty good at drawing people out. I tried to get Georgia to talk about San Antonio attractions, but would have settled for a discussion of her two-year-old's potty training. No dice. Every time I attempted to change the subject, Georgia would circle back to the Clintons. Finally, I said, quietly but firmly, "I don't agree with you about the President and First Lady. Can we talk about something else?" That did the trick.

A few days later, I indulged in what I thought would be a bit of harmless payback. Georgia was putting together a new press kit that she wanted me to have. I promised I would stop by and pick it up when I would again be in the area. By coincidence—I swear!—I arrived at the hotel to find a clutch of Secret Service men corralling a small crowd of people behind wooden barricades. The lobby had been cleared and everyone had been asked to wait until Hillary was safely inside. I was happy to stand by with her other enthusiastic admirers. The surprisingly petite First Lady arrived about fifteen minutes later, smiling and waving and leaning over the barriers to shake hands.

Secret Service blockade dismantled, I went on to Georgia's office. I apologized for being late, but said I hadn't been allowed in until after Mrs. Clinton had arrived. I added, just a touch perversely, that I was very pleased to have had the chance to see her. I figured Georgia wouldn't have anything to say in the sober light of day, especially since Hillary was now officially a guest. Sure enough, Georgia just gritted her teeth behind a rictus of a smile. But as she ushered me into the lobby through a long hallway, a woman wheeling a cleaning cart greeted her and said, excitedly, that the First Lady had stopped to shake her hand as she'd passed. Georgia turned to her and said, voice dripping bile, "You should cut your hand off and give it to a liberal. They'd like that."

🐪 🐪 🐪

That wasn't my only encounter with a toxic blend of PR and right-wing politics in Texas. The second was worse because it occurred in a dry county.

When I first sent a query to San Antonio and Austin about my Frommer's research trip, the two tourism bureaus passed it along to the nearby Hill Country communities that partnered with them. I got some enthusiastic responses, including ones from Fredericksburg, Bandera, and Uvalde. Without good guidebooks to consult, I hadn't known how to distinguish between the towns, so I accepted all invitations.

My newfound tourism friends in Austin and San Antonio were surprised to see Uvalde on my itinerary. It's not professional to diss other destinations, but a couple of them gently suggested that I might better serve Frommer's readers by going elsewhere. But, I protested, Uvalde had been so enthusiastic. I was too guilty to bail.

I regretted my decision almost as soon as Tanya Taylor, a thin young woman with a shield of big hair, greeted me at the Uvalde Chamber of Commerce. She handed me a plastic bag filled with press souvenirs, including a sun visor that read, "Uvalde, the soar spot of Texas." The town was a parasailing and hang-gliding center, Tanya explained proudly when I gaped at it in disbelief.

Uvalde's main claim to fame besides its aerodynamic activities was that it had been home to vice president John Nance ("Cactus Jack") Garner. Our first stop was the house museum dedicated to him. Garner had, I learned, served two terms under Franklin Delano Roosevelt. He eventually broke ranks with FDR over the New Deal, which he thought went too far in its largesse to the poor. Information later gleaned: John L. Lewis, the president of the United Mine Workers of America, called Garner a "labor-baiting, poker-playing, whiskey-drinking, evil old man." In the late 1940s, Garner's wife burned all his personal and public papers.

Tanya next drove me to the town's oldest store, a Rexall Drug with a soda fountain that featured the original 1950s Formica counter. I loved its muted yellow-and-turquoise boomerang design—which was why I'd bought a kitchen table and matching chairs with the identical pattern earlier that year at a second-hand store in Tucson.

The day ended at the National Fish Hatchery, billed as "the top-producing warm-water federal hatchery in the nation." It was the end of May and getting toasty in Texas. The place smelled like, well, a fish hatchery.

I'd explored the home of a union-busting politician I'd never heard of—maybe I've mentioned that my mother was a proud member of the International Ladies Garment Workers Union?—sat at a soda-fountain counter similar to one I had at home, and toured a fish-birthing facility. I could have left some sardines out on my kitchen table for a few days and recreated two out of three of those experiences.

Making the day even more excruciating, Tanya provided a running commentary on the evils of East Coast liberals and their ilk. I wondered how she had failed to recognize that I might number among their ranks, given that I worked for a New York publisher and we control the media and everything.

Finally, the ordeal was over and it was time for dinner. Tanya named a few casual local spots and asked which one I preferred. I joked that I didn't care as long as alcohol was served. This was when I discovered the existence of dry counties. At least with Georgia in San Antonio, the wine at dinner was a two-way street: It enabled Georgia's rant but also blunted its impact on me. I knew a little about blue laws; when I was growing up, you couldn't buy booze in New York on Sunday. I had no idea that there were places in the US besides Utah where you couldn't get alcohol, ever, much less that they could occur county by county within a state, much less that the state might be Texas, for fuck's sake.

I had to listen, cold sober, to Tanya's right-wing ravings at dinner. I was too tired and dispirited to protest.

I can't say I hadn't been warned about Uvalde.

I didn't include the town in the Hill Country section of *Frommer's San Antonio and Austin.* You can check. It's a hard concept to document, but omissions are as important as inclusions in guidebooks, which have limited space for listings. I don't think it would have made a difference if a progressive PR rep had slipped me a flask of whiskey and quoted chapter and verse from Ann Richards' speeches, though I can't swear to it.

🐫 🐫 🐫

Left to my own devices in the Hill Country, I meandered along back roads, stopping at whim without worrying about getting lost. Traffic was slow, and it was hard to go too far out of my way. My devotion to dromedaries, for example, led me to Camp Verde, the former headquarters of the short-lived United States Camel Corps. This attempt by the Army to introduce "ships of the desert" into dry Southwest terrain was doomed because of the widespread ignorance of camel habits and the onset of the Civil War, but many of the military brass had great respect for their humped charges. The Camel Country T-shirt I bought at Camp Verde's old general store doubled as an ad and a history lesson. It sported a sketch of the store and its founding date, 1857; the seal of the Official Historical Medallion of the State Historical Survey Committee of Texas; and the notation "Camp Verde, Texas 78010 (Site of War Departments 1857–69 Camel Experiment), 11 Miles South of Kerrville on Hwy 173." I only wish the apostrophe hadn't been left off "Departments," undercutting the garment's otherwise scrupulous attention to detail.

On other days, I wandered into a country store-cum-bar where pickled eggs—and heaven knows what else—floated in a jar on the counter; bought strudel at Haby's Alsatian bakery in Castroville; and hung around the dance hall of tiny Luckenbach, a two-store town immortalized in a song by Waylon Jennings and Willie Nelson. I'd heard that local musicians jammed in the hall on the weekends, but only the dress style of a few weekday stragglers suggested the presence of Willy's spiritual kin.

It used to be that the sound of a twangy guitar set my teeth on edge, but living in Tucson gave me a new perspective on the culture wars; the musical sides were not as sharply drawn between right and left as I'd thought in New York. Mainstream country singers like Garth Brooks emphasized their working-class roots; they were anti–fat cat, not anti–flower power. The Dixie Chicks did not stand by their men; "Good-bye Earl" might be the best revenge song against an abusive boyfriend ever written.

Also, I was far better suited to jeans, tailored shirt, and cowboy boots than I had ever been to flowing peasant blouses.

By the time I got to Texas, I was less inclined to see things in black and white. I wasn't as surprised as I once might have been to learn that Kinky Friedman, a macho cigar-smoking musician who once had a backup band called the Texas Jewboys, founded the Utopia Animal Rescue Ranch in the Hill Country.

Still, I hadn't expected to be converted to Lyndon Johnson love.

I had never gone down the conspiracy path with my mother, who had been convinced that Texas governor John Connally shot himself in the leg because he was in cahoots with Kennedy's assassin and wanted to install a fellow Texan in the White House. I just considered LBJ crude, especially compared to the dashing JFK, and I loathed his escalation of the Vietnam War.

Now, touring his Johnson City birthplace, I realized that LBJ was a local hero, and not just because he'd been elected president. In Congress, he had secured funding for a series of dams that provided a dirt-poor region with inexpensive water and hydroelectric power. His civil rights and anti-poverty legislation as president dwarfed anything that Kennedy had tried, much less succeeded, to get passed; LBJ was a reformer second only to FDR in the twentieth century.

By the time I visited the National Historical Parks at LBJ Ranch, where Johnson retreated to lick his wounds after public outcry made him decide not to run for a second term, I saw him as a tragic figure—and myself as a shallow thinker.

It wasn't only Lyndon I'd misjudged. Lady Bird (what kind of corny name was that?) beautified Texas highways with wildflowers before eco-decoration was trendy.

My gold membership in the Knee-Jerk East Coast Liberal Elite Club was in danger of being revoked.

Often, pondering these weighty questions while driving along bluebonnet- and Indian paintbrush–flanked roads, I thought, "I've got the best job in the world." I was getting a free continuing education, one far broader and more useful than the one that had cost a fortune at NYU.

If only I didn't have to produce a guidebook in return.

My relationship with that guidebook soon became more complicated. I was back in Tucson, slotting my observations into city-guide structure, when some upsetting news arrived on company letterhead that had changed yet again.

Simon & Schuster had acquired Macmillan Publishing Company. The Frommer's guides were no longer under the aegis of Paramount Publishing Consumers Group; they were now part of Macmillan Travel, a division of Macmillan General Reference, a division of Macmillan Publishing USA. The sower logo was still on the stationery, but Prentice Hall was gone and Paramount was no longer paramount—or even present.

This was not the disturbing part; I wasn't usually affected by corporate reshufflings. What alarmed me was the announcement that Richard Brooks, the former editor-in-chief at Fodor's, was Macmillan Travel's new publisher. He was Jaclyn's boss—and, in effect, mine again.

I had dealt amicably enough with Dick on the Fodor's bed and breakfast guides, but as the editor, not as an author. I wasn't sure that I would have chosen to write a new book for a company led by him. I was not only fond of Jaclyn personally, but I also appreciated her hands-off, no-nonsense management style. Once she made an assignment, she left her editors and authors free to work on a book together.

In contrast, as I learned when editing the *Wall Street Journal* guides, Dick took the male dog approach toward books: He needed to put his mark on everything.

Don't worry, several friends in the business said. Being a publisher is very different from being an editorial director. It's an administrative position, one that has little impact on the day-to-day details of book production. You'll have no reason to interact with Dick.

Imagine my surprise then to pick up the phone one day and discover Dick on the other end.

"You're the only person I know who is familiar with both the Frommer's and Fodor's formats," he said. "I'd love to get your input about the strengths and weaknesses of both series." He would fly me to New York. Or maybe I could write up a detailed analysis. Or possibly both. He wasn't sure. He just wanted to gauge my interest. He'd let me think about it.

I was flattered—and pumped. I hadn't learned many useful skills in graduate school, but one I mastered was textual analysis. And I could address the books from both an editorial and authorial perspective.

I asked around about the going rate for consulting. The consensus was that $50/hour was fair. It was a bit low in comparison with what I'd get in other industries, but par for the publishing course.

When Dick phoned again, I told him I was very enthusiastic about the project and quoted my rate.

He seemed surprised. "Oh," he backtracked, "I thought maybe we could just fly you out for some discussions."

"That would be great," I said, "as long as I get paid for my time there."

A written report?

"Sure," I said. "I'll send you an estimate of the number of hours I think that would take."

I did that. And never heard back.

I was also met with silence on another Frommer's front. I probably should have been relieved that Dick didn't gut the city-guide style before I finished my book—that happened later—but neither did I enjoy the opposite experience: almost no editorial feedback.

I'd worked really hard on the guide and felt proud of the end result. When I sent the book in, I got an acknowledgement of its receipt from Susan Ennis, the editor to whom the book had been assigned. She was fairly new to the company, and we had never met.

After this initial contact, crickets. Then one morning, a few months later, my fax machine churned out two pages containing thirty-one queries—for the entire book. I've since gotten more queries for a 700-word magazine article. I was glad not to have to spend days answering questions, but the lack of feedback was disconcerting.

Was the karma I'd accumulated from my days at Fodor's, when I operated from the principle that good writers know they are good and don't need to hear it, going to be worked out in this lifetime?

Susan disappeared again after I responded to her queries. Finally, a few months later, another fax:

Dear Edie,

After having edited your manuscript, I can ask you: Was it worth all the sweat and toil; all the hours spent calling hotels and restaurants and sundry attractions, doing painstaking research, sometimes far into the evening; answering queries from the editor; gathering essential information for maps; deleting, emending, and otherwise improving the text; pondering over style and format and debating whether an item belonged here or there or anywhere. Was it, pray, worth it all?

After reading your manuscript, I'd say yes.

I felt deflated. The message was oddly formal, and too little too late. And so my first book entered the world with little fanfare, not with a bang—or any *sturm und drang*—but a nice note.

Jaclyn would probably have cheered me on enthusiastically, but she was distracted by the personnel shakeup. Within a year or so, she left the company—whatever it was called at the moment. Her departure had nothing to do with Dick's arrival, she said. Her job had just gotten too corporate.

🐪 🐪 🐪

I revised *Frommer's San Antonio and Austin* every two years for another decade, until 2004. I fell hard for both cities. It became routine for me to consider relocating to one or the other every time I went—San Antonio for its diversity and culture, Austin for its university-town hipness.

Then one year I found myself feeling claustrophobic in Austin. I couldn't see the sky; all those trees were blocking the view. Around the same time, I started noticing how flat both Austin and San Antonio were. Their gently rolling hills couldn't hold a candle to the craggy mountains ringing Tucson.

It occurred to me, too, that I was already living in a hip, multicultural university town.

No, I decided, I wasn't going anywhere—and definitely not back to New York, though I would have preferred to have had that choice left open to me.

Three years after I started subletting my New York apartment, I got an ultimatum from the co-op board: Move back for a minimum of two years or sell your place. Rules were rules, they said; absentee tenants were frowned upon. This was ludicrous. All subtenants had to pass muster with the board. My apartment was on the eighth floor. Since the building's elevator was manually operated, it would be impossible for anyone who hadn't been vetted to hide unless they were willing to climb up and down many, many stairs every day. My board-approved subtenant and I were happy with our arrangement; I assumed she wasn't going to suddenly turn into a homicidal maniac or start stiffing the super on the tips required to get any maintenance work done.

It was official: My once-hip Greenwich Village building had gone all snooty Upper East Side.

The ultimatum hit me hard. I was making do as a freelancer in Tucson, but my on-again–off-again income couldn't be depended on to cover my New York mortgage and maintenance payments consistently. So I sold my beloved piece of Manhattan island—and for a song. The same housing slump that netted me my bargain home in Tucson kept me from making a killing on my East Coast domicile.

I was distraught for a while, but, like many types of bereavement pain, this one was blunted with time. New York will always be part of me. I'll always elbow my way through a crowd, interrupt friends in the heat of an argument, talk with my hands, and try to convince people to share food if they're not so inclined. But the instinct that led me to leave turned out to be sound. Like the houseplants that routinely wilted in my small, dark Manhattan apartment, I needed light and space to thrive.

PART THREE

🐪🐪🐪

SEMI-SUCCESS

CHAPTER 11

HONEYMOONING FOR MONEY
Costa Alegre, Mexico, 1996

Picture this, if you will. A coveted assignment for *Brides* magazine transports you to Las Jacarandas, an ultra-romantic getaway on Mexico's Costa Alegre. Perched on 1,200 acres between the azure Pacific and a pristine river estuary, the resort is miles from everywhere, and so exclusive that only ten luxurious casitas nestle on its lush, expansive grounds.

After a long journey, as dimming shafts of daylight soften the dazzling white sand to a golden glow, you enter a spacious room to find the word *Bienvenidos* spelled out in brilliant magenta bougainvillea petals on your ivory chenille bedspread. Candles in pressed-tin lamps lend the room an atmospheric shimmer, and two coconuts brimming with a fruity rum concoction perch on intricately carved twin night tables. There is nothing to distract you from the resort's natural allures—no TV, no Internet, no electricity at all, in fact. And no sounds intrude on this tranquil scene except those of waves lapping against the shore and the calls of tropical birds.

Everything is perfect except for one thing: You are alone, and every casita besides yours is occupied by a lovey-dovey couple. At first, you are extremely grateful for the mistake that landed you a second spiked coconut, but later, after your eyes hurt from trying to read by the light of those fucking flickering candles, you curse the extra trips to the bathroom, not to mention those deafeningly loud waves and those damned shrieking birds, all of which interfere with your only means of escape from this waking nightmare: sleep.

Ah, yes. Just another glamorous night in the glamorous life of a travel writer.

🐪 🐪 🐪

Don't get me wrong. I was thrilled to be writing for *Brides*. I'd been getting sporadic magazine assignments, including dining stories for a local lifestyle publication, but high-circulation *Brides* had become a regular client. And one of the best things about the gig was that it had fallen into my lap.

I was at the assignment stage of what had become the annual task of editing the huge *Fodor's Mexico* guide. After several years on the job, I felt like I was finally getting a handle on the sprawling, multi-author book—and on Mexico.

I'd phoned Val Lewin, one my favorite updaters—she wasn't only conscientiousness but pleasant to work with—to see if she wanted to take on a few chapters again. "Sorry," she replied, "I've just accepted a full-time job as the travel editor at *Brides*. But do you think you might like to work for me?"

I was no *Brides* browser but I knew the magazine was published by Condé Nast, which also put out glossy publications like *Traveler*. I figured its travel section was bound to focus on luxury resorts in gorgeous places.

True, my ex and I had honeymooned in $5 rooms in Afghanistan and the Soviet Union, our wedding had been held in the low-rent hall of a Brooklyn synagogue, and my dress had been a floor model from Gimbels that needed to be dry cleaned before the ceremony. But who cared if I didn't fit the audience demographic and I wasn't seeing anyone at the moment? If I could fake orgasms, surely I could fake honeymoons.

Every couple has its problems to work through. I was certain that *Brides* and I would make an excellent match in the long run. I told Val, "I do."

A few days later, she phoned, very excited. "We've decided to cover the Iditarod, and we've got an invitation to a press trip. Could you be ready to leave for Alaska in two weeks?

Could I? Yes. Did I want to? No way. High on the list of reasons I'd moved to Tucson was a fear and loathing of cold weather.

But I was eager to write for *Brides* and didn't want to blow my shot at it. If I turned Val down, I was certain she'd never ask again. "Sure," I said, trying to inject some enthusiasm into my voice. "I can go."

Luckily, Val was not only pleasant but perceptive. "You don't sound very excited," she said. "Don't worry. If you don't want to do this, we'll find you something else. What kind of places do you like?"

"Warm," I replied.

Val was true to her word. She called back a few days later and asked if I'd been to Cancun lately. I had, as the updater of several sections of *Fodor's Cancun, Cozumel & the Yucatán Peninsula*.

"We need a wrap-up of the destination in 150 words and then five honeymoon-worthy hotels at 100 words each. Do you think you could do that?" Val asked.

No problem. Although I'd been looking forward to a longer, more narrative assignment, I was sure I could gush in a tight format.

To my surprise, I enjoyed the exercise. It was tough making guidebook listings lively; I tried, but there were so many of them and I had so little time. For $1 a word at *Brides*, I could afford to be lapidary, to tease out witty little gems. My prose glittered and sparkled like Cancun and its resorts—I said witty, not cliché free—and Val was pleased.

She phoned a day after I sent the story in to tell me so, thus setting an unfortunate precedent. It led me to expect Val in particular and magazine editors in general to be more communicative than the guidebook editors I'd worked with.

True, I could have chalked up the personal attention Val was paying me to the fact that I'd known her from my in-house days at Fodor's, though I'd never met her. But this was my first inkling that relocating to Arizona had given me a certain clout. When I'd first contacted Val from Tucson, she had enthused, "You're so brave to move to the Southwest." I was discovering that being from New York and transplanting myself to someplace hip—not Santa Fe, but close enough for most East Coasters—conferred unanticipated cachet. Editors could indulge in relocation fantasies and real estate porn ("You got a four-bedroom house in the center of town for less than $100,000?") without having to give up their Manhattan apartments.

I'd gotten guidebook assignments because the editors knew me. Now I could also impress an editor through sheer geography. I'd been reinvented as an intrepid adventurer—I was, after all, living in a metropolis with only one art cinema and no decent cold sesame noodles—with big-city chops.

Big-city chops were the key. I thought about my own prejudices as an editor. I had a tendency to trust the opinions of correspondents from urban hubs like Atlanta, Chicago, Los Angeles, and Seattle, assuming that smarts and sophistication were natural byproducts of living in crowded places. Density was creative destiny! The writer whose clips I questioned for the *Wall Street Journal* guides? She was from a mid-sized city in the Midwest.

It didn't help that I was right in her case.

As with so many other things from that in-house era, my small-mindedness came back to bite me. These days, I'm annoyed to see major magazines send writers from New York to cover Tucson. But I understand the impulse. When I edited *Fodor's Arizona* from my Manhattan desk, I hired an updater from Phoenix for the Tucson chapter, heaven help me. Now that my New York roots are buried deep beneath two decades of Arizona residence, I'm not sure that I would hire me either if I were still a Fodor's editor.

In the six months following my first *Brides* assignment, I became a honeymoon maven. I began getting a taste of the good life that everyone outside the travel business assumed I had been enjoying all along. If I hadn't been to a place that *Brides* wanted covered or hadn't been there recently, the magazine paid my airfare and any expenses that weren't comped. Or else they got me a spot on a press trip, which was never a problem. Everyone loves a bride or a *Brides* writer.

I had a nice long run at the magazine. For maybe a dozen years, I was passed down as a recommended writer from editor to editor as they left, one by one, for better or less stressful jobs. I've heard people diss the staff at women's magazines, especially the stereotypically girly ones like bridal pubs, as temperamental and difficult to work with. That was far from my experience at *Brides*. Without exception, everyone I worked for was smart, friendly, and extremely professional.

I began patrolling my beat of the Southwest US and Mexico with newly romance-focused eyes. Santa Fe turned out to be surprisingly short on love nests, while Puerto Vallarta, which rose on the fame of Liz Taylor and Richard Burton's affair on the set of *Night of the Iguana*, still had plenty of sizzle. Los Cabos, Scottsdale, San Antonio, Acapulco, the Grand

Canyon (yes, sometimes nature was given a nod)… I mined them all for post-nuptial nuggets.

My most frequent scouting trips, however, were to Las Vegas. Sin City had become Brides Central, with drive-through weddings at cut-rate chapels giving way to full-family extravaganzas at posh hotels, and newlyweds staying on for high-energy honeymoons.

More than three days in Vegas would have driven me crazy; I don't gamble and have a neon light limit. But from the time I first explored the city for Fodor's, I was drawn to its excesses, its over-the-top architecture, and its anything-goes ethos. And now Las Vegas's restaurants called to me. The city was undergoing a dual revolution: At the same time as Las Vegas was morphing into an upscale bridal destination, it was also becoming a magnet for celebrity chefs. *Brides* loved celebrity in all forms, so the magazine had another reason to highlight Sin City.

Like editors at women's magazines, Las Vegas restaurants tended to be judged unfairly. Absentee chefs and lack of quality control were the charges I most commonly heard leveled against them. I beg to disagree. I had a better meal at the Coyote Cafe in Las Vegas than I had at the Santa Fe original, even though chef Mark Miller was on the premises in New Mexico. The competition is sufficiently fierce that Las Vegas restaurants that fail to deliver great service and food don't make it, no matter how famous the names behind them. The only thing I found missing from these dining offshoots was the attitude and the long wait to get a table.

I was excited to be invited on a press trip tailored to food journalists, and not only because of the chance to eat at great restaurants. As I'd discovered in San Antonio with Shannon, I really like people who really like food. Most of the foodies I encountered in these groups were enthusiasts, not snobs. We were grateful to be able to sample meals that would have been way beyond our price range, to dish about dishes with others who were equally geeky about textures and ingredients.

The foodies-are-good-company rule proved true on this Las Vegas trip, with one exception: Tim Naylor, the correspondent from a major food magazine. He was a complete prig. He didn't drink and had a tendency to lecture the rest of us on vegetarianism. When one journalist asked how he could evaluate a restaurant when he couldn't sample most of what was on the menu, Tim sniffed that he judged a place on how well it catered to the needs of vegetarian diners.

That seemed vastly unfair.

When I was in Austin for Frommer's, I was invited to dine at a Ruth's Chris Steak House. I accepted, even though I hadn't eaten red meat for the previous few years. I figured I could always order seafood or chicken.

But when I got there, the smell of the steaks sizzling in butter—the restaurant's signature preparation—whetted my appetite more than I'd expected. I was dining with the restaurant manager, who encouraged me to try one of their large cuts. That's way too much food, I protested, thinking I could wiggle out of eating meat that way. He suggested the petite filet mignon.

Resistance was futile.

Okay, I thought, after a delicious meal, I'm going to pay for this later. My body is going to be very unhappy. It'll be in shock after all these years.

My body, instead, said, "Screw you. Why have you deprived me for so long?" I had more energy after dinner than I'd had for a long time and didn't feel ill in the slightest.

Ah, yes, I think I read that somewhere: All things in moderation.

Which brings me back to Veggie-Man Tim. His holier-than-thou attitude was bad enough, but I don't think anyone in the group forgave him for spoiling our last morning meal together. Soon after we sat down to breakfast, he began regaling us with details of how the organic asparagus we'd enjoyed at dinner the night before made his pee smell. He used adjectives to describe its qualities that most people apply to fine wine: citrusy, floral, robust. You can't unhear that. At least he didn't claim he could judge restaurants by the effect of the food on the "nose" of his urine.

🐪 🐪 🐪

Most of the press trips I went on for *Brides* fell into my geographical areas of expertise, but every now and then I was sent to scope out a more exotic destination. Such was the case with Easter Island.

Confected by the PR firm representing Chile's national airline, the familiarization trip was a sampler of visitor temptations. Our press group touched down in Chile's capital, Santiago. It was a veritable cornucopia of *Brides* buzzwords: big city sizzle, grand Spanish Colonial churches, charming cobblestone streets, party-'til-dawn nightclubs, trendy restaurants. Especially *Brides*-worthy was Valparaiso, the nearby town where Pablo Neruda had lived on a hilltop overlooking the sea. Sitting in an intimate cafe, watching boats bob along the dock while sipping a pisco sour and reading Neruda's love sonnets to each other—now there was a made-for-romance scenario.

With its lush rows of grapevines blanketing terraced hills poised against the snow-capped Andes, Chile's wine country rose to *Brides'* standard too. The boutique hotel where we stayed couldn't have been cozier, and the dinner feasts, replete with wine pairings, were sumptuous. I wouldn't have minded lingering for a few more days—or weeks.

But I was even more psyched about heading to Easter Island. One of the world's most remote places, Rapa Nui (as the natives call it) is more than 2,300 miles off the coast of Chile, a 5½-hour flight from Santiago. The closest South Pacific island, Pitcairn, of *Mutiny on the Bounty* fame, lies some 1,300 miles away.

I was especially excited by the prospect of seeing the *moia*, the huge, brooding stone heads arrayed in rows along the coast. As my ex-husband—whom I'd dragged to every Mayan and Aztec ruin en route from Mexico City to the Yucatán coast—could attest, I've never met an archaeological site I didn't like.

My first impression of Easter Island was not auspicious, however. The island was lacking a few essentials.

Trees, for one thing. The place was almost entirely deforested. There would be no reason to celebrate Arbor Day here.

Theories about the eco-disaster abounded. Our native guide told us that the once-thriving palms were chopped down to serve as tracks and rollers for transporting the big heads to the coast from an inland quarry. More recent theories held that European visitors arrived in ships bearing rats that considered palm trees and their seeds a great delicacy.

Indeed, rats and chickens were two of the only land invertebrates left on Rapa Nui, according to *American Scientist*; many of the original bird species had been rendered extinct long ago. In addition, the publication said, "Strong winds bearing salt spray and wide fluctuations in rainfall can make agriculture difficult."

A dearth of island-grown produce and domestic animals—without grass, there's nothing for cows or goats to graze—meant that much of Easter Island's food had to be flown in from Chile twice a week.

Our group had arrived at the end of one of those delivery cycles. Travel writers are generally fêted and overfed with the best a destination has to offer. No fêting or overfeeding occurred here.

Also missing from Rapa Nui: dependably warm weather. *American Scientist* noted that Easter Island "lies just south of the tropics, so its climate is somewhat less inviting than many tropical Pacific islands." That's putting it mildly. True, we visited in the cold season, but in most popular South Seas getaways even the winters tend to be temperate. On Easter Island, there wasn't a day when we didn't bundle up in sweaters and windbreakers. On the bright side, this allayed any disappointment we might have felt about the lack of sandy beaches. You could only swim comfortably at one, Anakena.

I began to be concerned.

Okay, I rationalized. So what if the coastline is as inviting as Alcatraz Island, the food as exciting as the spread at a Weight Watcher's bash? Honeymoons are all about holing up in a great hotel. It didn't have to be posh, just loaded with style and character. Memorable.

That turned out to be a non-starter too. A few lodgings, including the one where we were staying, were pleasant but nondescript; others had character but were not overly clean.

I flashed back to my days at Prentice Hall Travel. I was editing *Frommer's Hawaii* and browsing readers' letters about the book. One man threatened to sue the company because, he said, the room he'd booked for his honeymoon based on a Frommer's recommendation was substandard: leaky sink, lizards on the ceiling, irregular towel service... His new bride was so upset by the ongoing problems that she denied him his conjugal rights.

No way did I want to be responsible for messing up someone's sex life.

Neither, I knew, did *Brides*. And so, when I returned, I ticked off the reasons that Easter Island might not be a dream retreat for their demographic. I offered a few alternatives. Chilean wine country got a nod from the magazine—and a genuinely enthusiastic write-up from me.

🐫 🐫 🐫

My *Brides* trips were fun, the paychecks large and swift in arriving. If the writing became less challenging once I got the hang of the formula, I didn't mind.

Still, I was pleased when Val contacted me to do a longer, more experiential story. "There's a very exclusive resort on Mexico's Pacific coast called Las Jacarandas," she explained. "Only ten casitas on 1,200 acres. I'd like you to stay for a couple of days and write about how it really feels to be there." She also wanted me to check out El Piloncillo, another luxury resort that was soon to debut in the area.

And that's how I found myself on a solo honeymoon in Mexico, stuck in the middle of nowhere, unable to escape to a town or to a less couples-oriented resort. Nor were there any staff members or marketing people on site to dine with me; it probably didn't occur to them that the *Brides* correspondent would arrive unaccompanied.

I've already mentioned the lack of electricity.

Good place for a fling, I'd thought as soon as my situation sunk in. As much fun as I'd had with various press groups, I'd been ignoring the physical part of the honeymoon experience.

I wasn't very good at flirting or, frequently, at knowing when men were coming on to me. Friends often pointed out guys who were checking me out. This time I vowed to try to pick up any signals being sent my way. At the slightest suggestion of interest, I would make eye contact and smile.

As far as I could tell, not a single waiter evinced any interest in post-prandial activities.

When morning light finally broke at Las Jacarandas, I was irritable from the lack of sleep and felt a cold coming on (how could germs have gotten to me? I'd had no human contact). I couldn't even lie out in the sun and wallow in my misery. I had an appointment to tour El Piloncillo, a few miles to the north.

A few miles as the crow flies, it turned out, not as Luis, the senior citizen in the equally ancient van assigned to haul me between resorts, drove. I approved of hiring the elderly in principle, but I was beginning to think that Mexico carried this policy way too far. Even if our progress had not been hindered by Luis's worrying eyesight—were those cataracts or just allergies causing that clouded-over look?—it would have been slowed by the road's abundant *topes,* speed bumps ubiquitous all over Mexico but especially closely spaced here. Maybe the ranchers of the Costa Alegre (the "Happy Coast" as the stretch of shore between Puerto Vallarta and Manzanillo had been optimistically dubbed) bribed the government to install more than its fair share of topes to keep speeders from crashing into their cows.

By the time I arrived at Piloncillo, more than an hour and countless kidney jolts later, I was definitely not a Happy Coaster. Nor was I in the mood to meet what I assumed would be a perky PR representative for a property tour. True, Mexican reps weren't nearly as relentlessly upbeat as their American counterparts, but they were often even younger, thinner, and more gorgeous—not what you want to face when, on the previous evening, you've been rejected by a dining room full of waiters with nowhere better to go.

Imagine my surprise, then, when a nerdy-looking guy came out to the guard barrier to greet the van; he had dark, disheveled hair, and his black-framed glasses were askew. "I am Miguel," he said, extending his hand. He spoke to Luis in rapid-fire Spanish, and then explained to me that he was the only one on site. "I am a marine biologist," he said. "We are doing tests here to make sure that the construction does not have a negative impact on the sea life."

I was impressed that Piloncillo was so eco-conscious—an anomaly in the mid-1990s—but dubious about this dweeb's ability to give me what I typically need in a tour for *Brides*: room statistics, information on luxury amenities, hype. Still, he assured me he had been waiting for me and was eager to show me around. And at least he wasn't perky.

Miguel sent Luis away with assurances that he would drive me back to Las Jacarandas, which was fine by me. Miguel was at least thirty years younger than Luis and therefore bound to have better driving skills—or at least faster reaction times.

"So, where would you like to start?" Miguel asked. "From the golf course? That has a view of the entire grounds."

"I don't care," I grumped. First, the lack of attention at Las Jacarandas. Now this snub. I had gotten used to special treatment as a *Brides* correspondent. Didn't I warrant a professional tourism person to show me around instead of the odd employee who happened to be available? "I'm tired and I'm not feeling well."

"I'm so sorry," said Miguel, sounding like he meant it. "Is there anything I can do? Nothing is open here yet, but I can make you a cup of tea at the little marine station where I work."

"That's okay," I responded, in my best martyr tone. "Let's get this over with so I can go back to Las Jacarandas and get some rest."

Undeterred by my testiness, Miguel continued to be relentlessly nice. He checked my health status, asked about my job and my life in Arizona—and listened to my answers, or at least made an excellent show of it. He told me a bit about his background, about the Mexican academic system, about the region's politics.

As we slowly made our way up the narrow path in a golf cart, Miguel pointing out rare native birds and trees in the surrounding thicket, it struck me that he was actually the ideal person to tour me around. I'd learned a great deal about the various plants and animals that could do me damage in Arizona, but my knowledge of tropical flora and fauna was limited, and this *Brides* story was going to require color, vivid background detail. I'd walked around Las Jacarandas that morning, trying to get someone on the staff to help out with names for the various growing and chirping things around me, with little success; they hadn't known the words in Spanish, much less in English. Now, in Miguel, I had my own personal field guide and translator. Asking him to stop and repeat his identifications, I took out my notebook and scribbled madly.

When I put the pad away and we resumed walking, I began to be aware that Miguel had a kind, intelligent face and that, although he was bordering on skinny, his arms were nicely muscled.

By the time we reached the golf course, terraced on a hillside overlooking the Pacific, I was feeling considerably more cheerful. I was having a stimulating conversation with an interesting man in a stunning setting, a huge bay flanked by acres of rainforest. The scenery was so gorgeous that I wouldn't have to exaggerate its allures in future articles—and I could identify its natural attributes if required to do so.

I must have been looking considerably more cheerful too. Miguel stood behind me to point out the prime diving and snorkeling spots and, next thing I knew, he was cradling my elbow and murmuring, "Oh, your arms are so soft, just like marshmallows."

"That's not something you should ever say to an American woman if you want to get to first base with her," I cautioned. "We spend hours in the gym trying to get rid of marshmallow arms."

But I was smiling.

🐫 🐫 🐫

Like most travel writers, I wasn't keen on inspecting hotel rooms, a necessary evil for both my guidebooks and *Brides* stories. It was a struggle to come up with creative riffs on a simple theme: bed, bath, chairs, desk. If a room were generic, you'd have to try to find something to distinguish it. If it had lots of character, you needed to pin down the buzzwords *du jour*. I'd ask, "So what do you call that fabric?" or "What's the name of that type of lighting?"—fairly basic questions that the PR person or hotel manager conducting the tour was rarely able to answer.

It didn't help that most of my own home furnishings came from thrift stores, which don't tend to identify their donated items in shelter magazine–style detail.

I suspected that the room inspection at Piloncillo would be complicated by something that didn't usually factor in: sexual tension.

As we descended the hillside to the complex of thatched-roof casitas, Miguel and I had moved into high innuendo mode. By the time we entered the model room, as organic–chic as the rest of the resort, the die was cast. It was just a question of where and when, not if.

I asked a few obligatory questions about the inlaid pebbles and the folk art, but was distracted by intensive neck nuzzling, which I made only desultory efforts to discourage. Finally, Miguel said, "You've seen enough, haven't you? I can answer any other questions later. Let me drive you back to your hotel."

But that wasn't really an option. I didn't want everyone knowing my business, and driving into a gated resort with a man who didn't depart immediately would ensure speculation about our activities. "Sorry," I said, "That's not going to work."

"How about the beach?" he asked. But, sensing my earlier grouchiness returning at the notion of getting sand up my butt, he quickly backtracked, lest the mood be lost.

Miguel didn't really need all that much encouraging to be convinced that we should stay right where we were. The bed in the model room at Piloncillo may not have had any bougainvillea petals spelling out *bienvenidos*, but it beckoned nevertheless.

Passionate lead-up notwithstanding, I tried to keep my expectations low. The only other time I'd had sex in Mexico, with Enrique the Copper Canyon hotel manager, it was "El Rapido," the south-of-the-border version of "Wham, Bam, Thank You Ma'am!" Still, I figured that Miguel's extended verbal foreplay (i.e., actually conversing with me) and the elements of danger and excitement (what if someone walked in on us?) would be enough to compensate for any lapses in technique.

But there weren't any. Let the curtains (damask? tulle? moire?) descend on this scene; bridal magazines like their sex gauzy. Let's just say that, three unfaked orgasms later, I could see why this was called Costa Alegre. All my cold symptoms had miraculously disappeared.

¡Viva Miguel! ¡Viva México!

CHAPTER 12
A COMPLETE IDIOT—AND A DUMMY
Coastal Mexico/Arizona, 1998–2001

It's the rare travel editor who hasn't encountered some form of this query: "I've always wanted to go to [name of appealing exotic country]. Would you be interested in sending me? I really like to travel."

"Sure," the editor thinks. "Who doesn't? But do you really like to write? And are you any good at it?"

Few writers really *like* to write. We do it because…well, for a variety of reasons, some less irrational than others. But more than a decade and a half after getting my PhD, I wondered if I would ever be good at it again.

Academia had knocked the bejeezus out of my prose and bitch-slapped my ability to ease words onto a page. I was like the frog in slowly heating water that doesn't know it's being cooked. One day I was turning out college papers praised for their clarity. The next, I was submitting a proposal for a dissertation titled "From Apocalypse to Entropy: An Eschatological Study of the American Novel." I switched thesis topics but didn't kick the jargon and passive construction habits, because that's how lit crit rolls.

When you're as far gone as I was, it's a long road to recovery. I never did regain my pre–grad school fluency. I did, however, learn to fake it far better—thanks, in part, to getting in touch with my inner Idiot. And Dummy.

When Macmillan Publishing became part of Simon & Schuster, the company brought with it a new reference subdivision, Alpha Books, which had recently rolled out the

Complete Idiot's Guide (CIG) series. A not-so-subtle imitation of the For Dummies line—*DOS for Dummies* was published in 1991; *The Complete Idiot's Guide to MS-DOS* appeared in 1993—it was conceived to explain computers to non-geeks. Success brought an expansion into lifestyle topics, and travel was a natural for the company that produced the Frommer's guides.

I had just finished updating *Frommer's San Antonio and Austin* when I got a call from an editor at Macmillan, Margot Weiss. Few of my former Prentice Hall colleagues were left at the company; Margot was as much of a blank slate to me as Susan the Silent, Queen of the Occasional Fax, had been. But she soon made herself—and her mission—known: to get me on board for one of the first books in the new series, *The Complete Idiot's Travel Guide to Mexico's Beach Resorts*. I was impressed at Margot's strategic use of the telephone, but had no intention of signing on to write another guidebook.

I wasn't unhappy with my Frommer's experience. I'd been paid the same amount for the second edition of my San Antonio and Austin guide as I'd gotten for the original. The tourism bureaus of both cities now bent over backward to help me. And I'd managed to piggyback several magazine assignments onto my San Antonio research. But the balance between editing, writing, and updating had been restored and I didn't want to tip the scales again. And a Complete Idiot's Guide? Seriously?

It didn't take long for Margot to change my mind.

Her enthusiasm for the new series was infectious, her collaborative approach unprecedented. My reputation as a writer and editor had preceded me, Margot said, without a trace of sarcasm. I was exactly the right person to help her create a new template.

The topic couldn't have been more appealing either. After years of combing Mexico's beaches for Fodor's and *Brides*, I knew and loved the terrain.

Flattery and a hefty fee will get you anywhere with me. The $25,000 that Macmillan put on the table sealed the deal. For the first time, I could cover my research costs and even make a profit. What a concept.

An unexpected bonus: I got plenty of practice crafting a light-hearted but authoritative voice and transforming disparate bits of data into witty, comprehensible prose.

🐪 🐪 🐪

Most general travel guides term themselves "comprehensive," but no book weighing less than ten pounds can come close to making good on that claim. Decisions about the regions, states, and cities to include and the number of pages to devote to each are based on conventional wisdom— and perpetuated over time. In several editions of *Fodor's Mexico*, for example, Monterrey got five pages to Guadalajara's thirty-three, even though the two cities are roughly the same size. Both have interesting histories and striking scenery; indeed, Monterrey is wealthier and a modern art hub. Why the disparity? Tourists will find far more to do in and around Guadalajara—or so I assumed when I edited the Mexico guide. Since Fodor's updaters are paid by the page, it wasn't cost effective for me to verify this by visiting Monterrey myself.

CIG takes a cut-to-the-chase approach to all its topics, and travel was no different. The beach-resorts theme pared down the book's scope, and my mandate was to winnow, winnow, winnow—and then dig in. My goal wasn't to direct readers to the most out-of-the-way places; it was to help them choose from among the ones they were likely to hear about, those to which the most flights went, and those that had the best tourist infrastructure. After much poring over statistics and backing and forthing, Margot and I settled on eight beach towns: Los Cabos, Acapulco, Puerto Vallarta, Ixtapa/Zihuatenejo, Mazatlan, Manzanillo, Cancun, and Cozumel.

The only one I lobbied for that didn't get in was Huatulco, the southernmost of the Pacific coast resorts. Although it was hellishly hot there the one time I visited, I'd been blown away by the pristine beaches—and even more by the cuisine. Huatulco is in the state of Oaxaca, land of a thousand *moles*: Think fresh seafood with wonderfully complex sauces. Oaxaca also distills the world's top mezcals, tequila's often maligned cousin. Appealing to fans of smoky dark spirits like Laphroaig, they substitute the taste of sun-kissed agave fields for damp peaty bogs.

If Huatulco had been in my guide, I might have included a text box titled "Don't Worry about the Worms." It would have explained how *gusano rojo* larvae ended up in some mezcal bottles by way of a perverse promotional campaign and how tequila's reputation was besmirched by association. I would likely have devoted another sidebar to Oaxaca's more offbeat delicacies, especially the crispy *chapulines* (little grasshoppers) that locals munch like potato chips. It might have had a cautionary "Yo, Gringo" heading—one of the stylized graphics used to highlight information that was slightly off-topic or that needed to be emphasized. The *chapulines* fit into both categories: One of my fellow writers on a Oaxaca press trip had downed an entire bowl of bugs before someone clued her in to what she'd been eating.

Huatulco aside, I didn't mind CIG's greatest-hits approach. Good tourism infrastructure meant good media assistance for me. But I had a hard enough time getting respect writing as an Idiot in the US, where the eye rolling of friends and associates at least came with basic comprehension of the concept. I couldn't begin to bridge the culture gap in Mexico. Why would a publisher gear guidebooks toward stupid people, my Mexican PR contacts wondered. Can they read? Do they appreciate nice things? Do they have money to spend? By this time, I'd banked enough good will working for better-known brands to be able to plead, "Trust me on this one." They did. I had little trouble lining up accommodations, excursions, and meals.

I also could have gotten comps for many aquatic sports, but my idea of fun in the sun is a throwback to teenage years spent baking on Brighton Beach. I can almost smell the baby oil and iodine my friends and I slathered on before lying back on our towels, sun reflectors poised for maximum impact. I shudder to think how many hours we spent motionless, absorbing damaging ultraviolet rays. At the time, it felt oddly soothing. Although fashionably darkened skin was the goal, the intense heat and light seemed to cauterize my free-flowing anxieties.

When we were ready to cool off, we hit the surf. Our exertions were largely limited to wave dodging, however. We were not an athletic bunch.

In Mexico, clad in shorts and a T-shirt, I flitted from one aquatic activity concession to another, asking how much it would cost to rent a waverunner or Hobie cat, what the price was for an hour of waterskiing, jetskiing, and parasailing—"for later, with my friends," I pretended. I eventually learned how to distinguish between these sports but grew no more interested in sampling any of them. I occasionally yearned to roast in the sand again; the dangers of tanning, while dire, lay in the future. In contrast, the bodily harm that could be inflicted by water sports, from concussions to close encounters with man-eating fish, were more grievous and more immediate.

My proximity to all those miles of gorgeous shoreline was far from wasted, however. I was tasked with finding the best sea-view restaurants on the Gulf, Pacific, and Caribbean coasts, and I took that job very seriously. I researched them all: the holes in the wall on the *malecón* in downtown Mazatlan where fresh shrimp, not atmosphere, was the draw; the cozy cafe in Puerta Vallarta serving pan-Mexican specialties; the fine dining room with a prix-fixe menu in the tony Acapulco Diamante district. Gazing out at the water with a margarita or a Negro Modelo in hand never got old.

Cigarettes were often involved too.

Through a quirk of body chemistry, I was able to smoke for limited periods of time—an evening, a day, a few weeks—and then stop cold turkey, with a minimum of withdrawal stress. I hardly ever indulged in Tucson because no one else I knew there smoked, but I pursued my closet vice enthusiastically in Mexico, where hotel mini-bars offered inexpensive packs and few people looked down on lighting up. Knowing I was doing something culturally taboo in the US made the cigarettes I puffed with my morning coffee taste even better.

I didn't expect my Mexican dalliances with tobacco to prove to be a research aid as well as a guilty pleasure.

Many of my sea-view meals doubled as networking sessions with tourism representatives. One evening, I was scheduled to meet three women from the Manzanillo visitors bureau at Las Hadas, the ultra-luxe resort made famous by the 1979 film *10*. The movie had spurred a surge of much-needed tourism in Manzanillo; Mexico's largest commercial port, the city is less picturesque than many more intimate beach resorts. It also inspired a spate of copycat architecture: White Moorish-style spires, towers, and domes cropped up like mushrooms.

Some of the movie's other effects were less salutary. Decades after a bodacious Bo Derek loped along the Las Hadas beach sporting blond cornrows, a pocket industry of al fresco beauty salons arose. Amateur hairdressers staked out stations on the sand all over Mexico, inflicting the hairdo on scores of pale white women. I came to dread the beaded, braided, and sunburnt heads I would encounter on flights back to the US from Cancun, Puerto Vallarta, and other seaside cities, knowing their bearers had only split ends and mockery awaiting them back home.

The Las Hadas dinner didn't start out well. I was accustomed to warm welcomes in Mexico, but the three women waiting at the table to which I was ushered seemed on edge, fidgety. I was certain that this was because I was new to Manzanillo and its tourism scene. Why would anyone want to dine with an unknown journalist writing a book for mental defectives? The trio's unease was contagious. Figuring I had nothing to lose, I asked, "Do you mind if I smoke?"

The mood lifted immediately, as all three whipped out packs of cigarettes. "Thank God," one of them said. "So many American journalists are Puritans. We can never usually smoke in front of them."

It soon emerged that the collective discomfort I'd sensed had nothing to do with my book title or me. One of the women was convinced that her boyfriend was cheating on her. The friends were eager to discuss his faithlessness rather than make small talk with a writer. No problem. I can dish infidelity and betrayal with the best of them. After a few margaritas, we abandoned any attempt to discuss Manzanillo's attractions and began spinning elaborate revenge fantasies. Some were crude and involved the removal of a certain body part; others were more creative, straight out of a *telenovela* plot. At least I recall them as being creative. The details of the evening are a bit hazy.

I may not have learned very much about Manzanillo that night, but women who scheme about castration together tend to form a bond. I didn't have to worry about getting Manzanillo tourism help after that.

Rule to live and work by: Know how to schmooze. Letting loose and being yourself will often get you further than trying to stick to a strict work agenda.

I later had a long run writing for a wine and spirits magazine because I did a camel imitation at a writers-and-editors conference. At one of my ten-minute pitch sessions earlier in the day—the journalist's version of speed dating—I'd proposed a tequila story to the publication's editor. I don't doubt that my Mexico expertise was the determining factor, but I'm also convinced my silliness at dinner got the editor to look at her notes and take a chance on me. Note: If you are a morose or mean drunk, abstain from alcohol and hone your listening skills instead.

🐪🐪🐪

I may have been able to keep up with their gossip and plotting, but I couldn't hold a candle to Mexican women when it came to style. Their hair, makeup, and clothing—even when casual—were impeccable.

By now I had realized that all of the women and most of the men I would meet in public relations (or in public, period) were likely to be far better put together than I could ever hope to be. Freelancers are notorious for letting their sartorial skills atrophy; it's an occupational hazard for everyone who works at home. But whereas many freelancers see clients face-to-face only occasionally, travel journalists by definition frequently leave their houses. They are sometimes expected to look respectable.

Organizers of press trips have good reason to be wary. Take the aforementioned writer who unwittingly downed a bowl of grasshoppers in Oaxaca. A full-figured woman to whom time and gravity had not been kind, she had a temporary skin condition that made putting on a bra uncomfortable. It happens. But instead of wearing loose-fitting cotton cover-ups, she chose clingy Lycra tops, often in bright colors. It was not a good look. Our group got stares everywhere we went, from cathedrals to upscale restaurants, and not admiring ones.

Friends in travel PR have confided that good personal hygiene is sometimes all they can hope for from writers. I figured that taking regular showers put me ahead of the game. After that trip, keeping my nipples concealed set the bar even lower.

I can't really blame all my fashion failures on freelancing, however. I am the world's worst packer, and traveling for a living didn't cure that.

It's hard to explain. I go into a kind of fugue state—or demonic possession—when faced with a suitcase. Call it fantasy packing. Recently, I took only one warm sweater, an unlined rain jacket, and lots of T-shirts along on a trip to the Pacific Northwest. I had decided it should be warm and sunny where I was going, weather reports to the contrary notwithstanding, and prepared my wardrobe accordingly.

Occasionally, I am inspired to take along clothing that has hung, unworn, in my closet for years, convinced it'll be perfect for the trip. Not until they're sprawled out on my hotel-room bed do I remember the reason I don't wear those pants at home is that they make my butt look huge. Because they were expensive, I couldn't bring myself to donate them to a thrift shop.

It would be bad enough if my clothing catastrophes ended with my journeys, but travel also has dire effects on my closet.

I've become convinced, for example, that native garb will delight and impress the folks back home. I once bought an ornately embroidered Huichol peasant dress in Puerta Vallarta, the type worn by Frida Kahlo. It was beautiful, but no longer in style except maybe in Berkeley. And even in the height of my hippie days, flowery flowing clothing made me look like I was in drag.

It could have been worse. At least I didn't take home a Xoloitzcuintli (show-low-eetz-QUEENT-lee), the hairless Mexican dog that appears in several of Kahlo's paintings—and in Manzanillo gift shops.

Chubby ceramic dogs were discovered in tombs throughout Colima, the Mexican state where Manzanillo is located, and reproductions are sold everywhere. The Colima dog, as it came to be known, played a variety of roles in Maya, Aztec, Toltec, and Colima Indian lore: guide to the underworld, hunting companion, sacrificial offering, and dinner centerpiece (hairlessness no doubt made preparation easier). Xolos were also prized for their healing properties: The canine equivalent of a hot water bottle, they exuded doggie body heat.

I was excited to learn that these multi-purpose pups were still around and little changed over some 3,000 years. I fantasized about getting one. I figured warm and sunny Tucson would provide the perfect climate for my non-shedding deity, which I vowed not to eat.

Maybe I should mention here that I also yearned for an *abuela*, a Mexican grandmother. I didn't know my actual Austrian grandmothers, who were killed in Europe, but I pictured them Germanic and judgmental, unlike my imaginary south-of-the-border nurturing nana. Never mind that I traveled too much to take care of a pet or that a traditional Catholic matriarch would chide me endlessly for getting divorced and not wanting to have children. I was besotted with Mexico.

That said, I wasn't entirely blind to my beloved's flaws. I'm not talking about corruption or drug lords—or even handsy tour guides. Mexico is no country for the klutzy. The pavements are often uneven and the curbs crazily high, even in new parts of the city. Some of the most opulent hotel rooms I stayed in were accidents waiting to happen. Making a good impression is important in Mexico, so marble is often the flooring of choice. This is especially ill conceived in beach towns, where people tend to come into rooms dripping seawater. Whoops.

Then there's the Mexican fondness for cobblestoned walkways—charming to look at but hazardous for those wearing high heels.

One of the strangest hotel features I encountered was the riser in the center of a guest room—sometimes a step, one time a thin metal strip. I'm not sure why you would need a physical reminder other than an actual door that the bathroom and bedroom areas function separately. Still, the possibility of slipping on a wet marble floor, tripping over a room divider, or tripping over a room divider onto a wet marble floor, paled in comparison with the fear I experienced in one posh room that had a patio overlooking a cliff and, beyond it, the sea. The view was unbeatable but the patio was missing an essential element: a railing. I kept the curtains drawn and the patio door tightly secured for my two nights there, lest I suddenly take up sleepwalking.

🐫 🐫 🐫

Returning to Tucson from my series of trips to Mexico, I often struggled with a sense of isolation, notwithstanding my growing conviction that I was temperamentally suited to living and traveling on my own. Getting together with friends who had little idea of what my work entailed was a far cry from the high of constantly meeting new people in another country—as part of my job, yet.

Margot helped smoothed those transitions. She proved as supportive through the final stages of compiling the book as she'd been in the first. And she was an excellent schmoozer. Knowing I could pick up the phone and discuss everything from my love life to the "Yo, Gringo" sidebars with Margot made me feel less disconnected as a travel freelancer than I'd ever felt before—and, for that matter, since.

This helps explain why, even before the beach resorts book went to press, I accepted Margot's invitation to write *The Complete Idiot's Travel Guide to Arizona*. My familiarity with the state helped; the money, again, was the clincher.

Margot and I hammered out a chapter outline and style sheet for the book, and then I sketched out a travel schedule. I decided to start with the Valley of the Sun, the twenty-two–city metroplex that most people know simply as "Phoenix," "Phoenix and Scottsdale," or "Greater Phoenix." I had volunteered to update every other chapter in *Fodor's Arizona*, but figured it would take someone who lived there—and actually liked the place—to do justice to the Valley.

It wasn't just the maze of freeways and abundance of golf courses that put me off, or even the conservative politics. It was my sense that Greater Phoenix was soulless, Los Angeles without water—except for its oceans of swimming pools—or historical depth.

I nevertheless looked forward to filling in the gaps in my Arizona education and maybe even overcoming a few prejudices.

I'd already visited several of Phoenix's top museums, but hadn't yet been to the Arizona Science Center. I was not especially keen to remedy that omission. Like many girls, I grew up with the sense that science was a foreign country, one I ventured into at my peril. I'd hated the grade school trips to Manhattan's Museum of Natural History, all those big, dead things in airless, high-ceilinged rooms.

With its light, bright spaces and playful exhibits—a giant sneezing nose! paper airplanes!—this science museum came as a revelation and a delight. As I was wandering around scribbling notes, a man working on one of the exhibits asked me, in a friendly way, if he could help me with anything. He was lean and rangy, wearing a work shirt and jeans but also wire-rimmed glasses. Because of his eyewear, I assumed he was a scientist.

Come to find out, Harry was a carpenter, hired to construct the exhibits, not conceptualize them. Even better: a blue-collar man who looked white-collar smart. When I explained I was writing an Arizona guidebook, he expressed surprise at the thoroughness of my research, at the fact that I was doing on-site research at all.

I was surprised by his surprise. Why wouldn't I be gathering first-hand impressions? Harry explained that his friend Clarissa ran an informal B&B and had recently rented a room to the author of an Arizona guide. Clarissa had complained that, instead of going out to do research, the writer had stayed holed up making phone calls while eating cold Spaghetti-Os out of a can. The room had begun to exude a sweaty-guy smell; she practically had to pry the writer out so she could change the sheets and throw out all the tomato sauce–encrusted cans, which had begun attracting bugs.

I knew the book Harry was talking about. It was part of a series lauded for its honesty and attention to detail. Clarissa's intel both gratified and galled me. It confirmed my suspicions that I was more conscientious than some of my fellow writers—emphasis on fellow—but that their books garnered more respect.

Maybe testosterone was a prerequisite for tackling a region known for its craggy, skyward-thrusting rocks and soaring cacti, its bellicose history of conquistadors, cowboys, and Indians. Whatever the case, most of the big-name Southwest and Arizona guides were written by men. Many lifestyle magazines celebrated the cosmopolitan New West, but the manly myths of the Old West still lingered in popular literature. They were not too tough to die. They were carefully nurtured.

I'm not suggesting that all the boys on this beat were macho—or slackers. I'd known Karl Samson, author of *Frommer's Arizona*, when I worked at Prentice Hall Travel; we cemented our friendship when I moved to Tucson and Karl came to town on annual research visits. He enjoyed many of the manly activities that authors of Western guides are expected to enjoy, but he was also an unabashed foodie and oenophile. Karl and I often tried the latest Tucson restaurants and watering holes together.

Similarly, I'd met Greg Ward, the author of the *Rough Guide to the Southwest*, when I worked in London; we'd reconnected in Tucson and Las Vegas. Greg was at once enthralled and appalled by the vast American region he'd opted to write about. I didn't agree with all of his takes on places we both covered, but our discussions about them were as respectful as they were bracing.

That wasn't the case with Jeb Krasnowski, the British expat author of a rival Southwest guide; he lived in Tucson and was married to a doctor. Greg knew Jeb a little and, on one of his visits to town, arranged for the three of us to have a meal together.

Our dinner started off pleasantly enough, but after a few drinks Jeb started sneering about the superficiality and bourgeois nature of *Fodor's Arizona*, which I was updating at the time. Ah, yes, I knew that British superciliousness well. Now, however, I was on home turf and a lot more confident than I'd been in London.

What exactly was bourgeois about the book? I wondered. That it recommended nice restaurants? We were sitting in one. Superficial? Fodor's authors ventured to as many off-the-beaten path places as other guidebook writers. The three of us began reeling off the most remote outposts we'd visited in Arizona. Slot canyons beyond the most famous one, Antelope Canyon? Check, check, check. Colorado City, home to Warren Jeffs and other creepy polygamists? Check, check. Fort Bowie National Historical Site? Aha! Although Jeb had been in the vicinity, I was the only one who had actually hiked out to the fort.

You don't need a penis to win a pissing contest.

Now, however, I was writing an Arizona guide that had the word "Idiot" in its title. I would have lost that contest by default.

Its name notwithstanding, the book covered my adopted domicile and I wanted it to be a knockout—especially the restaurant listings, an increasing area of expertise. I felt woefully uninformed about the Phoenix/Scottsdale dining scene, however. I decided to enlist the help of the Valley food writer I admired most: Nikki Buchanan.

Nikki and I had a slight professional connection. The previous year, I'd been hired to critique restaurants for a new city magazine, *Tucson Monthly*. Its consulting editor had helmed *Phoenix Magazine*, for which Nikki wrote. I'd pored over her columns as models for my own future reviews.

Typically, I'd felt intimidated by Nikki's stylistic verve, her range of culinary knowledge. Atypically, I swallowed my insecurities and approached Nikki as a peer. I explained that I was working on a new Arizona guide and needed a list of Valley restaurants to start with. I offered her a small fee and assistance with dining in other parts of the state.

Nikki not only agreed to help me compile a list but volunteered to meet with me and chat informally. She turned out to be almost exactly my age, pretty and petite, with blond wiry hair. Like me, she was struggling with a freelance career and with a tendency to look for love in the wrong places. We bonded instantly. We've lost touch in recent years, but I have no doubt that, if I phoned her today, we would pick up our conversation where we left off.

And we'll always have Palm Springs in the nude.

My relationship with Harry of the Arizona Science Center turned out to be far shorter and less significant than my connection with Nikki. Harry drove down to Tucson to see me a few times, but I soon discovered that his room-renting friend Clarissa was actually his room-renting fiancée Clarissa. It was for the best. Harry had fudged when I'd asked him, perplexed, about the crude LOVE and HATE tattoos on his knuckles. By the time I found out why Phoenix was off limits for our trysts, one of my friends had explained that Harry had doubtless gotten the ink in prison. What can I say? This was before knuckle tattoos had gone mainstream and before *Oz*, *Orange is the New Black*, and other forms of incarcero-tainment had become popular.

I never did learn what Harry had been in for. Maybe that was for the best, too.

🐫 🐫 🐫

About six months after I signed the contract for the Arizona CIG guide, I received the following in the mail:

> Dear Edie,
>
> This letter is being written to inform you of several changes related to the Macmillan General Reference Group ("MGR") and how these changes will affect you.... As of August 2, 1999, MGR became a wholly owned subsidiary of IDG Books Worldwide, Inc., publisher of the "...for Dummies" brand of books.... This transaction did not include the Complete Idiot's Guide series, though a subsequent deal did include the rights to certain travel books, one of which is the Work you were contracted to write.
>
> Therefore the Work which was originally to be published by MGR under the CIG imprint will now be published under IDGB's "...for Dummies" brand.

Translation: The Idiots had been bought out by the Dummies.

Until further instructions arrived, I was in writing limbo.

The massive style memo that finally materialized several months later dictated changes that were largely cosmetic. The light-hearted but authoritative voice was identical in the two series, which meant I could use the Arizona dining, hotel, and attractions reviews I'd already written; only the service information was affected.

Still, there were a few more substantive differences. The author-generated breakout boxes like "Yo, Gringo" that provided visual emphasis for quirky information were replaced by series-wide icons designating topics like child friendliness, a move back toward the more boring Frommer's model. There was a new section with an oddly generic name, "The Part of Tens." The required series of items—the Top Ten Crafts to Buy in Arizona, for example—struck me as silly. Little did I know that I was being prepared for a future of *BuzzFeed*-style listicles.

I also hated the cartoon guy with the crewcut, googly eyes, and triangular head who was plastered over all the Dummies books.

Those were still quibbles. The CIG/Dummies transition would have been smooth if it weren't for two things: Authors weren't given much of a deadline extension, in spite of the delay in receiving revised style sheets, and Margot was no longer my editor.

She hadn't yet left the company—that would happen in another six months—but she wasn't involved with the Idiots-to-Dummies transition. I was assigned a far less congenial taskmistress whose comments on my copy were a far cry from the constructive suggestions I'd always received from Margot.

In the end, I was happy with the published *Arizona for Dummies*. I updated it three times, until travel guides were cut from the For Dummies lineup. I even had an intern to help me with research for subsequent editions: Kate Davis, a friend of a New York friend, sought me out. I was delighted to be the beneficiary of her top-notch assistance—and foodie enthusiasm—and pleased that someone thought I had skills worth teaching. Maybe I was a real author after all.

That possibility lay behind my decision to turn down the next job offer from Macmillan: to transform my *Complete Idiot's Travel Guide to Mexico's Beach Resorts* into *Mexico's Beach Resorts for Dummies*. I would receive the same fee as I'd gotten for the original book, but there was a catch. In order to avoid copyright infringement, I would have to rewrite 75 percent of the text. Could I have done it? Probably. But I didn't want to. It had taken me a great deal of effort to get the words just right.

Besides, I don't think I could have withstood the embarrassment. It was bad enough going to Mexico as a Complete Idiot. How would I explain to my south-of-the-border friends that I had suddenly become a Dummy?

CHAPTER 13
WHEN TRAVEL WRITERS GATHER
Assorted Exotic Places, mid-1990s–the (occasional) present

Once I started writing for magazines, my job-complaint credibility hit the skids. If getting free hotels and meals while researching guidebooks made others suspect I was living high on the hog, going on press trips convinced them I was a freeloading slacker.

I wish.

Every now and then, I was invited on a journalists' jaunt that fit the "junket" stereotype, down to the lavish suites, umbrella drinks, and large swaths of free time. Far more often, however, my familiarization (fam) tours resembled sleep-away camps run by speed freaks. In an elaborate juggling act, trip organizers would try to anticipate every conceivable interest of an eclectic group of writers while satisfying the publicity demands of the destination or hotel picking up the tab. It was a lose–lose proposition. Running journalists through a frenetic gauntlet of activities only made them irritable and thus less likely to pen glowing reviews.

The first press trip I went on fell somewhere in between the poles of decadent and forced march.

I was working for Prentice Hall Travel and had recently started seeing Bill Taylor, a "real" travel writer, as I thought of him: He was published in magazines like *Travel + Leisure* and was always being dispatched to far-flung places. Bill was a departure from my usual unavailable and/or bad-boy type: He lived in the same city as I did, and he was nice. Really nice. He was in touch with his feminine side, crediting luck, rather than hard work and talent, for his success. And he encouraged my confided-in-bed writing ambitions—through deeds as well as words.

Tourism Business magazine had asked Bill to cover a new safari-and-surf package to Kenya and Mauritius created by Aquarius, a tour operator. He was busy for the dates of the associated fam trip; after clearing it with his editor, he asked if I would like to take his place. I was blown away. PHT editors weren't given time off for press trips, but accepting them wasn't against company policy, and I had two weeks' vacation coming to me.

I was excited about the upcoming trip, less so about the accompanying assignment. Forget imposter syndrome. I actually *was* an imposter, filling in for real-writer Bill. I was relieved that my article would appear in a limited-circulation publication geared toward industry insiders rather than in a high-profile newsstand magazine. Less pressure.

My fax machine soon churned out an eight-day itinerary and cast of characters. There would be eight of us— two representatives from Aquarius and five writers besides me—and we'd spend the bulk of our time in Mauritius. Kenya safaris were already popular with American travelers. Aquarius wanted to promote a destination less known in the US than its Indian Ocean rival, the Seychelles.

Our three days in Kenya sped by in a blur, but I can't forget the name of the Nairobi restaurant where we dined the first night: Carnivore. It resembled a Brazilian barbecue, with formally attired waiters stopping tableside to slice off pieces from large spits of meat, but here zebra, giraffe, and other exotics stood in for beef and lamb. I was hesitant, but I partook. This was the mid-1980s. Fear of being thought a wuss ranked far higher in my mind than wildlife conservation.

At least elephant wasn't on the menu. Bumping along the dusty roads of the Masai Mara Game Reserve the next day, we gazed, awestruck, at gazelles, lions, cheetahs, and other fleet exotic creatures. A slowly moving pack of pachyderms turned out to be the most attention grabbing, however. It took a few seconds for the first in our group to register that one of the lumbering giants we were ogling seemed really happy to see us—or, more likely, to see an attractive female of his species. The impressiveness of an elephant erection cannot be overemphasized. The engorged member reached past its bearer's knees, almost to the ground. The sound of camera shutters opening and closing soon overtook the sound of our initial embarrassed titters.

Another oversized rarity caught my eye at the gift shop of the tiny Madagascar airport, where we stopped en route from Nairobi to Mauritius: a foot-long praying mantis carved out of alabaster. I hadn't researched Madagascar since we weren't staying there, so I knew very little about the country; I associated it only with humongous hissing cockroaches, which could reach three inches in length, according to the *Encyclopedia Britannica*. The praying mantis souvenir fed my fear that the island was a sanctuary for giant mutant insects. What can I say? I lived in a city where nature discussions revolved around pigeons, rats, and roaches.

The mutant part turned out to be true. Having been severed from the east coast of Africa some 160 million years earlier, Madagascar and its fellow Indian Ocean islands teem with plants and animals found nowhere else on the planet. The best known of them was the dodo, which once thrived on Mauritius. By the 1660s, Dutch colonists had rendered these flightless—and apparently tasty—birds extinct, conferring on them the dubious distinction of being the first recorded species to be wiped off the Earth by humans. They were immortalized on T-shirts and other dodo-a-bilia sold all over the island.

Happily, our group wasn't offered any endangered species to eat on Mauritius. Indeed, our dining experiences were far less adventurous than they should have been, given the country's history. First settled by the Portuguese, Mauritius was in turn conquered by the dodo-destroying Dutch, the French, and the English, from whom the country gained independence in 1968. Indian and Chinese workers joined the fray in the nineteenth century. The result was a culinary mix-it-up, an East-meets-West buffet of curries, seafood stews, chili-dusted fruits, and *crème brûlées.*

Because we were expected to check out the lodgings that Aquarius was planning to feature on its new tour, we dined in a succession of upscale but indistinguishable hotel restaurants. Like most people schlepped around in groups, we were rarely allowed to order à la carte. Our meals soon became predictable. Both lunch and dinner almost invariably produced an appetizer of smoked marlin and hearts of palm. It got so that whenever one of our hosts proclaimed they had a "local specialty, just for you," one of us would pantomime sketching a heart on our palms.

What with being shuttled around to hotels on different parts of the island, we had little time to do what tourists do: laze on beaches, browse local markets, take wildlife photos. This didn't bother me, since my assignment was to write about the Aquarius tour; I was glad to be earning my keep. Most of the other journalists were far more frustrated, however, especially Roger, a newspaper stringer from Detroit and an avid birdwatcher. He'd been eager to check rare species off his life list and to use the ever-present absent dodo as a writing hook. He finally managed to finagle an afternoon off from hotel-tour duty, and a rental car.

The only one without an assignment or a plan to nab one was Dana, an editorial assistant from *Cosmo*—which, at the time, didn't have a travel section. The vetting process to ensure that journalists will "produce" is far stricter these days; few writers who don't have an assignment in place or their own high-traffic blog get invited on press trips. It's still hard to screen for personality flaws, however. There's almost always one prima donna or don on every trip, someone who turns up late, is overly demanding, is rude to the hosts—who makes life miserable for everyone else.

Dana did double duty as professional deadwood and group irritant: She was unlikely to ever place a story, and she annoyed the hell out of everyone. She wouldn't stop talking: her job, her boyfriends, her hair...whatever crossed her mind passed through her lips, unfiltered. No one had to share rooms in Mauritius, but in Kenya I drew the short straw and got Dana as my safari-hut mate. The only upside: Her white-noise droning drowned out the scary, unfamiliar jungle sounds—Is that a lion? Can he climb the stilts up to our room?—and put me to sleep.

Most of my companions were sharp, genial, and funny, especially Roger and Leslie, another Detroit newspaper stringer. I would have happily chosen to travel with them, even if we hadn't been semi-arbitrarily thrown together. I was surprised to discover how closely you can bond in a short period with strangers toward whom you haven't developed an instant antipathy.

Good company notwithstanding, I was eager to return home to Bill. I wanted to tell him all about the trip, to convey my gratitude in person.

I phoned him almost immediately. He avoided making plans to meet, pleading deadlines. A week or so later, Bill finally bit the bullet and admitted he had gotten back with his old girlfriend. Aha! The trip had been a pre-emptive apology, meant to soften the blow Bill knew he was going to inflict. Apparently he was my type, after all: not so nice and not so available.

It took a while for my anger to dissipate. I refused to speak to Bill again, even though he tried to see me the following year at Rough Guides in London, and even though a contrition-filled American friend would have been a welcome break from my condescending British co-workers.

I could still win Olympic gold in the Nose Biting to Spite Face and Marathon Grudge Holding events, but my pique over that particular blow to my pride now seems wildly misplaced. Men I'd dated far longer had stopped seeing me without so much as a farewell phone call. Given a choice of being dumped by someone I barely knew and getting a free trip halfway across the world, I'll take the consolation prize every time.

🐪 🐪 🐪

I didn't become a press-trip regular until nearly a decade later, when I became a *Brides* correspondent. As I expanded my client file to include in-flight magazines, luxury niche publications—one for people who owned Steinway pianos, for example—and big newsstand players like *Sunset*, PR people increasingly sought me out.

It was my repeat appearances in *Wine and Spirits Quarterly of Pennsylvania*, the gig I got by doing camel imitations at a writers-and-editors conference, that secured me a place on the invite list for trips hosted by the International Distillers Group (IDG). They were a hot ticket: You got to sample some of the world's premier spirits in the regions where they were produced without ever having to call a cab or designate a driver.

My favorite IDG excursion was to the Mexican state of Jalisco, source of most of the world's genuine tequila. By day, we toured distilleries, several of them on vast haciendas in and around the town of Tequila, others in the highlands. At night, we dined in some of Guadalajara's top restaurants and slept at the luxe Quinta Real hotel.

We were feted like royalty: met with mariachi bands, even in the agave fields; plied with margaritas (my favorite was tamarind, rimmed with Tajín spice); and encouraged to compare sips of *plata, reposado,* and *añejo* tequila while dining on endless rounds of Mexican specialties. I was on assignment for *National Geographic Traveler,* which got me props with both my hosts and my fellow journalists. Press trip? Comps? I just told the editor I pitched that I was going to Tequila; she didn't ask how I was getting there, and I didn't enlighten her.

Although most of our five days in Mexico were devoted to tequila, we also shopped for crafts in Tlaquepaque, known for its ceramics, and toured Los Guachimontones, an archaeological site in remote eastern Jalisco with rare circular temples. Good drink, good food, good folk art, and an ancient ruin. It doesn't get much better in my book.

My next trip with IDG, to the Cognac region of France, was so appealing on paper that it seems almost churlish to complain about it. Almost.

It had all the hallmarks of the Mexico tour: The countryside was idyllic, the food and drink first class. There were no bands with a big brass section to greet us, but the French are less effusive than the Mexicans.

We also had lovely—if slightly plumbing-challenged—lodgings, in converted nineteenth-century chateaux. Unfortunately, we didn't have time to enjoy them: We had to move rooms five times in six nights. A single afternoon picnic on a barge plying a slow route along the Charente River fulfilled our chill-out quota. On our final day, the schedule was so tight that, before going to dinner at a Michelin two-star restaurant, we had to change clothes in the bathrooms of a La Rochelle aquarium, where—sorry, no time—we hadn't looked at a single fish.

Our breakneck pace left me tired and crabby during the many hours we spent standing in damp cognac cellars listening to lectures about barrel aging and blending. After a while, every time I heard the phrase "angel's share"—the amount of cognac lost to evaporation—I wanted to pipe up, "So when does the devil get his due?"

My resulting article, in the annual desk diary for the International Club for Rolls-Royce & Bentley Owners, was accurate about the spirits and the scenery. The leisurely pace? Pure fabrication.

The final trip I took with IDG, along the American Whiskey Trail, promised to be less exotic but no less spirits-soaked. It kicked off in Washington, DC, where George Washington's rye distillery had been re-opened, and then continued into Kentucky and Tennessee.

I loved Scotch whisky of all stripes but was not a big fan of the American variety (and not only because the different spelling, "whiskey" with an "e," was a copy-editor's nightmare). Most of the bourbon I'd sampled was a bit too sweet. My experience with Tennessee whiskey was limited to Jack Daniels, which I liked—maybe too much. After I woke up one morning to find my keys in the bathtub, I decided Jack and I should part ways.

Always the consummate professional, I was willing to set aside any preconceptions in the name of research.

The trip started out promisingly enough. Flight schedules made it easier for me to join the group in Louisville, Kentucky, rather than meeting them in DC, so the writers on the large bus I boarded had already bonded. I don't mean that they deliberately excluded me, just that they had the boozy experiences of the previous evening to rehash. As a result, I was taken under the wing of one of the two IDG reps hosting the trip, Sarah Rosen. We clicked instantly: She was originally from New York and, before she took the IDG position, had been the director of communications for the Arizona Democratic Party.

We gabbed about growing up in the city and about the presidential election, how bummed we were that John Kerry had lost in a squeaker. As we traveled from distillery to distillery, Sarah tutored me in bourbon. I learned that even the best-known brands had boutique productions, small barrels of reserve spirits. Chatting companionably with Sarah, watching the rolling green hills of Kentucky slip by on a warm late-September day, nodding off now and then with a bourbon buzz... Sometimes my job was as cushy as people thought.

We had one final stop planned in Kentucky before crossing over into Tennessee. I was looking forward to my first taste of an artisanal brand that several friends had touted.

Kentucky distillers are a close-knit community, and a PR representative from one of the brands we had already visited was also headed over to the tasting room we were headed for. The rep was driving her own car, and Sarah offered to leave the bus and ride with her to keep her company.

We were all in a jovial mood when we got to the distillery and waited for Sarah to rejoin us. A cell phone rang; Madison, the other IDG rep, excused herself to take the call. From a few feet away, we could hear her voice change. I glanced over and saw the color drain from her face.

I'm not sure exactly what happened next. We waited for what seemed a very long time in limbo, aware that something was terribly wrong. Finally, someone broke the news: A truck rounding a blind curve had sideswiped the car Sarah was riding in. She had been killed instantly. We later learned that the car's driver was shook up but otherwise fine; she was released from the hospital the following day.

There are worse places to get horrific news than a distillery. As Madison conferred with the IDG office about what to do with our group—in the end, we were all sent home as soon as flights could be booked—we held an informal wake for Sarah, who was twenty-eight. None of us knew her well. She was new to the IDG job. But we had talked that day, Sarah and I. She had lent me a pair of rubber-soled shoes—flip flops? sneakers?—because the floor of one of the distilleries was slippery and I was wearing leather soles. I offered to give them back. No, she told me; hold on to them. Were those her last words to me?

I hesitated to dredge up these disjointed memories. What sense could I make of these events, what wisdom impart? I decided it was enough to write that my path had crossed with that of a thoughtful, smart, and funny young woman on the last day of her life.

And to raise a metaphorical snifter to Sarah Rosen. I might have found bourbon unpalatable because of its associations with the tragedy. Instead, I came to savor the distinctive spirit as a reminder of Sarah, of all such fleeting connections. *L'chaim!*

🐫 🐫 🐫

Much as I bonded with many of the people I met, the enforced camaraderie of press trips pushed the boundaries of my social comfort zone. I've never been much of a joiner but decided that, if I was going to be a professional travel writer, I should work a bit on the professional development part.

The most prestigious group I knew for that purpose was the Society of American Travel Writers (SATW). Entry requirements, based on a point system more complicated than the IRS tax code, were stringent. Those who made the cut were deemed dependable sources of stories, so destinations vied for the right to host conferences, dangling desirable activities and deep discounts in front of us.

Self-improvement and the company of my peers were undeniable bonuses, but the prime draw of SATW conferences was the guilt-free travel. Because I was paying my own way, albeit a pittance compared to what the average traveler would spend, I didn't feel remiss if a trip didn't yield immediate story results. I almost always managed to get something published sooner or later, but the urgency that kept me on edge during press trips was muted at these gatherings.

The more intimate Western chapter conferences I attended, held everywhere from Albuquerque to Vancouver, BC, made it easier to chill out with simpaticos. In contrast, the annual organization-wide confabs were a bit of a zoo, with complex travel arrangements and cutthroat competition to get in on the most desirable post-trips, as the after-conference excursions were known. But they were usually held in foreign places that, without the low, low conference rates, few of us would have been able to afford.

Which is how I found myself in Bangkok. I'm not as keen on the Far East as I am on other parts of the world—the interminable flights to get there don't help—but I couldn't pass up the chance to go to a country where Thai is the default cuisine.

I wasn't disappointed. I could pile my plate with pad thai, green papaya salad, red curry, and the like morning, noon, and night if I so desired. I so desired.

Another of the country's specialties, Thai massage, was less to my taste—to put it mildly. Sitting on a bare floor mat in a large room, I waited nervously with a few dozen other SATWers in loose clothing who'd signed on for the experience. Finally, the cadre of young women assigned to minister to us arrived. Whoa. My masseuse, who spoke no English, began twisting my arms and legs into positions for which the human anatomy is not designed. She was a slip of a thing, but able to exert at least twice her body weight in pain. Maybe I just got stuck with a sadist or a political activist—take that, capitalist American tourist pig—but I couldn't imagine why anyone would actually pay to subject herself to this torture. Except, of course, a masochist.

It was extremely hot and humid, so I was glad to leave crowded Bangkok for smaller Chiang Mai, where temple cruising and elephant riding were on the agenda. A bonus: Jean, a friend and colleague from Tucson, had chosen the same post-trip as I had. Meeting new people energizes me. Having an old pal with whom to gossip about them is the icing on the cake.

I've mentioned the "There's always one" rule of press trips. The same holds true for conferences, where you can count on a thorn in the collective side to turn up among the attendees. Sure enough, in Chiang Mai, we had Doris to play the part, and she was a doozy.

She couldn't stop *kvetching*. We didn't stay long enough in the shops en route to town and they were too commercial (a variation of the old Borscht-belt complaint about Catskill resorts: The food is terrible, and they don't give you enough of it). The bus was too large and touristy; couldn't we have gone in smaller vans? We were cruising past lush thickets of mango and coconut trees and flowering hibiscus and stopping at some of the world's most beautiful Buddhist temples on a trip that was practically handed to us as a gift. All Doris could do was complain.

When it came time to pair off for the elephant ride through the jungle, no one volunteered to sit with Doris. Who wanted that irritating whine to drown out the calls of tropical birds? Luckily, there were an odd number of people in our group, so Doris had one of the two-seat *howdahs* that the elephants bore on their backs all to herself. Jean and I were directly behind her in the line of beasts making their way down the banks of a shallow river; we had a front-row seat when Doris's elephant lowered its head, turned around, and thoroughly spritzed her.

Instant karma.

We laughed uproariously at the time and for many years afterward when rehashing the incident. Looking back now, it's less funny—not because an ungrateful woman got her comeuppance but because I've since learned about the cruelty of these elephant excursions, the harsh methods used to subdue the animals into accepting riders, and the pain of the combined weight of the box frame and passengers on their spines. Solo-rider Doris had less heft than the rest of us; maybe friskiness, not cosmic payback, was the source of her soaking.

Yes, constantly viewing the past through the prism of the present is the way madness lies. But it never hurts to reconsider what we thought we knew in the light of new data, to admit that it's impossible to predict how any one *kvetcher* might fit into the scheme of things—if there is a scheme.

I'm glad to report that my SATW trip to Ecuador gave me no cause to flagellate my less eco-conscious earlier self. Quite the opposite.

It was humans who were subject to duress at the main meeting in Quito. It wasn't intentional, just a lack of foresight. The conference organizers might have anticipated that holding a conference in a city perched at more than 9,350 feet might result in mass altitude sickness. Advance warnings to our group of travel professionals notwithstanding, attendees began dropping like flies. I had a slight headache on the first day; on the second, I took to my bed with what I was convinced was a fatal case of a dread tropical disease.

Still, much as I would have liked to see more of Quito, my prime reason for signing on for Ecuador was the post-trip to the Galapagos Islands. I'd long dreamed about visiting this peaceable kingdom, a land free from human predation—at least after 1934, when the islands were declared a wildlife sanctuary. Before then, the docile Galapagos dwellers were literally fair game.

The islands were everything I'd hoped for, if slightly more surreal than I'd imagined. Strolling amiably among creatures that were unafraid of humans was odd in itself; "Flee," I found myself thinking, "before it's too late and we humans turn on you." Odder still was the sense that many of these creatures were just a bit off-kilter, especially the large birds: the magnificent frigatebird, with its puffed-up, screamingly scarlet throat pouch; the blue-footed booby, whose appendages were psychedelically bright; and the flightless cormorant—shades of the ill-fated dodo. What, I wondered, channeling Alfred Hitchcock, if they turned on *us*? Scary—but no doubt spectacular on the big screen. I would never again think of bird watching as boring.

By the time we were done touring, I'd glimpsed every rare creature I wanted to except for one: The Great White Travel Writer (TGWTW).

The presence of TGWTW at the conference was anomalous to begin with. Not to denigrate any of my former fellow SATW members, but we were a mid-level lot. Many of us published guidebooks and articles, some in top-rated magazines, but no one on the scale of Bill Bryson, say, or Pico Iyer belonged to the organization.

Neither did TGWTW. He was in Ecuador as a plus-one, married to a woman whose excellent PR firm I had worked with several times. Spouses and partners, who paid their own way—at a higher rate than members but still a greatly discounted one—were usually genial, glad to be along for the bargain ride. TGWTW, however, didn't deign to engage SATWers in conversation. At least that's what I'd been told by several colleagues who'd been on GWTW watch in Quito.

I was not an admirer, mind you. In fact, the great man's most famous book, highly recommended by a graduate-school friend, had put me off travel literature for years. More accurately, the book confirmed my biases against the genre as a worst-of-both-worlds hybrid. I liked well-crafted fiction with a strong sense of place, and nonfiction that taught me something I didn't know, but I balked at the idea of viewing a country I might want to visit through the eyes of a stranger. Sure enough, I found TGWTW's persona unsympathetic—he seemed to disdain most of the people he encountered—his observations pretentious and overly metaphor heavy.

Still, I wondered whether my informants were just jealous of TGWTW's success and were judging his natural reticence as standoffishness. I was curious to see for myself.

The Galapagos post-trip was more fragmented than most. Usually, there was a central hotel where everyone slept and where the group gathered after dark. This time, most attendees opted for one of the array of cruise ships that docked at different islands at the end of the day. Being seasick-prone, I chose the only bunk that didn't move even slightly at night, a modest eco-lodge on the island of Baltra. And because the size of groups that were permitted to gawk at the fragile ecosystems was limited and island visits were staggered in two-hour shifts, once you chose your place to sleep, you chose your constant companions. My hopes for a viewing at the Charles Darwin Research Station on Santa Cruz Island, where group size wasn't restricted, didn't pan out. I saw plenty of rare giant tortoises, but no GWTW.

No biggie. It was just an idle interest that I quickly forgot about. I was thus unprepared for my chance encounter with the man in the Panama airport. I hadn't realized he was on my flight from the Galapagos to Los Angeles until passengers were instructed to disembark and take our carry-on baggage through customs—after having gone through the process a few hours earlier in Ecuador.

Over the years, I've developed the journalist's habit of engaging strangers in conversation, especially in public places like airports and banks where the boredom potential is high, and I am generally only rendered tongue-tied by people I admire. I wasn't fazed, then, when TGWTW queued up directly behind me. I turned around and suggested, laughing, that he might want to choose another line because I had an individually wrapped banana tree in the garbage bag I was clutching. The customs agent was likely to be spending a long time with me, I explained. It had taken me forever to get through the search at the Ecuador airport.

Banana tree in a garbage bag, you ask?

I had become enamored of this bit of wooden faux foliage at a Quito souvenir shop. It was brightly colored, reasonably priced, and surprisingly lightweight. The only reason I hesitated to turn over my credit card was that it was large, about two-feet high; it would not only be awkward to carry, but I was afraid the leaves would break off, no matter how carefully I managed to pack the item. The store clerk assured me this would not be a problem: The leaves and fruit were attached to the trunk with metal pins. He demonstrated how the tree could be easily disassembled and put back together again. Sold. I was excited by my purchase, less so with the clerk's subsequent wrapping method. I had expected the pieces to be boxed together. Instead, each leaf and fruit cluster was individually enfolded in newspaper and deposited in a large garbage bag, which was then knotted closed at the top rather than secured with a tie. When I complained, the clerk's English suddenly failed him.

Perhaps TGWTW's English failed him at the Panama airport too. He didn't respond to my jest about a possible banana-tree delay. He didn't ask me what I meant or even throw me a quizzical look. His face didn't register that I had spoken. I didn't persist, and the rest of the wait was spent in stony silence.

I was annoyed by the snub at first, but not for long. This was one of those rare occasions when I was able to bypass hurt feelings and go straight to story. I immediately started fleshing out the details of the encounter in my mind. I dined out on the tale of The Great White Travel Writer whose unpleasant personality matched his books' unpleasant persona for years—or rather dined in on it. The banana tree has a prominent place on the sideboard of my dining nook, and anyone who has ever directed a glance at it has heard this story.

At least my version of it. Maybe TGWTW had his own spin on The Great Banana Tree Incident: He was stalked by an insane woman clutching a garbage bag at customs and the only way to head her off was to ignore her. He or she who writes the better-selling book gets to be the arbiter of reality.

CHAPTER 14
STAR STRUCK
Tucson, January–March 2001

"Oh, man, did I get loaded last night." I didn't need to check my watch to know that it was approaching 10 a.m. Mallory Merlowe, my fellow assistant Features editor, could be depended on to begin braying about her latest booze-a-thon as soon as she arrived in the *Arizona Daily Star* newsroom— roughly an hour after everyone else. Also dependable: Mallory's uniform of camouflage jacket, scruffy jeans, baggy T-shirt, and Doc Martens, in ludicrous contrast to her perfectly shaped pink nails and expensively tinted blond hair. Rude to everyone except the high mucky-mucks, Mallory was a working-class wannabe who punched down and sucked up.

It was *déjà vu* all over again. After a decade of freelancing, I'd set aside both my writing ambitions and my wanderlust to work at Tucson's largest daily newspaper, where I was a travel editor who couldn't travel—shades of Frommer's—as well as a food editor who couldn't review restaurants.

What had I been thinking?

I'd been thinking that I was really worried about money. Once I'd started writing books for Frommer's/Idiots/Dummies, I lost my Fodor's connections and the editing jobs I'd relied on for financial backup. When a friend phoned to tell me that the *Star*'s Food and Travel editor was retiring, she'd caught me at low tide in the freelancing ebb and flow, a period when fears of becoming a bag lady would snap me awake at 2 a.m.

I had more exalted motives too. I'd come of age during Watergate and still believed in the power of the press to change the world for the better. None of my previous employers could claim anything but the power to send forth badly behaved hordes of tourists—if they were successful. True, the *Star* hadn't won any reporting awards for decades, but it was a venerable Pulitzer-owned paper. My stints at Simon & Schuster and Random House hadn't made me any less of a sucker for a status-y publishing name.

Anyway, I didn't really think I'd get the job. What could it hurt to apply?

My interview with managing editor Scotty Long was not promising. I arrived at the appointed time to find the *Star's* newsroom oddly depopulated, though I was directed to a man identified as Scotty sitting in a glass cage of an office. He looked more like Ned Beatty in *Deliverance* than Jason Robards as Ben Bradlee in *All the President's Men*. He seemed friendly enough, however, smiling as he said, "I forgot all about the holiday party when I made this appointment with you. Would you mind talking with me there?"

Ah, that explained the deserted newsroom.

Scotty steered me through several long, grim corridors into a fluorescent-lit lunchroom made all the more depressing by a few droopy streamers and other nondenominational decorations. One voice echoed above the general din. The center of attention—or at least of volume—was Tom Turner, the retiring Food and Travel editor. A repertory theater buff with the faded looks of a former leading man, Tom was in the midst of an annual holiday party tradition: his dramatic reading of *How the Grinch Stole Christmas.*

Not many people appeared to be listening, including Scotty, who gave a general wave to the room and then proceeded to ply me with questions. I tried to convey the impressiveness of my credentials while shouting over lines like "All the Whos down in Who-Ville will all cry Boo Hoo," and "Pooh-pooh to the Whos."

The questioning wound down soon after the Grinch reformed and Scotty decided he needed to mingle. Soon, he was deep in work-speak. I couldn't offer any suggestions about how to fill tomorrow's Features hole—I didn't know what a Features hole was, but it sounded ominous—so I thanked Scotty for his time and told him I'd find my way out.

Maybe it was because I had managed to keep a straight face during The Grinch. Maybe it was my 1980s black power suit, an anomaly in the *Star*'s laid-back atmosphere, that made him take pity on me. Whatever the reason, I was hired.

🐫 🐫 🐫

Mallory was hardly the only contributor to my hostile work environment; she was just the loudest and the one seated closest to me, separated from my desk only by a cubicle barrier. But she was one of the known unknowns; you can expect to encounter irritating co-workers at any office. The unknown unknowns: This was Tucson, not New York, and a newspaper, not a book publisher. I had no template to guide my worrying.

It turned out that, along with minor irritants like not being able to unzip my pants if I was full after lunch—having to wear pants with zippers, period—one of the greatest annoyances was the busywork: fielding phone calls from *Star* readers and, especially, sitting in on endless staff meetings with mysterious agendas. My first day on the job, for example, two editors forced the freelance reviewer for my Food section, Christine Highland, to quit.

The editors—Dolores Baker, in charge of Accent, the daily lifestyle section, and Barbara Rand, who ran Friday's entertainment insert, Caliente—had brought Christine in to discuss our restaurant coverage. The *Star* had a good dining writer on staff, but she couldn't do justice to Tucson's burgeoning food scene. I knew Christine slightly, socially as well as professionally. It would be fun to work with her, I thought, albeit within the constraints of the *Star*'s peculiar reviewing policy. The newspaper paid for its critic to go to a restaurant with a companion, but only for a single visit—and alcohol wasn't covered.

I had contributed a few dining reviews to the city's alternative paper, the *Tucson Weekly*, and had been required to try the venue twice, once for lunch and once for dinner. The *Weekly*'s budget wasn't large, but what you spent it on— including booze—was your business.

Since I wasn't going to be doing the reviewing, I decided this wasn't my concern.

At least not until the meeting with Christine. Almost immediately, Dolores and Barbara gave me my marching orders: I would accompany Christine on all her future restaurant reconnoiters so I could monitor her choices and make sure she wasn't getting preferential treatment.

Christine reddened as implications of misdeeds were piled on suggestions of incompetence. After sputtering defenses at first, she shut down. I trailed her to the elevator when the meeting broke up, apologizing profusely, explaining over and over that I was as blindsided as she was. Christine assured me that she understood.

There was probably nothing I could have said that would have kept her from resigning the next day; I couldn't blame her. On the other hand, maybe I should not have told Dolores and Barbara that the meeting had been awkward, that

I would have been happy to do as they had asked—had they only asked behind the scenes.

Rule to live by: Don't question the actions of your supervisors on the first day of a new job if you want to keep that job, however unprofessional and unfathomable those actions may seem.

I spent the next few weeks interviewing unqualified freelance dining reviewers, all the while wanting to shout, "Me, me, me! I should be doing this. I know the restaurant scene cold." I never did find a replacement for Christine—or learn why she was forced out.

And so most of my allotted Food section duties involved standardizing the font sizes of recipes culled from a variety of sources, then fielding phone calls from irate readers when said recipes turn out to be incorrect.

Which was fairly often. As is probably obvious by now, I believe cooking is best left to professionals—or to amateurs who enjoy it. (Hey, no one ever asks movie reviewers why they don't make films.) Common sense might suggest that a pound, as opposed to a pinch, of salt would be a lot to put into a quiche, but anything subtler than that was likely to get by me.

🐫🐫🐫

In contrast, I was qualified in every way to edit the Travel section. I was plugged into all the tourism trends and, if I hadn't personally visited a place, it had likely been covered in a book I'd edited.

I also knew the golden rule: no comps. I didn't need the stern lecture I got from Dolores before the debut of my first Sunday Travel section: "We don't run pieces based on hosted travel, you know." I knew, I knew. It had been drummed into my brain for years that, unlike guidebooks and many of the magazines for which I'd written, newspapers had Integrity. I suspected purity might be tough to achieve, but I planned to try.

Maybe the surprise wasn't that I failed but the rapidity with which it happened.

I soon understood that advertising, or the general lack thereof, distinguished my Travel section from those in larger newspapers. Tucson is a second-tier city in the middle of the desert. Cruise lines didn't advertise with the *Star*; neither did the larger land-tour operators and airlines, which saved their Arizona ad budgets for the Greater Phoenix papers. The *Star* mostly got small buys by local travel agents and bus tours to Laughlin, Nevada—not even Las Vegas!—along with occasional crumbs from Sea World, Disney, and other southern California theme parks.

The dearth of ads not only meant that my section was small; it also freed me from the constraints of an editorial calendar, the ad-driven, planned-in-advance schedule of big-city Travel pages. One October, for example, I had been commissioned by a major Chicago newspaper to write a spa story. It was no coincidence that my piece and several other Arizona-themed articles ran alongside promotions for the state and for major resorts in Scottsdale and Phoenix.

Not having an editorial calendar to follow meant my decisions about which destinations to cover were governed in part by my sense of where locals might want to go at a particular time of year. For example, you wouldn't want to highlight a warm-weather inland destination in January, temperate winters being the reason that many of us choose to live in southern Arizona. But a Mexican beach resort, especially one that many local airlines fly to, would be a good bet, as would ski slopes, or easy-to-reach places to travel with kids.

The other component that went into my choice of a Travel feature was, naturally, the article's quality. Heaven knows I had quantity. Torrents of manuscripts and queries poured in—at least 200 each week. They arrived in every format: rumpled typewritten pages stapled together and stuffed into hand-written envelopes; neat computer-generated manuscripts accompanied by slides and computer disks (this was pre-CDs and digital cameras); and succinct email inquiries sketching an outline of an available story.

With scores of rejections, nonresponses, late payments, and bad contracts under my belt, I had nothing but sympathy for my freelance brethren and sistren. Indeed, when I took the *Star* job, I had intended to make up for all my abruptness at Fodor's, to be a nurturing editor like Margot Weiss at Macmillan had been for me. I vowed to send encouraging notes to writers whose work was promising. I would make sure to get writers paid promptly.

It didn't take long for me to discover that I rarely had time to answer emails for story pitches that didn't quite cut it, much less write notes and address envelopes in response to the almost-there manuscripts that arrived by snail mail.

Hounding Accounting turned out to be my greatest *Star* achievement.

🐫 🐫 🐫

I was relieved to receive as many excellent prospects for features as I did, primarily from established travel writers. Not only was their writing skilled, but they often tailored their pitches to the *Star's* market. I was perplexed at first. The paper paid $100 per article, including photographs—a fee that is not atypical today, sadly. Who could afford to write at that rate?

Then I recalled a session at an SATW conference about self-syndication.

Newspapers had one advantage over magazines: Many of them didn't require exclusive publication rights. Rather, they asked only that a contributor not sell the same piece to a paper in a competing market. If someone submitted a story to the *Star*, say, it was understood that she would not also market it to the *Arizona Republic* in Phoenix, though a paper outside the state was fair game. By the time a single article completed its selling cycle—often short in the case of pieces tied to specific, newsy events or to travel trends—it might net $2,000 or more.

But only writers who had the system sussed could earn that type of money. Among other things, they had to keep careful track of their work, following up with editors to pin down rejections so they could try another publication in the same state if necessary. It was time-consuming, painstaking, and often frustrating, what with the frequent turnover of editors whose tastes they had just gotten to know or budget cuts that eliminated the purchase of freelance writing altogether. I was terrible at this type of administrative account-keeping—and grateful now that others weren't. These low-cost stories made my section credible.

Credible but not ethical, strictly speaking. If I knew through tacit agreement that writers who pitched me wouldn't sell stories I ran to competing markets, they in turn depended on me to keep up my end of a more nefarious pact: I wouldn't ask them if their articles were based on hosted travel.

I'd had an inkling that the no-freebies rule was permeable as early as the first week, when I was instructed to pull stories from the travel news wires to fill space in the Sunday section. I had no guarantee that contributors to the wire services to which the paper subscribed hadn't romped around on a client's tab. After all, my free trip to Kenya and Mauritius had included two stringers for Detroit newspapers.

It wasn't until I encountered a feature I wanted by a writer I'd personally met on a press trip, however, that I knowingly broke my vow about hosted travel.

I'm not suggesting this rule was flouted everywhere; I can only speak for my own editorial practice and past experiences. Some of the larger newspapers ask potential contributors if a proposed article is based on subsidized travel; others send elaborate forms for writers to complete, having them swear on their first-born child that they didn't take comps. I once received such a form *after* I submitted a commissioned story. I neglected to fill it out. If the editor wanted to pull my piece at the last minute, I was okay with that; the pay wasn't great and I wasn't willing to perjure myself. But the editor neglected to follow up when the form didn't arrive. Oops. We were both busy people.

I imagine I could have found another story for the *Star*'s Travel section that week, one that I didn't know for certain was based on a press trip. I blame my moral downfall on the fact that the article came with great pictures.

🐪 🐪 🐪

In the *Star*'s universe, the art department ruled.

Several times I'd found a terrific story, only to be told at the last minute by the photo editor, Toni Layton, that it wouldn't work visually. She, in turn, was only following the lead of her boss, Scotty, notorious in the newsroom for once having referred to the text that took up space around the pictures—i.e., the articles—as "gray goo."

After a few bouts of scrambling at the last minute to substitute another piece when Toni rejected the original, I started playing the odds and submitting two or three groups of pictures at the same time. The strategy worked. One of them always passed muster.

About six weeks into my tenure, however, I discovered that even art department approval was no guarantee I'd have the last word on what ran in Travel.

Although I'd searched for backup stories, I really hoped to get the nod for my favorite, a piece on Hedonism II, a Jamaican beach resort known for...well, the name is self-explanatory.

In spite of its title, "My Week of Living Wickedly" didn't allude to any X-rated activities. The writer, Ron Anderson, had gone to the resort with his wife, and they had stayed at the "other" beach—the one where people kept their clothes on. The most risqué details of the story were a wet T-shirt contest and, at the end, a description of Ron's wife mooning the people on the beach as their boat pulled away from the shore.

It was witty and well written; Ron was one of the journalists I'd quickly come to rely on. His accompanying photos were invariably newspaper-suited, too; in fact, I was confident enough in them to phone Ron and tell him I was going to run his piece that Sunday. True, one of the best scenes included a tiny nude figure, but it was off in the distance and not in sharp focus.

Late Wednesday afternoon, I got the call: All the photos had passed muster, even the one with the tiny nude in it. Whew. When Toni scrutinized the slides on the light table with her magnifying eyepiece, she must have deemed them nipple free.

Satisfied that I'd cleared the photo hurdles and nailed that week's feature without incident, I was packing up to go home at 5:45 when my phone rang again. This time, it was Scotty, summoning me to his office.

Shit.

Scotty was always friendly when I ran into him in the hall, but he was not disposed to calling his underlings into his office for social chats.

Sure enough, his demeanor wasn't typically genial. "What were you thinking?" he asked sternly. "This is a family newspaper." I tried to explain that the pictures had been vetted by the art department, and that there was nothing in the story that could possibly offend anyone, but he wasn't buying it. "Substitute something else," he ordered.

I wandered, dazed, back to my desk. I was less upset that I had to use one of my second-choice features than worried that my editorial judgment had headed south.

I phoned Ron the next morning, exhausted from a sleepless night, to explain why I couldn't use his piece as planned. I felt relieved as well as vindicated by his response: sympathetic, but slightly confused.

"Lots of newspapers went with that story," he mused. "I wonder why the *Star* is having a problem with it." He rattled off names, including *The Dallas Morning News*.

"Oh yeah, the major porn rag that turns up on all those Texas breakfast tables," I replied.

🐪 🐪 🐪

In spite of my many frustrations, I wanted to succeed at the job. Not only did I crave the regular paycheck, but I also reveled in the status of working at the *Star*. Along with the meanest and pettiest, the newsroom also bustled with some of the best and brightest. I especially liked Elena, the third in the trio of assistant Features editors, and Bryn, one of the reporters who supplied Accent stories.

And running the Food section had its perks. I was constantly receiving samples, some of them weird, some of them wonderful. A national pizza chain was introducing a new crust? Send a sample pie to the newspaper. It's National Kiwi Day? Deliver a fruit basket. The table behind the Food editor's desk was a popular gathering spot.

Since I no longer had time to go to the gym, I tried to offset the effects of this largesse by chipping in with some colleagues to take a group class with the personal trainer who was on call at the *Star's* poorly equipped exercise room. I was more impressed by the tiny woman's huge, immovable breasts than I was by her training techniques, but the workout was better than nothing.

The weekly Features meeting, held less than twenty-four hours after my Hedonism debacle, made me suspect I might be headed back to the far superior classes and exercise machines of the Tucson Racquet and Fitness Club very soon.

Conducted by Dolores, these gatherings were part news briefing, part pep rally, part public shaming session. As usual on this Friday morning, she was standing between the two clusters of desks that divided the Features editors from the Features reporters. With the exception of Mallory, who was an equal opportunity antagonist, these groups got along well, united against management's many insults.

This time, for example, in the pep-rally portion of the session, we were forced to listen to Dolores exhort everyone to "kick it up a notch"—the appropriated slogan of a corporate effort to raise circulation by getting employees and their friends to subscribe to the *Star*.

It was not an easy sell.

Why would we subscribe when we could pick up a copy of the paper as soon as we walked into the newsroom, and were annoyed anyway at not getting home delivery as a job perk?

I braced myself for Dolores to parrot Scotty's "this is a family newspaper" party line in the shaming segment of the meeting. It came, right on schedule—a nice segue from the "kick it up a notch" portion of the meeting.

"I can't emphasize enough that we're trying to expand our readership," Dolores said. "That's why we wouldn't run a story in Travel that might offend anyone."

She didn't mention me by name, but she didn't have to. I was the only Travel editor around. She did look pointedly in my direction, lest anyone who hadn't heard about my run-in with Scotty miss the reference and neglect to ask me about it after the meeting.

But I put on my best blank look and even managed a slight knowing smile. "You can't rattle me," I said silently. "I'm ready for you."

I was not ready, however, for what Dolores singled out for the meeting's praise portion: the cover page of that morning's Accent section, featuring two local radio DJs wearing nothing but sombreros over their tequila spouts.

"We like to push the envelope here," she gushed, punctuating the statement with her maniacal high-pitched laugh.

Huh? I was genuinely perplexed. I blurted, "Why are pictures of naked shock jocks okay, but stories about a married couple having fun together at a beach resort off limits?" I genuinely wanted to know. But my tone probably wasn't quite as neutral as I imagined, and questioning one's supervisor in public is even worse than questioning her in private.

Dolores assumed I was just being insubordinate. She flushed angrily and refused to answer, pretending she didn't hear. The meeting wrapped up quickly, class dismissed.

So much for my vow to keep my head down. Still, I was just a few weeks away from the three-month mark, when I would be eligible for health benefits. Hang in there, I exhorted myself.

I hadn't counted on how much good will I had squandered in that spontaneous dustup with Dolores.

Whatever slack she had been willing to cut me as a newbie was about to tighten into a noose. That morning marked the beginning of the end of my very brief and not so brilliant newspaper career.

🐫 🐫 🐫

The incident that sealed the deal occurred the following week.

I was searching the news wires for filler for the Travel section when one of the staff photographers, Kit Roberts, came over to my cubicle. "Will you do me a favor?" he asked, smiling.

Laid back and athletic looking, Kit was not only a terrific photographer—when he was not working for the *Star*, he was freelancing for publications like *National Geographic*—but also a really nice guy.

"Anything for you," I teased, but meaning it. Ever since my run in with Dolores, I sensed that I was wearing an expired "sell by" date on my back; my co-workers didn't seem eager to get too close to me, perhaps to avoid the whiff of spoilage. But Kit worked in a different department and was not inclined to gossip. I was grateful to have the chance to demonstrate to someone at the *Star* that I was really a pleasant, helpful person.

"I'm just back from a ski trip to Taos with my friend Joanne," he said. "Would you consider looking at the story she wrote about it?" Perhaps I looked slightly dubious because he added, "Don't worry, she's a professional travel writer" and—the clincher—"I took lots of pictures to go with the piece."

I assumed she'd accepted a few Taos freebies that she needed to repay with some newspaper ink. I didn't ask.

"Sure, Kit," I said.

How could I go wrong? Kit was so talented that even the suits wanted to keep him happy. I trusted his judgment about his friend and figured that even if the piece wasn't perfect, I could whip it into shape.

It turned out to be a fun, offbeat story, one that linked the town's art scene with its ski scene through the snow-white canvasses of Taos artist Agnes Martin. It was spare and lyrical, without the gush of adjectives rampant in travel writing.

I did have to do a bit of editing, but of the kind I really like: helping a talented writer convey her ideas as clearly as possible. It was one of the few times at the *Star* that I felt as though I was using my skills.

When Scotty phoned and asked me to come into his office the Monday after the piece ran, I was psyched. I was sure I had finally done something right, and that I was going to be praised for it.

Not exactly.

Scotty was furious, much more so than he had been about the Hedonism story. "What was that?" he shouted. "We've never run such purple prose in the paper before."

Jeez. Scotty ("gray goo") Long was suddenly a literary critic?

If having a PhD in literature wasn't generally a confidence booster, it made me certain I could recognize good writing. It was hard to take Scotty's critique seriously.

That wasn't all, though. "I hear you're not a team player," Scotty said. That intelligence had to have come from a revenge-bent Dolores.

Once the sports metaphors get hauled out, you know you're screwed. I saw the writing—or should I say the gray goo?—on the wall.

🐫🐫🐫

A week or so later I got a call at work from a representative of a PR firm that included eastern Australia among its clients. "Does your newspaper let you take press trips?" she asked. "We've got a group going next month. I can give you a press rate if you need one." That deep, deep discount was another beard for journalists seeking to claim they were never comped.

I looked across my cubicle at Mallory, sporting her smug "I'm such a bad girl" smirk.

I heard Dolores' high-pitched laugh a few desks down.

"They don't let me travel, press rate or otherwise," I said. "But how about if I ask *Brides* if they're interested in a story?"

"Even better," the rep replied.

And so, two days short of qualifying for health insurance, I gave my notice. It was time to cut my losses before my freelance contacts evaporated and my passport expired, unused.

For many years, I remembered my departure from the *Star* as a huge defeat. I pictured myself slinking out of the building, saying good-bye to no one. I realize now that the truth had been staring me in the face—more accurately, hanging on the wall behind my back—in the form of a large caricature by David Fitzsimmons, the *Star's* award-winning political cartoonist. Depicting me standing defiantly, hands on hips and wearing a "Born 2 freelance" T-shirt, the cartoon has a word bubble coming out of my mouth that reads "@#$% this."

And Bryn, my favorite Features reporter and still a friend, recalls that she followed me out into the *Star's* covered parking lot that day and gave me a verbal high-five. "Many of us admire you," she'd said. "We wish we had the nerve to leave too."

As usual, I was being harder on myself than anyone else could be on me—with one notable exception. Leave it to

Mallory to torment me even after I no longer sat across from her.

Maybe half a year later, I had gotten my first assignment for Southwest's *Spirit* magazine, a piece on the five best places to sip tequila in Tucson. I was pleased with the way it turned out; very few changes had been made to my copy. The editor seemed satisfied with the piece too—until she got an email from a staffer at the *Star*, questioning its accuracy. Mallory claimed that another bar, not the one I cited, had the most varieties of tequila in town.

Just my luck that either Mallory or one of her cronies had flown on Southwest the month my story was slotted into the airline's seat-back pockets.

Mallory was wrong, naturally. I had assiduously fact-checked everything. But who was the magazine editor going to believe: an unknown freelancer or someone who worked at the largest local paper? I never got another assignment from *Spirit*.

My nemesis was eventually laid off in one of the waves of personnel cuts at the *Star*, though she held on longer than many who were far better editors—and human beings—than she was. I suspect Mallory had dirt on someone in management and was kept on until that person got the boot and could no longer protect her.

That's pure speculation, of course, nothing I would ever publish as fact.

CHAPTER 15
MY LIFESTYLE BEARS NO RELATION TO MY INCOME
Everywhere (but mostly Arizona), 1992–2004

Emerging from the rabbit hole of the *Arizona Daily Star*, I welcomed the return to sweatpants and solitude—but not to my *mishegas* about money. Witching-hour anxieties notwithstanding, I didn't really believe I would end up on the street. I had a small safety net from the sale of my New York apartment, I never racked up credit card debt, and I always paid my health insurance bills on time.

Yet my still small voice whispered, "If you were any good at what you did, you would be wealthier. Not all artists starve. Only the ones who suck."

And poets.

Most confusing: My lifestyle and my bank balance couldn't get their stories straight. My earnings sent me scrambling to a second-hand appliance store when my washing machine died, while my restaurant meals and hotel stays proclaimed I was as successful as Stephen King.

This disconnect snuck up on me. Just as I hadn't set out to be a travel writer, I had never aimed to specialize in high-end tourism. But writing guidebooks meant covering lodging and dining in all price ranges, and my beat for *Brides* and other honeymoon-centered magazines brought me once-in-a-lifetime experiences. Add an address in Arizona, land of resorts and spas. I suddenly found myself an expert in the upscale.

I wasn't remotely ungrateful for my nobby job perks, but I was out of my element, the little girl with her nose pressed up against the fancy department store window who gets invited in without quite knowing how to behave.

That was especially true of lodgings. By the time I got to Tucson, I knew a little about fine dining but not about luxurious places to stay. I'd only once gone on vacation with my parents, to a low-rent bungalow colony in the Catskills. My later bunks ranged from fleabags in Afghanistan and cramped pensiones in Italy to cheap chain motels in the US.

When I was on a press trip or hanging out with friends, playing rich was a hoot. One time, working on *Fodor's San Diego*, I was given a suite in a Del Mar golf resort that was larger than my Manhattan apartment. I bought beer and snacks and threw an impromptu party for several of my grad-school pals. I felt like a rock star—except that no one trashed the room.

But far more often, when I traveled solo, I would have been happier staying in a motel that was clean, had cable TV and an empty refrigerator, and included continental breakfast; these days I'd add free WiFi. I especially craved the freedom of movement that came with being able to park near your room. At high-end digs, I often had to walk miles to the self-parking lot in the heat to retrieve a forgotten item from my car, or else wait for valet service—which was pricey to boot.

There was the rub: My comped resort stays often cost me more than a night at a Motel 6.

For one thing, I had a habit of guilt tipping. I tried to heft my own luggage, but couldn't always evade the bellhops— and felt bad when I managed. They had to make a living too. Although my unfashionable threads pegged me as a freelance writer, I had key cards to rooms that cost five times what I paid for the worn Easy Spirit clogs I was wearing. Had I stinted on gratuities, I would have looked like a cheapskate.

Along with tipping and parking, other incidentals that weren't comped included nighttime snacks. Because most rooms came only with stocked and locked mini-bars, getting a nosh after I'd gotten undressed and settled in to watch TV was expensive and/or complicated.

Room service was tempting because of the larger selection, but it had several drawbacks, including the lack of instant gratification. You always have to wait for your food, ten minutes at a minimum. And when it finally arrives, it's a big, formal production. I had to clear away work papers and clothes to make room for the giant tray with a pitcher of ice water and an unwieldy metal plate cover, sided by white cloth napkins wrapped around heavy cutlery. I know some people believe in maintaining a civilized atmosphere when dining alone, but I don't walk among them. Never did.

Both of my parents worked, my father often into the evening; he was a self-employed dental technician and made his own hours. Aside from Thanksgiving and Passover, we very rarely ate together as a family. It was a good night when my sister and I could agree on a show and eat in tandem on separate TV trays, eyes glued to the screen, chewing in silence. Most evenings, I had my head in a book at dinner. My mother didn't object. It was not until much later that I learned this practice is generally frowned upon.

Not only was the room-service rigmarole unnatural to me, but it didn't come cheap. No matter if I tried to order the least expensive item—maybe a $13 BLT. The tab ran at least $20 when you figured in tax, room-service charge, and tip; I always felt compelled to top off the already generous included gratuity. In comparison, grabbing a beer and can of Pringles from the mini-bar was a breeze—and a comparative bargain at about $12.

Happily, mini-bars were usually only a nighttime temptation—except for the one in San Diego that punked me by masquerading as a gift basket.

I discovered early on that one of the perks of being a travel writer was being greeted with food gifts—usually a fruit-and-cheese plate or local specialty like chili-coated pecans, but now and then something a little more unusual. A few months before I moved to town, I stayed in an upscale Tucson resort with Laura, a friend from San Diego. Laura had become an associate professor since I'd first met her, but she hadn't abandoned her enthusiasm for pot. Marijuana isn't my drug of choice—paranoia and hunger are not my idea of recreational— but I'd decided to indulge since our room opened onto a patio and it was a quiet day in early fall, with no one around to narc on us.

Suddenly, we heard a knock at the door. Crap, I thought. Busted. My life as a freelancer would be over before it began. But no. Cheerily announcing "Amenities, ma'am," a fresh-faced young man entered the suite bearing a tray of Bailey's Irish Cream and still-warm chocolate-chip cookies— the perfect stoner combo. We laughed so hard when he left that we had trouble catching our breath.

Most of the welcome munchies arrive after check-in so they won't get warm (or cold) in case you're delayed, but I've occasionally had them waiting for me upon arrival. This was the case in San Diego—or so I thought when I rushed into my room. I was running late for an appointment with the hotel's PR rep and had just driven over the terrifying Coronado Bay Bridge, so I was doubly rattled. I was also weak from low blood sugar; I'd been rushing around all morning and hadn't had a chance to eat. Eureka! A goody basket with a note on it was sitting on the bureau next to the TV. I was struck by the generosity of the selection, but didn't think much about it. I stuffed my face with pretzels, shortbread cookies, and turkey jerky without bothering to read the card propped up against a half-bottle of red wine.

The hotel's PR person was just the first of several appointments I hustled to that day; I also had a late dinner meeting at the Hotel Del Coronado. I was exhausted, not hungry, when I finally returned to my room. It wasn't until I was awakened at 5 a.m. the next morning by the irritating sound of my bill being shuffled under my door that I realized the ignored welcome card was, in fact, a mini-bar price list. Sneaky. At least I hadn't guzzled the wine.

My worst experience with a mini-bar was entirely NOT MY FAULT.

One of my best clients, a Tucson-based publisher, had hired me to write promotional copy for a new spa at a well-known Phoenix resort. I was to stay overnight and spend two days getting slathered, pummeled, and smoothed, then transmute the experience into golden prose. The fee was good, and the resort had agreed to pick up meals and incidentals as well as the room and spa treatments.

In spite of my intensive bout of relaxation, I was nervous at checkout. Occasionally, due to a communications glitch, I would discover that my credit card had been charged the full rate for a room and other items that were supposed to be comped; the tab for all my spa treatments would have pushed my credit limit. Having learned the hard way that it was an ordeal trying to get charges removed after the fact, I never left a resort without making certain the fees were voided.

Sure enough, there was a mistake, though not the one I'd worried about. I'd been stuck with a $300 mini-bar tab. I planted myself in reception until the front desk could track down someone with the clout to clear up the error.

I didn't have to wait long. The marketing director was there in a flash. She had been waiting for the call that I was leaving, so she could speak sharply to me. The mini-bar in my suite—one designed for business travelers and therefore stocked with an especially large supply of alcohol—was empty, she said. From this she inferred that I had downed twenty-five airplane-sized bottles of spirits and two half-bottles of wine and disposed of the evidence. She had phoned my Tucson client and reported my behavior. The resort could not possibly pay for my excesses.

Had I not been rendered momentarily speechless, I might have snapped, "If I had actually consumed that much hooch in one night, do you think I would be standing here arguing about my bill, rather than lying sprawled on the floor of my suite passed out in a pool of vomit?"

The irony: I hadn't touched a single tiny bottle. My spa treatments, including a sweat-inducing wrap and steam, had left me feeling purified. I was determined to maintain that state—at least for one night. I hadn't even peered into the mini-bar, much less imbibed all its contents. My uncharacteristic lack of booze curiosity turned out to be my downfall. For some reason known only to housekeeping, all the bottles had been shifted into another suite before I'd checked in. I just hadn't noticed.

Did I get an apology when the facts emerged? I did not, only a grudging acknowledgment of the "mistakes-were-made" variety. As for the editor to whom the marketing rep had complained, she claimed that she had defended me, offering assurances that I was very reliable and it was unlikely I would drink that much. I noticed that she said "unlikely," not "impossible," and that she sounded like she was stifling laughter over the phone.

🐪 🐪 🐪

I once wrote, "Where else besides a spa can you spend an hour of bliss in a dimly lit room with a stranger—guilt free?" It was a good line but not strictly true for me. I rarely emerged blissful from that dimly lit room.

The two Phoenix spa days that led to the mini-bar fiasco were an anomaly. Typically, a treatment was just one item to tick off a lengthy roster of unrelated activities. After the ministrations, instead of taking a leisurely *schvitz* or even a long shower, I had to bolt for a hotel tour or dinner.

Nor did most treatments relax me while they were happening. During a massage, you're expected to stick your head into a face cradle while your back is being prodded. Those padded donuts slant slightly downwards, which always made my sinuses drain. By the time my muscles were thoroughly kneaded, my nose would be stuffed, at minimum; at worst, my head would be throbbing. Using a pillow for elevation helped my sinuses but gave my neck a crick.

The need to make conversation with the stranger who was touching me also kept me from staying in the sometimes-soothing moment. I couldn't overcome the double whammy of people-pleasing genes and the journalistic habit of trying to draw out interview subjects. Every now and then I would try staying silent but it made me tense. It also worried the spa techs who were constantly taking my mental temperature. My promise to let them know if something hurt or made me particularly happy didn't seem to satisfy them. Small talk was the path of least resistance—except for the time when, as I lay on my back, the therapist placing hot stones on my outstretched arms punctuated her sentences with industrial-strength garlic breath. I pretended to sink into a meditative state to keep her from exhaling in my face. I was in fact contemplating the item that was heating the sacred river rocks. It looked suspiciously like a turkey-roasting pan.

So, you might wonder, if I was so spa-averse, why did I continue to accept free treatments? The short answer: Spas are a popular topic for upscale lifestyle stories. I pitched, editors bit—and eventually began contacting me as an expert.

The more complex, extra-credit answer: Women are supposed to like spas. My lack of domestic urges—cooking, cleaning, cohabiting, procreating—made me feel a bit like a misfit. It was easy enough to take one for Team Girly Girl.

But the longer I observed the spa scene, the more cynical about it I grew. In the mid-1980s, when I edited the ill-fated spa book at Frommer's, few hotels had facilities beyond steam bath, sauna, and a handful of massage rooms. Over the years, opulent temples to self-indulgence became *de rigueur* in any resort worth its exfoliating Dead Sea salt.

Pampering was billed as personal growth, and spa treatments took on a religious tone, but without the strictures of established belief systems. Cultural traditions were mixed indiscriminately, centuries-old practices taken out of context. The so-called Thai Yoga massage, for example, combined movements from India with manipulations from Thailand—neither of which bore much resemblance to the Eastern originals. One session of Shirodhara, where warm oil is dripped onto an invisible eye in the middle of your forehead, can only be expected to yield greasy hair, not Ayurvedic enlightenment.

For my articles, I mastered a lexicon designed to relax the spa-goer's hold on her wallet. "Ritual," "sacred," "healing," "ancient," "wisdom," "peaceful," "holistic," "wellness," "energy," "natural," "deep," "aura," "journey," "balancing," "tranquility," "vitality," "pathways," "revitalize," "aroma," "rhythmic"—all were mixed and matched to create a word salad of soothing.

Speaking of salads, food also became part of these elaborate sessions. One called Hammam that I recently spotted on a spa menu involved the application of coffee, sugar, almonds, lemon oil, quince, cardamom, clove, and tangerine fig butter in various configurations. I'm not sure what this fruit cake-and-espresso combo had to do with Turkish steam baths; I know I would prefer to have ingested them rather than be anointed with them.

Of course, it's unlikely that a treatment with Middle Eastern overtones like Hammam will stick around for long. Only a few favored nations, regions, and landscapes weather shifting geopolitical trends. Asia is always in, encompassing everything from Japanese Reiki to Tibetan meridian-based medicine, the more obscure the better. Among the evergreens in Europe were France, featuring any cream that has a circumflex over its name, and Sweden, whose no-frills massage remains the most popular vanilla option.

Lucky me. The hands-down favorite landscape for spas was the desert. There were some caveats, of course. Mud from the Negev, where bikini-clad Israelis know from moisturizing, thumbs up; sun-damage products from burka-wearing nations like Saudi Arabia, thumbs down. If an arid region had indigenous inhabitants, that was a bonus. Southern Arizona with its rich Native American heritage: Ding, ding, ding!

The possibilities were endless, and not always restricted to that small dark room. At one resort, for example, you could pay to meditate with a shaman in a tipi. No matter that these tent-like dwellings were only used by the American Indians of the Plains and the Great Lakes; they looked marvelous in the Arizona sun.

As for the shaman, I blame Carlos Castaneda and his best-selling *Teachings of Don Juan* for the widespread practice of shamanism without a license. Castaneda claimed to have learned his secrets from a Yaqui medicine man he talked to in Mexico and at a bus depot in Tucson. Rule to live by: Never trust spiritual guides named for fictional libertines who divulge their secrets at a Greyhound station.

I steered clear of shamanic types after an energy healer in Sedona told me that *all* my chakras were blocked—who knew? I had severe psychic constipation—but I did sample a few Native American–inspired treatments in addition to Halitosis Hannah's hot rock massage. The most memorable was in Scottsdale, where I signed up for a signature turquoise oil ritual.

I had the routine down. I stripped to my panties in the locker room; stuffed my clothes into a narrow box and input a combination code that I would immediately forget; donned the oversized white robe that sometimes dragged to my plastic sandals; made my way to the lavender-scented room with its bowl of apples and dispenser of cucumber water; and waited to be called. If I were lucky, the name announced would not be "Eddie." Although I have resigned myself to answering to Eddie in restaurants, the mispronunciation always sends me into a "double letter short vowel, single letter long vowel" funk.

Sure enough, my male alter ego was summoned. I tried not to let it annoy me; after all, I was there to relax. Also, I was distracted by a mystery. Serena, the short, dark-haired young woman who led me down the hushed corridor, looked very, very familiar. But from where? I asked her, but she didn't think she knew me.

Usually, spa therapists provided a synopsis of coming attractions, detailing the treatment in the reverent tone usually reserved for servers describing the day's specials in a celebrity-chef restaurant. Serena only asked if the room temperature was okay. I was on assignment and needed information so I pressed her: What was the significance of turquoise to Indian culture? Which of Arizona's twenty-two native nations inspired the treatment?

Flustered, Serena grabbed the aquamarine bottle of oil like a life preserver, desperately seeking illumination from the label, which she started reading aloud to me. No help there. Never mind, I said. I figured I would call the spa director later. I lay down and tried to relax. It was only when I turned over to my front and saw her breasts at eye level that it struck me: I was being turquoise-oiled by my former fitness trainer at the *Arizona Daily Star*. I would have recognized those huge immovable boobs anywhere.

I decided not to tell her that I remembered how I knew her.

Serena did not give a bad massage but she—and it—bore no resemblance to anything remotely Native American.

First we took their land. Then we took their spa treatments.

I didn't call the spa director but turned instead to the Internet for answers to the questions I'd posed to Serena. I learned that fish oil and the fat of raccoons and eagles, not turquoise oil, were the emollients of choice for the indigenous people of Arizona. Turquoise is indeed prized in many native cultures but worn as a gemstone, not pulverized and dissolved in a solution. Instead of shelling out for a spa treatment—$200 for ninety minutes, if I recall—those seeking an authentic experience would be far better off investing in a turquoise-studded Navajo silver bracelet, signed by the artist.

One heartening development on the spa front: Native American–owned resorts have begun taking a page out of the white people's playbook. Members of the Pima and Maricopa nations, who own and operate the Sheraton White Horse Pass Resort near Phoenix, have carefully adapted their native traditions to a program of spa treatments.

They're the real deal—and the only one I know of. Others just adopted the rhetoric. The catalog of one native-owned spa describes its Peaceful Healing treatment thusly: "Raw Pima cotton poultices are filled with steaming desert herbs to produce luxurious aromas that bring your mind to a state of rest. Rhythmic pressure is applied along energy pathways of the body, offering renewed feelings of vitality and balance, and finished off with a soothing massage of warm, reviving oils. This treatment was traditionally used to heal the farmer, the hunter, and the weary traveler."

Pima cotton is indeed grown in Arizona—it was one of the state's major exports—and maybe it was used for poultices in the past. But I suspect if anyone had tried to apply rhythmic pressure to the energy pathways of a hunter, farmer, or weary traveler, they would have gotten shot in their root chakras.

More power to the native people, though: If you can't beat 'em, join 'em. It may be too late to rectify the land grab, but Big Spa is showing no signs of slowing down.

🐪 🐪 🐪

Not only is the spa world accelerating—it's getting odder. Offshoots of the personal development trend now include such tough-love treatments as Muscle Melt for Road Warriors, which sounds like something you might have nightmares about if you watch too many zombie movies. Especially popular in the shape-up-or-ship-out sector are challenge programs: supervised group activities like walking across a tree-limb-width tightrope, leaping off a telephone pole, or ascending a giant ladder.

Because many of these involved heights, my greatest fear, I believed I might benefit. At one destination spa, I signed on for the relatively wussy climbing-wall challenge. It was so traumatic that I have blocked out much of the experience. I know people encouraged me and cheered me on, which only made me more self-conscious, but I can't for the life of me recall whether I got to the top or chickened out. One thing I know: I'm still afraid of heights and regret having wasted an hour of my life scaring myself silly.

I also took a challenge called the Equine Experience, because I thought it might be useful. Writers based in the West are expected to include riding in our repertoires. I wasn't exactly afraid of horses, but I'd never bonded with them either. My equine encounters in Arizona were decidedly more comfortable than the one in the Copper Canyon, insofar as not having to worry about my horse slipping on ice or my guide keeling over dead were concerned, but the animals seemed to sense I was from New York and that I'd learned most of what I knew about their peers from watching *Mr. Ed*. Every horse I rode in Tucson would stop next to a clump of cactus, daring me to try to make him move. I couldn't bring myself to do any prodding or poking, and not just because it seemed cruel. Those mothers were big. They could throw me and then stomp on my head.

My hope for the Equine Experience was that I would arrive at a détente with horsekind, achieving mutual respect if not abiding affection. It didn't quite happen that way. I managed to get my assigned horse to allow me to brush his mane and clean his hooves, which seemed to be the goal of this "trust" exercise. Becoming a horse's hairdresser and manicurist didn't move me any closer to getting equines to recognize me as ride-worthy, however.

Ah, the wringers I put myself through to get my words in print.

Which brings me back to my nudist resort story for *More* magazine.

I said I took the assignment because the money was good, but that wasn't my only motive. I was eager to write for *More* because it was one of the few publications I contributed to that I actually read. The magazine's other contributors included the likes of Wendy Wasserstein, Molly Ivins, Pam Houston, and Francine Prose. I hoped that regular appearances would help me upgrade my own literary credentials, if only by association.

Nearly a year after my visit to Desert Shadows, *More* printed a version of the piece that was mildly amusing, but bore little relation to my actual experience—or to my writing. Along with self-censoring, I'd had to add a bunch of pop-culture references and speculate about the changing role of nudity for different generations. That might have been interesting had I dug deeper into the question, but here the additions were superficial, intended only to make my story appeal to a larger demographic.

The article won a Lowell Thomas Award—the so-called Pulitzers of travel writing—but that only made me feel more like a fraud.

I did get a few things out of my foray into the land of the unclothed besides a paycheck: the confirmation that I am, in fact, shameless, lots of synonyms for nudity, and the realization that writing for a magazine I hadn't considered fluffy might be no more satisfying than writing for *Brides*.

Indeed, it was more frustrating.

With *Brides*, my role was straightforward: I was pushing romance fantasy. Just as spa treatments hid their venality behind an aura of spirituality, *More*'s feminist gloss was insidious. Because the magazine was selling "empowerment," all the forty-plus women featured were beautiful, self-motivated, inspirational, or brave, like my story's persona. Or else their experience led them to some kind of life-changing revelation. Women like me who were just muddling through, constantly repeating the same mistakes, were represented only in the medical-advice section, where they tended to die from some dread disease because they hadn't had the smarts to get a second opinion.

My disappointment in the *More* story was just a symptom of a larger malaise. Amidst the wall climbing and the horse whispering, I had lost sight of the real challenges and fears I had conquered: giving up a steady paycheck, moving to Tucson without knowing anyone, and learning to drive though I was phobic about it. I was too busy trying to work the angles, pitching and accepting assignments on popular topics, to delve into anything I really cared about.

By taking the path most traveled, I had lost my way. Enviable as it might have looked from the outside, this was not my beautiful life.

CHAPTER 16
THE ACCIDENTAL DOG WRITER
Tucson, October 2004–the present

Less than two months after my *More* story ran, I adopted a small disheveled dog named Frankie. He turned out to be just what I needed to rouse me from my career crisis, though no one could have predicted that at the time.

Frankie immediately made it clear that I was not what he was seeking in a caretaker. He cowered when I approached and declined to move off my couch, not even to eat or use the backyard facilities. He lay tightly curled in silent reproach, a depressed, compressed comma.

Rule to live by: If you're not sure that you want a dog, never tell an animal rescuer that you like dogs but.... The next thing you know, you'll be palling around with terriers, ready or not.

I was not. Not by a long shot.

I grew up in a dog-averse household. Make that animal averse; my mother feared all creatures great and small. She barely tolerated the dime-store turtles my father brought home—and, I later learned, secretly replaced when they died—and actively loathed my escape-artist hamsters. Nor did any of my childhood friends have dogs. Our urban Flatbush neighborhood was a far cry from Lassie country. Our parents cautioned us about falling down elevator shafts, not wells, and I wasn't allowed to cross the street by myself until I was ten. Had I spotted a collie speeding down my block, I probably would have peed my dungarees.

I nevertheless wanted a dog in much the same way as I wanted to be a writer—secretly and vaguely. I didn't have any idea what kind of dog I craved and had very little information on which to base an opinion.

I first began making the acquaintance of dogs on a regular basis in Manhattan, where several of my building's residents had canine companions. I was especially drawn to Rose and Louise, the black pugs that kept company with playwright John Guare. Although it was their owner I had a crush on—or so I assumed—I was always tickled to encounter the pair of lively, inquisitive clowns in the lobby.

But I was too busy with graduate school and, after that, publishing jobs to think seriously about getting a dog. By the time I settled into a house with a backyard in Tucson and met some pet-inclined friends, I was traveling a good part of the year.

At one point, I made a timid foray into the world of dog adoption. Since pugs had grabbed my attention, I chose that breed. I contacted a pug rescue. A few weeks later, I got a call; they'd found me a dog. The only caveat: She had an eye infection, so I would have to administer drops twice a day. No way. I didn't want to meet my first dog in the guise of Edie the Eye Poker.

I then did what I should have done initially: researched the breed. Apparently, eye problems are not uncommon for pugs. Neither are breathing issues. I wasn't ready for that responsibility.

I sat back on the fence, more ambivalent than ever. I felt no social pressure to get a pet. "Don't you think your life would be more fulfilled if you had a few cats or a couple of pugs?" said no one to any woman, ever.

No one except a rescuer.

I met Rebecca Boren, transplanted Seattle journalist and pet proselytizer extraordinaire, at a lunch of women food writers. It was over an arugula, candied walnuts, and bleu cheese salad that I made my fateful "I like dogs but…" remark. Rebecca immediately sized me up as "open to persuasion" and started to pitch: companionship, love, fun, exercise, yada, yada. She was a pro, but I didn't succumb right away. I was about to leave town to research the sixth edition of *Frommer's San Antonio and Austin.* I couldn't possibly deal with a dog.

Rebecca had to wait another six months before nailing me, and even then I resisted mightily.

Yes, the scruffy terrier mix in the picture Rebecca emailed me was adorable, but Frankie was about five years old when he was found skittering around the streets of Phoenix, where Arizona Schnauzer Rescue had pulled him from the pound. When his first adoption didn't work out, he had been brought down to Tucson to be fostered. I'd always imagined myself with a newer-model dog and not one from the Valley of the Sun who had been named for the golf partner of his original rescuer's husband.

I didn't mention my Phoenix and golf aversion to Rebecca.

Older dogs were much mellower than puppies, Rebecca said, and therefore a better fit for a newbie like me. She noted that dog-sitters were plentiful in Tucson. When I was in town, holed up writing, I could provide my new best friend with quality time.

"Don't worry," she argued in closing, playing to the judge and jury's obvious insecurities. "You'll give Frankie a great home."

In the end, it was Frankie himself who sealed the deal. When Rebecca brought him over for a meet-and-greet, he proved as cute as his picture, perky and friendly. He was so fetching, in fact, that I decided to forgo the original plan: for Rebecca to give me time to consider whether or not I was going to adopt him after a short introductory visit. "Let him stay," I said.

Famous last words. As soon as Rebecca left, Frankie went into mourning.

I was certain that I was doing something horribly wrong or that I'd gotten a lemon; hadn't someone in Phoenix found him wanting? Either way, it was humiliating. Between bouts of weeping, I consoled myself with the knowledge that Frankie and I were together on a two-week trial basis. If need be, I could make us both happy by returning him to Rebecca.

When a travel-writer friend phoned and heard my tale of woe, she encouraged me to do just that. "Give it back," she said, referring to Frankie. "It's not too late. You don't have to do this."

That's when I realized I *did* have to do this. I was frustrated, sure, but Frankie was not an "it," to be returned like a purse. I was determined to win him over, if only to prove to myself and everyone else that I could.

🐫 🐫 🐫

Pride and obstinacy have their rewards. I don't think I ever worked as hard to make a relationship work as I did mine with Frankie. Slowly, ever so slowly, he came around.

I began to understand that Frankie was a serial monogamist, a one-woman dog. Once he understood that I wasn't going to injure him, at least not deliberately—when you live with a klutz, small objects rain from the sky—he transferred all the affection he'd had for Rebecca to me. It got to the point where, when she visited, Frankie would regard her with mild interest, as though to say, Do I know you? He was no fool. It just took him a little while to figure out which side his kibble was buttered on.

So much for the myth that dogs are forever bonded to their rescuers.

A great many other popular myths fell by the wayside as I started a course of intensive reading. Getting a dog proved more intellectually stimulating than getting a PhD. As part of my continuing education in applied biological science, I pored over scholarly articles about wolf-pack behavior as a model for canine family structure and cited dolphin studies to support my advocacy of positive reinforcement–based training.

Combined with my empirical observations of Frankie and a small sample of his fellow canines, I concluded that:

- Not all dogs enjoy the company of other dogs.
- Some dogs are picky about food and don't eat when they are nervous.
- Many dogs don't like loud noises.
- Not all dogs like riding in cars.

As you might imagine, this last was a problem. Frankie didn't drool, throw up, or manifest other signs of car sickness, but he shook in fear during every journey, short or long. I tried everything—soothing music, car-seat elevation, open windows, closed windows. Nothing worked. I couldn't afford to get an Escalade to see if better suspension might be the key to his comfort.

The irony of overcoming a driving phobia only to adopt a dog scared of riding in cars was not lost on me.

By then, however, I was well beyond caring about anything except Frankie's happiness.

I barely recognized myself. I'd always been annoyed by men who expected me to prepare food for them; not only did I not enjoy the activity, but they could bloody well do it for themselves. Frankie did not have the opposable thumbs required to use a can opener, and he was too short to reach the microwave. I had no choice. What started as duty soon morphed into pleasure. I found that I enjoyed hunting for healthy food my finicky pup would deign to eat.

I also sought out toys that he particularly liked. He had a fondness for a squeaky chili that was taken off the market. To compensate, I bought a plush carrot intended for a cat, removed the feathers, and inserted a squeaker—bought separately for that purpose—into the Velcro compartment designed for catnip. I'd become the Martha Stewart of the dog world.

Frankie made me feel like a natural woman. A mildly deranged natural woman.

Our life together began falling into a routine, as I learned to adjust my expectations. Most of the challenges Frankie's anxieties posed were manageable, some of his responses to them even admirable. For example, Frankie didn't pre-emptively lash out at other dogs or humans, a common fear response; instead, he shied away. I myself could have benefitted from more conflict avoiding, less barking. Frankie's disinclination to eat when he was stressed was another trait I gladly would have emulated.

His need for daily walks turned out to be a boon too, and not just because they provided exercise. The sounds of traffic made neighborhood strolls uncomfortable for my nervous charge, so I started taking Frankie to a car-free zone near my house.

Over the years, without knowing it, I'd largely forgotten why I'd moved to Tucson. That magical city in the desert that drew me from New York had become a way station between trips, a sunny, inexpensive place to hole up and work. Now I joined the bicyclists, strollers, and occasional horseback riders on the Rillito River Park Trail, a twelve-mile path that snakes through the north-central part of the city. Gazing up from the small creature tethered to me, I saw it all again: the Santa Catalina mountains soaring against the vast swath of sky, cactus wrens building nests in saguaros, scrubby gray-green creosote shrubs that smell like desert rain when you pour water on a sprig...

I formed new impressions too. Although I rose early, I never used to go outside right away. Now, on summer days, when it grew too hot to walk after 6:30 a.m., Frankie and I watched the sun streaking purple-pink as it peeked up over the horizon.

My circle of friends began to expand as I met a new, canine-oriented cohort—one that had its own rules of engagement. It was bad form to inquire about the names of the people you met, for example, though you were expected to ask what their four-legged friends were called. Especially at first, an unspoken rule said that conversation was to be limited to dog-related topics—or the weather.

That's not to suggest that our chats were free of controversy. Far from it. We tut-tutted over the woman who let her large, muscular dogs run wild to terrorize other people and pooches, and I didn't always hold my tongue when the topics of electric fences and harsh training methods came up. Mostly, though, we engaged in friendly information exchanges: a javelina up ahead, a recall on treats from China, the least expensive place to go for a doggie dental.

I began to look forward to seeing certain people, especially members of Frankie's small but loyal fan club. Frankie became a favorite with many who didn't try to overwhelm him or get upset when he didn't respond to their overenthusiastic greetings. By all indications, he savored our excursions too. When, on certain coyote-safe stretches of the trail, I let him off leash, he would follow behind me with a happy, prancing gait—or so I'm told; he always stopped when I turned around to check on his progress. I walk briskly, so I'm picturing us, my tiny Lipizzaner stallion and I, striding together in a rousing two-person parade.

While my Tucson life was becoming revitalized, my travel-writing career was tanking.

Taking Frankie on overseas press trips had never been an option, but at first I tried toting him along him on research jaunts around Arizona. Rather than relaxing into our car rides as I'd anticipated, however, he shook through the duration of the journey. The tremors sometimes diminished in intensity but never abated entirely. Although Frankie was fine once we got to our destination and loved leaping around our hotel room—unlike me, my dog appreciated the trappings of luxury—he didn't enjoy the attention that was invariably lavished on his cute self. "I love dogs," a bellhop might boom, while barreling over to try to roughhouse with Frankie, who was having none of it.

Within a few weeks of adopting him, I took Frankie to a travel writers' conference in Scottsdale that I'd attended in the past. It was not a success. Frankie wasn't entirely sure he could trust me yet, and I was still laboring under the delusion that he would straighten up and fly right if only he were exposed to enough new situations. Travel writers are not a particularly scary bunch—unless you get in their way when the free bar opens—but Frankie was so stiff with fright at meeting a variety of ogling strangers that one of the attendees remarked he looked like the stuffed dog in *There's Something About Mary*. It was cruel, but sadly true.

In the end, leaving Frankie at home while I hit the road proved easier and less distressing to us both. Sort of.

Rebecca had been right about the availability of pet care, but Frankie was not open to all options. The one time I tried to board him, he was miserable. Getting someone to stay with him in our home worked far better for Frankie, though not for my budget, and there was no guarantee of the caretaker's quality. Pet sitting has become a more reputable—if still not very tightly regulated—profession in the last decade, but it was strictly amateur hour when I started engaging enthusiastic University of Arizona students for the job. Several of them were great, but one young temporary guardian filled the dog bowl with so much food that Frankie puked all over the house.

I found myself becoming more selective about my travel, accepting trips only to places I really wanted to go and taking their duration into account.

Then, some three years after I adopted him, Frankie developed diabetes.

Canine diabetes is similar to type 1, or juvenile, diabetes in humans. It's caused by a complex of genetic factors not yet fully understood, but it has nothing to do with being overweight and is not reversible with diet. The only way to keep a diabetic dog regulated is with insulin, administered twice a day on a regular schedule.

I was devastated—and terrified. Frankie was going to go blind. He was going to go into insulin shock. And he was going to hate me because I kept sticking him with needles and following him around to collect his pee to test its sugar levels.

For the six months or so that it took to get Frankie's blood sugar regulated, I went slightly mad. I refused to believe the science. I was certain all would be well if only I could find the right woo-woo remedy. It was not until the right insulin dose was finally established that I became semi-rational again. Caring for Frankie became rote, though never quite routine. If he got too much exercise or something else caused his glucose levels to dip, Frankie could get hypoglycemic. I took to carrying Karo syrup—the official brand of the quick sugar fix—with me on all our walks.

Even short road trips with Frankie became difficult. I had to gear my schedule around administering insulin, which couldn't be done in the car because Frankie was too stressed to eat. Leaving him at home also became more complicated. Having a special-needs dog upped the price of pet sitting—and my worry quotient. I no longer felt confident in the ability of most caretakers to keep Frankie safe. One pet sitter, for example, assured me over the phone that she had given Frankie his insulin on time before she left, but I came home to discover that his food bowl was full. This meant she hadn't waited to make sure he had eaten before giving him the shot. I was horrified to think that he could have been in an insulin coma by the time I arrived, several hours later.

I started limiting my travel schedule even more.

🐫 🐫 🐫

Here's the odd part. In a revelation as gobsmacking as the notion that I could become besotted with a small furry alien, I realized I was relieved to have an excuse to stay home.

I had often returned from trips and thought, "Well, that was interesting. If only I didn't have to write about it." I longed for the days when I traveled for adventure or relaxation rather than for work. And loath as I was to admit it to myself, much less to anyone else, 9/11 multiplied the pre-trip anxiety I'd always experienced. I knew I was supposed to take the endless lines and shoe removals in stride; I was a seasoned, intrepid traveler who didn't want the terrorists to win. In reality, my dread of the prolonged airport experience was just one more thing that undercut the excitement I used to feel when embarking on a new adventure.

My newfound domestic arrangement provided me the cover to cut back.

But that still left the question of what to do about my writing career. I'd been telling myself that my traveling days were just on hold. Frankie's illness forced me to stare that delusion in the eyes.

I could write a book, I thought, an original book, not part of a series, one that would earn royalties. I already had such a book on hold, a humorous travelogue from a single woman's perspective. I had put together a proposal and a few sample chapters and had even managed to get an agent—two, in fact, though not at the same time.

The first agent, based in San Francisco, decided at the last minute that she didn't like my persona (um, that would be me). The second, a high-powered New Yorker, stopped answering my emails and phone calls after the first round of editors he sent the package to turned it down. Incredulous that he would have so little faith in my book—and be so rude—I dispatched a friend to his Upper West Side building to find out from the doorman whether he was dead or at least deathly ill. He was neither.

As a result, I didn't have much confidence in the project. In addition, I now found the idea of writing about adventures I was unlikely to have again upsetting.

But what else did I know besides travel?

Food? I had become the contributing dining editor for *Tucson Guide* magazine and the Tucson correspondent for the Zagat guides. My stories about the city's restaurant scene appeared in national publications. But in order for books about dining to have any authority, you need to be: a) a member of the ethnic group whose food you are celebrating; b) a restaurateur; c) able to provide recipes; d) all of the above.

I didn't cook and knew no more than the average New Yorker about Jewish food. Anyway, there were no good delis in Tucson, so a book on that topic would just make locals feel bad.

And then it struck me. I was inhaling every book and article I could find to help me unlock the mystery that was Frankie. I could write about dogs from a newbie's perspective, a kind of Complete Idiot's or For Dummies guide without the constraining format or the intelligence-insulting title.

Every semi-depressive will recognize this pattern: You have good days, days when you are your best self, days when you are capable of doing the things that seemed entirely impossible the day before. On one of those good days, I emailed Mike Sanders, the editorial director of Alpha/Penguin, which publishes the Complete Idiot's Guides. I had met Mike at a Tucson writers' conference a few years earlier, when, on another of those good days, I sat down next to him at breakfast instead of hiding in a corner as I was tempted to do—even though I was there as his equal, getting paid to give a talk on travel writing.

Mike had been very enthusiastic when I introduced myself to him. He said he'd really liked my *Complete Idiot's Travel Guide to Mexico's Beach Resorts*. There was a possibility that Alpha/Penguin might resurrect their travel series now that the five-year moratorium on producing travel guides that the Dummies had imposed on the Idiots was over.

I hadn't followed up on Mike's suggestion to get in touch if I was interested in writing another travel guide, because I wasn't, but I'd held on to his card. And on the good day that occurred a few years after the good day when I first chatted with him, I emailed Mike and asked him if he would be interested in a dog book, a lighthearted manual for first timers.

Send me a proposal, he said.

There then ensued a series of bad days, days when I wondered what the hell I had been thinking. There were hundreds of dog books out there. What could mine possibly add?

Deep breaths.

In addition to the perspective of a first-time dog owner who was learning along with the reader, I could offer a track record of being able to write and organize a book that was useful but not deadly dull. And although I rarely hauled out my PhD as a credential, when you are proposing a reference-type book, a few letters after your name can't hurt.

As for the sheer number of dog books on the market, I decided to look at the glass as half full for a change. The existence of a large quantity of dog books could be construed to mean that a lot of people buy dog books.

I came up with a format: a hundred questions, divided into ten chapters. I wrote some sample listings and provided an outline for the rest.

I pushed Send.

I waited. I sent a nudging note. And waited some more, for Mike to talk to the publisher.

Then I got the word: It was a go!

🐫 🐫 🐫

The result, a little more than a year later, was *Am I Boring My Dog? And 99 Other Things Every Dog Wishes You Knew.* I created a blog to publicize the book and called it *Will My Dog Hate Me,* which was short for "Will my dog hate me if

I dress him?"—another of my hundred questions. If I had it to do over again, I would have given my dog blog and my dog book the same name, and preferably the one starting with "A." I have no idea why I ignored the core principles of alphabetization.

Never mind. Both book and blog were semi-successful, the blog more so than the book because reading online is free and I was constantly adding new content; it was fun to write the stories I wanted to write and to see them appear immediately.

I even became a pet travel correspondent for a local TV station; Frankie was cute and you couldn't tell by looking at him that he hated to travel.

I expanded my community of the pet-obsessed. There was a whole new world of smart, interesting, and empathetic people, one that was not entirely virtual; I met several of my favorite pet bloggers in person. There were controversies, certainly, as there are about every subject that makes people passionate, but we could all agree about one thing: The shortness of a dog's life span is painful. As Frankie grew old and canine cognitive dysfunction set in, blogging about him grew emotionally draining.

Then, through a quirk, I became interested in my family's history. I've mentioned my mother's sadistic, meat-selling uncles in Vienna; I'd long known that one of them had a famous customer, Sigmund Freud. What I didn't know, until a friend googled it, was that my relative's butcher shop was at 19 Berggasse. My great uncle Siegmund Kornmehl had shared that address with Freud for forty-four years.

I started another blog, *Freud's Butcher*, with the eventual goal of writing a book. The research was fascinating at first, but I couldn't avoid the part of the story where the Nazis destroyed my family. Between that and the decline of my beloved Frankie, I was getting very dispirited.

One day, a friend tagged me on Facebook to join a poetry discussion that was about me—sort of. Its focus was Paul Blackburn, whose collected poems I had edited. One of the participants wondered what had happened to me. Another chimed in that I had "become a professional dog person." Thank you, Google.

I got it. People intersect with you at different times of your life and think they know who you *really* are; at heart, they're convinced, you're interested in whatever it is they're interested in. That was a key reason I'd moved to Tucson: I wanted to be a different person than the one solidified in the minds of my friends. But en route from editing Paul Blackburn's poems to becoming a dog writer, I had also been a travel editor and travel writer. More recently, I had been blogging about Jewish genealogy.

Seeing myself described as a professional dog person was like reading my own very short, very inaccurate obituary.

Some of the omissions were of the variety never cited in newspaper death notices: That I was happily single—if a self-flagellating semi-depressive could call herself happily anything. That I was a Western badass progressive of the type I had been looking to befriend, a loud New York voice in the wilderness.

Obituaries very rarely use the word "badass."

Most of all, what I wished my mini life summary had said was that I was a writer. Full stop. If, for a long time, I didn't have any idea what type of writer I wanted to become, I now knew at last: the type of writer who doesn't like to be typecast.

Rule to live by: Don't decide prematurely—as in, before you are dead—who you are, or who you think you should be. It's never too late to change. Corollary: Ignore all the rules to live by that you've concocted for yourself if they no longer apply.

Nevertheless, the fellow who declared me a professional dog person did me a favor. I now had enough distance from it—and enough confidence in myself—to resurrect that earlier book about my on-the-road adventures. It would set the record straight about the twenty-five years I'd spent as a travel editor and writer.

Here it is.

ABOUT THIS BOOK

It's an odd experience, writing a memoir over a long period of time, especially one focused on publishing, an industry changing at the speed of light. As I sent this book to the copy-editor, for example, *More* magazine, which ran the story that inspired the book's title and its first chapter, folded. Fodor's/Random House—the record holder for longest lasting relationship between brand and publisher of the companies I worked with--was sold to Internet Brands while this book was being proofread.

In addition, many other details written early on took on layers of meaning they didn't originally have. These include the vignette of my encounter with Hillary Clinton in San Antonio and the fact that the Gulf + Western building—where I worked for Prentice Hall Travel—had been gutted to make way for the Trump Tower.

In the end, I stopped trying to keep up. If some details are products of an earlier era and several contexts have shifted, there are universal elements that I hope will make the specifics less crucial. And one development has obviated the need for a lot of explanation: If you don't understand a reference, google it.

I kept a few names intact, but used mostly pseudonyms to protect the guilty, the easily embarrassed, and those who I thought might not want to be associated with this book for a variety of reasons, valid or not. I changed the names of several businesses for similar reasons.

ACKNOWLEDGEMENTS

This book wouldn't have seen the light of day had it not been for my successful Kickstarter campaign. My contributors buoyed me in ways far beyond the financial one.

The print version was made possible by:

Marita Adair, Jennifer Alford, Rae Armantrout, Nadine Baker, Charles Bernstein and Susan Bee, Rebecca Boren, Amy and Rod Burkert, Ann Cochran, Kate Davis, Joseph DiLorenzo, Denise Dube, Martin Dunford, Jen Fischahs, Shelli Hall, Adrienne Halpert, Sara Hammond, Lee Hilton, Erica Hunt, Debbie Jacobs, Christopher Knight, Lesley Kontowicz, Hilary Lane, Valerie Lee, Tatum Luoma, Gwen Matear, Jennifer Mauger, Kathy McMahon, Karen Norteman, Shannon Oelrich, Mary Peachin, Heidi Ravven, Laura Reese, Jeannine Relly, Jillian Robinson, Matt Russell, Karen Samuels, Ron Silliman, Miriam Stern, Jessica Vogelsang, Pamela Douglas Webster, Mike Webster, Janos and Rebecca Wilder, Charles Williams, Manfred Wolf, Debbie Wolfe, Marilyn Wood, and Karyn Zoldan.

Those who really, really helped me reach my financial goal include:

Susan Anderson, Sharon Balinsky, Peggy Bendel, Jo Bobb, Lori Chamberlin, George E. Davis, Steve Dyer, Elaine Glusac, Barbara Greenhalgh, Roxanne Hawn, Charles and Judith Hibbard, Miriam Hughes, Kate Kaemerle, Christie Keith, Margo Kesler, Maryrose Larkin, Daniela Lax and Linda

Snyder, Karen Luthur, Carol Kornmehl, Gloria McDarrah, Jeanne Muir, Leslie Olyott, Mary-Alice Pomputius, Elaine Raines, Simon Rosenblatt, Frankie (Cheesesteak) Santos, Leo and Merete Scheltinga, Elaine Schmerling, Janet Simmonds, Paul Starrs, Jill Stephen, Michelle Streeter, Marilyn Sutin, and Robyn and Jeff Timan.

And then there are the Platinum Club contributors:

Jeff Atwell, most excellent fross/briend (cross between boss and friend); Colby Cavanaugh, surprise patron who left town way too soon; Cynthia David, happy hour pal and partner in dog-springing crime; Lydia Davis, longtime friend and literary consigliore; Bonnie Kay, cat patron extraordinaire; Renee Kreager, Queen of Kind and Director of Yum at Renee's Organic Oven; Shana Oseran, force of nature behind the Hotel Congress, Cup Cafe, and Maynards Market & Kitchen; and John Peterson, PhD, BMAD (best movie and dining companion).

Several people went above and beyond the call with social media boosting and/or fund raising: Vera Marie Badertscher, Ellen Barone, Sharon Balinsky, Beth Blair, Jane Boursaw, Kate Davis, Judith Fein and Paul Ross, Mary Haight, Judith and Charles Hibbard, Miriam Hughes, Renee Kreager, Adam Lehrman, Anna Redsand, Hilary Lane, Diane Schmidt, Leo Scheltinga, Debbie Wolfe, and Marshal Zeringue.

Tony Baril and Maggie Adams made my Kickstarter video possible, while Alana Björn edited it down to its essence, focusing on its canine star, Madeleine.

A shout out to Mike Webster, who won the better sex scene contest (you'll have to ask him what that means); to Steve Dyer, who volunteered to design the book, though it didn't work out; and to Lydia Gregory, who helped me come up with some terrific Spanish-language pseudonyms.

Finally, major thanks go to friend, web guru, and all-around awesome person Laura Kelly, who helped me with the campaign in every possible way: getting my website ready for the launch, enlisting people to contribute, creating badges and banners, and providing moral support.

🐪 🐪 🐪

But there was life before and after Kickstarter.

Many people helped guide this book over the years—too many to enumerate. For this final incarnation, I thank Alice Peck for her excellent big picture editing and Lisa Anderson Cooper for her laser-like attention to detail at the end.

Although several friends looked at bits and pieces of the book along the way, Elaine Glusac and Kate Kaemerle were the most persistent in convincing me that, yes, they really did want to read it—as well as the most helpful and encouraging.

I am grateful to you all. I'm sure I've missed several people and will wake up in the middle of the night full of guilt and regret after this book is printed. Consider that your revenge.

ABOUT THE AUTHOR

Edie Jarolim earned her PhD in English and American literature from NYU and worked as a guidebook editor at Frommer's, Rough Guides, and Fodor's before moving to Arizona to become a freelance writer (or, as her mother might have put it, "You left your good job in New York to go where? To do what?"). She is the author of three travel guides, *Frommer's San Antonio and Austin*, *The Complete Idiot's Travel Guide to Mexico's Beach Resorts*, and *Arizona for Dummies*, as well as one dog guide, *Am I Boring My Dog? And 99 Other Things Every Dog Wishes You Knew*. Her articles have appeared in publications ranging from *Brides* and *Sunset* to *National Geographic Traveler* and *The Wall Street Journal*. She currently spends most of her time in Tucson, where she is best known as a dining reviewer, but her terrier mix, Madeleine, is showing signs of restlessness.